Greg has been a baker, bank teller and English teacher in Japan. He has climbed in the Himalayas, hitchhiked over 40,000 km and paddled 500 km down the Congo River in a dugout canoe. But Greg's real passion is politics. He grew up in a family completely uninterested in anything political and struggled to understand why no one around him was interested in politics. So in 2018 he undertook the first ever academic study on people who don't give a toss about politics, which has formed the basis of this book. At least now he knows why he is strange.

Neil got an early introduction to politics in a pram at anti-Vietnam War marches, and later in the front line of US nuclear ship and Springbok rugby tour protests. After stints as a farmhand, fruit picker, postie and piano teacher, he left New Zealand to bus, hike, hitch and cycle around the world. Highlights include canoeing PNG's Sepik River and getting shot at and arrested while cycling from China to Pakistan. Neil now lives relatively uneventfully with his partner and children. He teaches writing at Auckland University, an institution he barely graduated from due to all the time spent protesting.

Author relationship
Greg and Neil met travelling in Papua New Guinea in 1987 and went on to trek the Baliem Valley in West Papua together. They met ex-cannibals, caused an inter-village dispute over a pocket-knife, stumbled blindly through the middle of a local war, and survived on the local diet of sweet potato. What struck most though, was the genuine kindness and warmth of the West Papuan people. They staggered out of the jungle several weeks later, 10 kilos lighter and with one shoe each, and have been firm friends since.

For Thomas and Travis: May you stand up and be counted when they work out right from wrong. And thanks to Brigid for living this book with me.

—Greg Kramer

For Naoko, Wakana, Gen and Kaze. Kia kaha in your own way.

—Neil Matheson

Greg Kramer and Neil Matheson

THE APATHETIC COUNTRY

Why Ignorant Voters Dominate
Australian Politics

AUSTIN MACAULEY PUBLISHERS™

LONDON · CAMBRIDGE · NEW YORK · SHARJAH

A CIP catalogue record for this title is available from the British Library.

ISBN 9781398449435 (Paperback)
ISBN 9781398449442 (ePub e-book)

www.austinmacauley.com

First Published 2023
Austin Macauley Publishers Ltd®
1 Canada Square
Canary Wharf
London
E14 5AA

I would like to thank Professor Clive Bean for overseeing my PhD, which this book is based on. Clive's mentorship and gentleness, along with his thoughtful input, made the PhD a joy. But mostly I would like to thank my wife Brigid who read the PhD and book countless times, always offering thoughtful and helpful advice. It takes a lot of time to write a work such as this and I thank her for her patience. I would finally like to thank all the people who are interested and engaged in politics who attempt to make the world a better and fairer place - quite often to their own detriment.

—Greg Kramer

To my family; thanks for your immense patience during the writing process. Grateful thanks also to the University of Auckland for study leave at a key time in the project. And to Greg, whose 15 years of study forms the basis of the book, and whose vision and passion drove it to fruition.

—Neil Matheson

Table of Contents

Introduction

This book is about a group of little-known Australians with enormous political influence. One was approached by a television reporter after leaving a polling station during the 2018 'Super Saturday' by-elections and was asked how he'd voted:

> "Yeah, I don't even know who I voted for."
> "You don't know who you voted for?"
> "Yeah, people like me shouldn't even be allowed to vote if you don't know who you're voting for."
> "So, you just ticked some boxes down the line."
> "Pretty much."
> "Like a donkey vote."
> "Yeah. I'd like to know who and what-not, but I've got enough things in my own world going on."[1]

While most wouldn't be as honest as this guy, it is a common situation for many voters. At least 20 per cent of Australian voters are not interested in politics. Their knowledge of politics is minimal, they don't browse the media for political news, they don't talk about politics, and like our friend leaving the polling station, many don't know who they vote for. But that doesn't matter to them—because they don't care who wins.

Voters who are not interested in politics are very different political actors compared to interested voters. Interested and knowledgeable voters are generally rusted on supporters of one party or the other and it often takes a dramatic event for them to change. In contrast, politically uninterested voters are highly fickle. Studies continually show that uninterested voters are generally swinging voters who are more likely to change their vote from one major party to the other at differing elections.

Australian academic Ernest Chaples described swinging voters as:

> the airheads and drongos, they are the apoliticals of our society. They do not know much about politics, and they care even less. If it were not for compulsory enrolment and voting, the airheads would hardly matter as they would seldom be enrolled and would hardly ever show up to vote. But in the Australian system, airheads do vote.[2:363]

If Labor can get enough uninterested votes, then they form government and vice versa. These voters have been characterised as "Howard's battlers", called "working families" by Rudd, and "hard working early-alarm-setting Australians" by Gillard, while Morrison rebadged them as the "quiet Australians".

Whatever they're called, election campaigns and a lot of politics is oriented towards catching the attention of uninterested voters, which is why catch phrases such as "moving forward", "stop the boats" and "jobs and growth" are repeated over and over in the hope that an uninterested voter will stumble across the slogan and be influenced by it. This is also why fear campaigns are so prevalent in election campaigns. A fear of Medicare being privatised or refugees throwing their children overboard may be the only 'information' some voters have.

Uninterested voters may also be influenced by politicians wandering around with fluoro vests and hard hats during elections while others treat elections like a popularity contest, voting for the politician they most like. Voters with little interest in politics generally decide who to vote for in the last couple of days of the election campaign, which is why major parties concentrate the majority their advertising in the last week of campaigning. It is aimed fair and square at the people who decide who governs.

This book is based on a PhD written by Greg Kramer in 2018, which was the first study to quantify the electoral impact of politically apathetic voters in Australia. This book expands on this research and is the only book written that focuses solely on Australian voters who are apathetic about politics. It is provocative because we highlight the political shortcomings of these voters and the fragility of our democratic system. We are not trying to denigrate these voters. Almost every citizen has the cognitive capacity to engage in politics if they so desire, and it is not the fault of uninterested voters that they are forced to vote. But it is shocking to realise that our politicians are most interested in the voters who are the least interested in politics.

If uninterested voters were fully informed on the social and economic issues that have the most impact on their lives, it is likely election outcomes would be quite different, and the social and economic systems in place would be more responsive to their needs. As it is now, their uninformed voting choices mean they may well be making things worse for themselves, with implications for the whole system of government in Australia. Given many uninterested voters are from lower socio-economic groups, the serious concerns they have about health, education and economic equality are hijacked by issues that have little influence on their lives. It is the fear of differing races and religions which has been highlighted in order to win people's votes. A vote based on fear may elect a government that acts directly against the needs of these voters.

Where Do the Numbers Come from?

To demonstrate the influence of uninterested voters, we draw on the views of individuals from the Australian Election Study (AES), which has surveyed about 2,300 people after every federal election since 1987. This book is, therefore, based on the views of about 27,000 voters over a period of 32 years. The survey asks a range of political questions and a lot of the academic research on Australian politics is based on these surveys.[Annexure 1]

Surveys such as the AES are carried out in most developed countries and results are similar in all the surveys, so Australia is not a special case. The US was the first to undertake the study in 1948 in an attempt to understand why Germans had voted for Hitler. The researchers believed that a Hitler-style leader could never be elected in the US and set out to prove it. The results, however, showed a third of Americans were uninterested in politics and if they did engage in politics, they would vote for a strongman authoritarian figure, as evidenced by Trump's election. Academics fell over themselves to reassure people that political apathy was not a problem as long as apathetic citizens didn't engage in politics. It's a very different situation in Australia where we compel these apathetic voters to vote.

It is important to note that it is the AES respondents themselves who are telling us they aren't interested, or don't care who wins, or don't know which party they voted for. If they say they are not interested in politics, then it's a fair call to believe them. Think about the last conversation you had—was it interesting? Was the last party you went to interesting? Are you interested in 15th century music, cooking or tennis? We can all quantify our level of interest in something and can equally recall knowing who we voted for—if we are interested enough.

Like any large public survey, there are a few concerns with the AES. It has become increasingly difficult to get people to complete the survey. In 1987, 63 per cent completed the survey; this dropped to 23 per cent in 2016. However, if you received a survey asking your opinion on something you have no interest in—it could be say, crochet, curling or Carthaginian architecture, it is more than likely you'd bin it too. It's no surprise that politically uninterested voters bin the AES survey meaning, if anything, the results under-report the lack of political interest. Political apathy is, therefore, likely to be worse than described in this book.

The AES, however, remains the most reliable survey available for studying political interest in Australia and is used extensively in this book together with other research findings. The picture of political apathy we paint is already so disturbing that we can afford to be conservative in our estimates of the problem.

Overview

To explain the impact of uninterested voters in Australian politics, we explore unchartered territory, as even within academia there is a 'surprisingly scarce' amount of research on apathetic voters.[3:73] We document just how little interest apathetic voters have, their lack of knowledge, their demographic and the reasons why they don't care about politics or who governs them. And we show how their votes have affected electoral outcomes and political discourse.

Winston Churchill famously said, "the best argument against democracy was a five-minute conversation with the average voter." If we were more interested in politics we would be more likely to elect intelligent and forward-thinking politicians. We would have experts making decisions on our economy, the environment and health. Instead, we allow self-serving politicians to claim the carbon tax would wipe Whyalla off the map, that Vegemite is funding terrorism, and that there is a link between abortion and breast cancer. We elect someone who jokes about Pacific nations disappearing under water and another who reasoned that marriage equality would mean people could marry the Sydney Harbour Bridge. We leave crucial decisions on our economic, social and environmental future up to politicians pandering to the fears of apathetic voters.

Chapter One
Democracy: A Long and Glorious History?

Mention the word 'democracy' and what often springs to mind is a rich history of government by the people, for the people, in a tradition linking all the way back to the ancient Greeks. Modern democratic governments are seen to be carrying on a tradition of democratic rule developed across millennia.

The reality is, however, quite different. Democracy as we know it is a relatively recent way of deciding who governs and how we are governed. This is because there has always been a concern that ordinary citizens lacked the interest or knowledge to make reasonable political decisions. Plato, Aristotle, Socrates and pretty much every leading thinker until around 150 years ago thought the idea of democracy as we conceive it today was rule by the 'poor, the ignorant, and the incompetent'.[4:9–10] This argument has been used to exclude groups such as women, the young, the uneducated and the poor from participating in democracy until relatively recently. It was due to this distrust of the masses that democracy came about slowly and cautiously in Western countries.

We can trace the roots of democracy back to Athenians with their concept of 'demokratia'. Derived from 'demos', meaning the people, and 'kratos', meaning power or to rule, it is the rule of the people, and it is the people who decide political outcomes. While government decides things on a day-to-day basis, responsibility for political decisions rests entirely with us. We have the power to kick politicians out if they've done a poor job or if better people or policies are available. The defining feature of democracy, in other words, is that elected officials can be replaced without bloodshed by simply casting a vote.

Many traditional societies had some system where people contributed to collective decision-making, but Athens is seen as the birthplace of democracy. However, Athens was far from what we would consider democratic today. In order to vote, you had to be a citizen, and only around 40,000 out of a population of

250,000 were allowed to participate. Slaves, women, merchants and labourers were denied citizenship and property qualifications denied others until around 450 BCE. Aristotle justified this on the basis that there was a hierarchy of citizens, with some born to rule and others born to obey.

Plato agreed that most Athenians were incapable of contributing to democracy, while Socrates believed that in order to participate in politics, people had to have knowledge rather than just opinions. For Socrates, you had to know something about the topic in order to have the legitimacy to open your mouth and speak about it. Interestingly, technical issues that required experts were depoliticised in Athens, with Socrates stating:

> When we gather for the assembly, when the city has to do something about buildings, they call for the builders and advisors and when it is about ship construction, the shipwrights, and so on with everything else that can be taught and learned. And if anyone else tries to advise them, whom they do not think an expert, even if he be quite a gentleman, rich and aristocratic, they none the less refuse to listen, but jeer and boo, until either the speaker himself is shouted down and gives up, or the sergeants at arms, on the order of the presidents, drag him off or remove him. That is how they behave on technical questions.[5:46-47]

Can you imagine how political debates in Australia on issues like climate change or 'clean coal' might be different if we adopted this Athenian strategy? The average Athenian citizen did, however, have a say on many issues even if they had little idea what they were talking about. One such issue was war with citizens voting to send a military force against Sicily in 415BCE.

Thucydides commented that most Athenians had no idea how big Sicily was, how many Sicilians there were, or what may be needed by Athens to invade successfully. It seems that a jingoistic fervour overtook the Athenians to such a degree that those who actually opposed the war were afraid of being thought unpatriotic if they voted against it.[6:22]

The war was hampered right from the start because Athenians understandably did not want to tax themselves adequately to prosecute the war.[6] As you might expect, the war didn't go as Athens hoped; they lost over 200 ships and their entire expedition was captured or killed.

The defeat proved to be the turning point in the long running Peloponnesian war and for Greek democracy. Naturally, Athenians looked for someone to blame and pointed the finger at Pericles, their leader at the time. Pericles, however, reminded the Athenians that they had voted for the war. Can we imagine an Australian political leader nowadays castigating the public for making bad political choices?

Socrates also chastised Athenian citizens for failure to rule their empire correctly, stating "The persons to blame are you…who go to see an oration as if it were a sight, take your facts on hearsay."[7:65–66] This criticism of the public for being ill-informed got Socrates into trouble. He was put on public trial and ended up having to down a jug of poisonous hemlock. This seemed to work in silencing him—permanently.

The disastrous war illustrated the central problem with Athenian democracy— citizens lacked the capacity to make reasonable decisions. It was not just the war in Sicily where Athens failed. Athenians continually voted to make war on former friends and allies, formed alliances with Greeks who had collaborated with the Persian enemy, extorted financial payments from weaker neighbours, and imposed governments on the people they did not support.

They increased state welfare to themselves and when the treasury was getting low, invaded neighbours to replenish their coffers. Rich people also paid poorer citizens for their vote—pork barrel politics, at least, has a long history—and leaders simply told the electorate what they wanted to hear in order to stay in power.[7:63] This sounds especially familiar.

With Athenian democracy in its death throes, the only way to coerce citizens to gather and make decisions was to pay them, yet as Athens had little money left, corruption also became rife. Plato thought the primary reason for democratic failures in Athens were "decisions made by an unenlightened majority."[8:96]

Plato, Thucydides, Aristotle and Socrates were all harsh critics of voting rights for citizens, doubting their ability to make rational and informed decisions. Considering Socrates' fate for voicing criticism, it's surprising the other three survived. Perhaps it was because of Athenian apathy. Democracy did, however, prevail in Athens for nearly 200 years and in comparison, the autocratic rule, which subsequently took hold can hardly be viewed as enlightened or fair.

Rome also embraced democracy at a similar time as Athens. They called it a 'respublic' with 'res' meaning thing and 'public' well, public, so a republic is a public thing. The Roman parliamentary system was very complicated and has never been replicated, though elements of the US democratic system can be traced back to the Roman version.

Initially, the Roman republic was limited to elites, but eventually the 'plebian' commoner males were also allowed to participate. Women, slaves and non-citizens, however, were still excluded and the military dominated the Senate chamber. The Roman republic endured longer than the Athenian democracy, in fact longer than any democracy in history, and they did manage to introduce some useful concepts such as 'equality under the law'. Another good idea was providing citizenship to the people whose lands they had conquered—a clever way to stave off rebellions across their empire.

But it all started to unravel around 60 BCE. Imperialism had left the republic over-extended, which led to local governors usurping control and undermining central Roman government. Pompey, a successful military commander, along with the mega-rich Crassus, dominated government which had become chaotic and dysfunctional.

Corruption was also rife as elites become even wealthier. Understandably these aristocrats saw no reason to change as they drank wine and had grapes peeled for them in their heated baths. The republic finally ended when Julius Caesar crossed the Rubicon with his legion and convinced the Roman Senate to anoint him as emperor in 44 BCE.

Given their reputation for lawless mayhem on their overseas jaunts, it may come as a surprise that the Vikings also had a limited form of democracy or popular rule. As early as 600, free men with hereditary status would gather at a 'Ting' (the origin of our word 'thing', meaning 'thing' or 'assembly'). This was an open field area often marked by large vertical stones.

Many Tings are still standing today. The Ting in Iceland is a spectacular place of pilgrimage for anyone interested in the history of democracy. Located right on the junction of the American and Eurasian tectonic plates, it overlooks Iceland's largest natural lake. A large rock feature creates a natural amphitheatre, allowing for good acoustics.

Situated on land confiscated from a convicted murderer, the Ting was relatively close to where people lived with citizens only having to travel a maximum of 17 days to attend. Can you imagine Australian voters giving up 17 days to go to parliament? And in Iceland they had to cross rivers, glaciers and volcanic ranges—not a bad effort to have your voice heard. At least, they held it in summer!

Anyone attending a Ting had the right to make political arguments from the 'Lögberg', or law rock. They would accept laws, settle disputes and even vote on changing their religion. Kings also swore faithfulness to the laws adopted by the Ting.

However, there was a Law Council that only chieftains, nobles and later Christian bishops belonged to and this was the body that effectively settled disputes and decided new rules. The Ting remained Iceland's effective parliament until 1271 but inevitable wars between Icelandic chieftain families led to Norway taking over and the Ting being abolished.

Around 1100, some city states in Italy began to experiment with popular rule. They were initially dominated by elites, but over time the middle class demanded the right to participate. And since the middle class were more numerous, effectively organised and could threaten violent overthrow of the upper-class elites, they eventually gained the right to participate. City states such as Florence and Venice flourished for around 200 years, creating extraordinary wealth, art, music and architecture. Sadly for the history of democracy, around the mid-1300s these centres began to give way to the perennial enemies of popular government: corruption, economic decline, war, and the seizure of power by authoritarian figures.

These same issues also plagued the French Revolution. While the revolution promised a more open and egalitarian form of government, it actually confirmed that most people were unprepared for political rights. Many were ignorant about democracy, irrational and prone to violence. The rule of law was suspended and anyone deemed to be an enemy of the people executed by guillotine.

The revolution unsurprisingly led to Napoleon, a charismatic authoritarian figure, usurping power. He attempted to have his rule legitimised with repeated plebiscites based on universal male suffrage—not exactly what we would call open and egalitarian government.

No state listed above fulfilled the democratic requirement expected today of allowing the participation of virtually every adult citizen. We think of popular government and democracy in positive terms, but it has had a chequered history and has never ended well.

With the downfall of Athens, the term 'democracy' effectively disappeared from the vocabulary for over two thousand years. Indeed, the British Prime Minister William Gladstone only 130 years ago was deeply offended at being called a democrat by a political opponent.[9:15]

The French revolution showed that the people were not ready for self-rule, and many were desperate to come up with ways to counter the perils of democracy. They realised that if democracy was to work, there had to be the rule of law and the guarantee of individuals rights, term limits for politicians and above all, educated citizens.

This is why James Madison framed the American constitutional system as he did with separated powers, checks and balances, divided electorates and limited terms of office. The whole constitutional structure was designed to mitigate the effects of mass participation in the system and the ambitions of politicians.

Nothing highlights the fear the framers of the American constitution had of the average voter than the establishment of the Electoral College to elect the president. In the US, voters technically elect 538 people to represent their state at a meeting (the Electoral College) and it is these people who choose the president. This only changed in 2020 when the Supreme Court ruled that Electoral College members must support the popularly elected candidate in their state.

The US founding fathers were afraid that American voters would be wooed by some dastardly tyrant lying and manipulating their way into power. Alexander Hamilton, one of the founders of the American constitution, argued the Electoral College would ensure only qualified people became president. Essentially the founders did not trust the voters to make the right choice. We can only wonder how Hamilton and Jefferson would view the phenomenon of white, uneducated and religious folk coming together so strongly to elect Trump.

The Long and Winding Road to Political Inclusion

Until around 150 years ago, many leading thinkers and writers believed that democracy just wasn't possible because most people were not interested enough in political affairs or lacked the capacity to engage in sound political decision making. These arguments have been used to exclude the majority of people from voting until very recently. It was due to this distrust of the masses that democracy came about slowly and cautiously in western countries.

Hobbs argued way back in 1651 that the majority of the populous had dangerous and destructive passions.[10:41] Edmund Burke thought that the lower socio-economic class should not be afforded the vote arguing "You think you are combating prejudice, but you are at war with nature."

Adam Smith argued that workers suffer "drowsy stupidity by the mind-numbing division of labour, the worker is the victim of nurture rather than nature but a fallen creature nonetheless. Of the great and extensive interests of his country he is altogether incapable of judging."[11]

Even the great John Stuart Mill, a giant of liberalism, was concerned about "the danger of a low grade of intelligence in the representative body and in the popular opinion, which controls it." Mill's 'natural' or ideal position was to allow people who had a good education more votes than those with poorer education, going as far as to require a literacy test. Mill also argued to exclude paupers without property, men who laboured for a living, and those receiving benefits and bankrupts as they did not pay taxes. Remember that Mill was writing in an era when most people were poor and unable to read so his suggestion meant that the vast majority of citizens would not have been able to vote.[12:474] As this shows, a number of enlightened thinkers were alarmed at the prospect of allowing people to vote who were uninterested or seemed to lack the ability to make rational political decisions.

It wasn't just enlightened thinkers of course. Adolf Hitler rejected democracy because he thought voters were ignorant and easily manipulated. In *Mein Kampf*, he wrote "the receptivity of the great masses (to information) is very limited, their intelligence is small, but their power of forgetting is enormous."[13]

Hitler's solution was to institute a dictatorship and invade Poland, which as we know didn't work out so well. We're not advocating such extreme measures to cure Australia's democratic ills—though invading New Zealand could be worth a shot.

Chapter Two
Who Gets to Vote in Australia?

There has always been resistance in Australia to granting certain people the vote. In the early 1800s, only men who owned or rented a property could vote, with John Macarthur's view that "representative government would seal the destruction of every respectable person here" typical of the time. The New South Wales (NSW) Legislative Council wanted the minimum rent paid to be 20 pounds per year before a man could vote, meaning only men renting expensive properties would be eligible to vote.

However, ex-convicts were starting to make a pretty penny and free, respectable English immigrants who were yet to establish themselves were excluded from voting. It seems the Legislative Council was afraid former convicts would be voting at the expense of respectable Englishmen because it reduced the minimum rental to 10 pounds per annum. This was the same minimum as in England and since it successfully excluded most working men there, there was no reason to believe it wouldn't work here.

That changed when gold was discovered in Victoria, resulting in the economy booming and many men suddenly became eligible to vote. Universal male suffrage gradually permeated through the colonies. South Australia guaranteed the vote for all adult men in 1855 followed by NSW, Victoria and Queensland in the 1860s.

Anyone receiving aid from a public or charitable institution was, however, excluded from voting in NSW, Western Australia (WA) and Queensland. If this were applied today, anyone receiving welfare, such as unemployment benefits or the old age pension, would be barred from voting. And until 1900, Tasmanian men had to have property or a job paying more than 40 pounds a year before they could vote. This association between wealth and voting rights was widespread. WA, Victoria, Queensland and Tasmania even allowed men plural voting (more than one vote): they were able to vote wherever they owned property. The *Brisbane Courier Mail* justified this, saying:

> Men are possessed of property because they are possessed of the industry, and enterprise, and foresight and thrift which is invaluable to the State, and which in an eminent degree qualify a man to vote helpful to his country. Even when property has come apart from any personal quality of the possessor, as by inheritance, the very possession confers an interest in public affairs which by itself is valuable as a qualification to vote. [14:17]

Curiously, plural voting still exists in most states, with people allowed to vote in local government elections if they own property there, even if they live on the other side of the country. There were other odd voting rules before federation. These included police and people working in the military not being allowed to vote in NSW or Queensland, and men who failed to pay maintenance to their wife and children were also denied the vote. [15]

On January 22 1856, Fanny Finch, a London-born businesswoman of African heritage and a single mother of four became the first woman to cast a vote in an Australian election. Finch ran a restaurant and lodging house at Victoria's Forest creek goldfields alongside 25,000 men and a sprinkling of women. Her next establishment was a lodging house in Castlemaine, which was, according to the local newspaper, "the only one in which any person could get respectable accommodation."

Finch was a strong character who dressed in bright blue silk with artificial flowers in her black hair. She was known for remedying injustice either with her words or fists, and on one occasion was fined 50 pounds for the illicit sale of alcohol. The trial lasted a month and included 'scandalous cross-examination' of miners and the police who were all caught up in the libation of sly grog. It seems Finch's lodging house may not have been so 'respectable' after all.

Because of her business, Finch paid rates and because the Municipal Institutions Act of 1854 granted the vote to rate-paying 'persons', she was theoretically able to vote in the Victorian election. Finch, therefore, wandered along to do her democratic duty and cast a vote. However, her ballot was disavowed by election officials on the grounds that she "had no right to vote" and the *Melbourne Argus* passed it off as "an incident of the day."

Finch's ballot paper is on display in the Castlemaine Art Museum. In a little-known fact, a handful of women did actually vote and had their votes count in the 1864 Victorian election because they were 'persons' who paid rates and this so shocked men that the Act was re-written with 'persons' becoming 'male ratepayers' in 1865. It would be another 54 years before another woman cast a vote in a Victorian election.

In the 1880s, women began to agitate for the right to vote. One argument was that women needed the vote to make the male-dominated parliaments properly protect women from vice and devious, sexually-driven men. However, it was argued that women couldn't make rational decisions and they were given the same political status as the "idiot and the criminal."[14]

In 1886, a bill to allow women over the age of 25 to vote was defeated in South Australia. The proposer of the bill justified the age qualification, stating that women "had been in the past somewhat handicapped in intellectual progress and were a few years behind men in matters political."[14] The bill was opposed on the grounds that "true women, virtuous, modest, and shunning publicity would not be interested in voting. She would be content to have as her mission in life the welfare of her husband and children."[14]

Well-worn arguments were that women would be degraded if they brushed up against the nasty world of politics or that female suffrage would deprive men the responsibility of protecting women. Even though women were agitating for the vote, men argued that women didn't want it and that it was a "new-fangled fad espoused by a few noisy, carping, dried-up old blue stockings."[14]

Other arguments were that women would inevitably vote the way their husbands told them to, giving married men an unfair advantage over bachelors or that women would vote for good looking guys over ugly ones. This last argument was put to bed when women first voted and it was pointed out that none of the elected politicians were "particularly handsome."[16]

Some women were against female suffrage; Queen Victoria called it "mad wicked folly...with all its intended horrors."[14] Vicky doesn't seem to have had a strong grip on irony; she was the head of the largest empire on earth yet thought women lacked the capacity to vote for a political representative.

In 1894, a bill to allow women the vote looked likely to pass the South Australian parliament, so in an act of desperation, conservatives introduced an amendment not only allowing women the vote, but also to stand as candidates, a right suffragettes had not asked for. Conservatives believed the idea of women standing and possibly entering parliament was so ridiculous the bill would be defeated. To their horror, the bill passed 31 to 14 votes, one of the biggest political belly flops in Australian politics. South Australia would proudly go down in history as the first parliament to allow women to stand as candidates and the second, after New Zealand, to allow women to vote. Within four months, women would have their chance to vote, with the *Adelaide Observer* noting that women voters added a civilising element to the election, which was calmer and more respectful.

Ultra-conservative Western Australia was the next state to allow women the vote. When gold was discovered in the early 1890s, a large number of impoverished diggers rushed west with radical political ideas like republicanism, socialism and unionism. Giving women the vote was a desperate act by a conservative government to stymie the influence of these miners.

Women won the right to vote federally in 1902, with all states following suit except the aptly named Victoria which refused women the vote until 1908. The "mad wicked folly" didn't seem so mad once in place. After viewing the Australian national election, an Englishman noted, "women's part in politics is taken as quite natural…and crucially they do not neglect their husbands' meals nor are they in any way unwomanly in appearance."[16:309]

Indigenous Australians and other non-white people were also denied voting rights as they were thought to be "uneducated or uncivilised."[17:523] Some Indigenous people were allowed to vote in some state elections prior to federation, although the 1902 Franchise Act that enfranchised women also stated that "no aboriginal native of Australia Asia Africa or the Islands of the Pacific except New Zealand shall be entitled to have his name placed on an Electoral Roll."[18] Senator Alexander Matheson, who had championed the bill said:

> It is absolutely repugnant to the greater number of the people of the Commonwealth that an aboriginal man, or aboriginal lubra or gin—a horrible, dirty, degraded creature—should have the same rights, simply by virtue of being 21 years of age, that we have, after some debate today, decided to give to your wives and daughters.[19]

Some non-white people were given the vote in 1925 after the Commonwealth was challenged in court by Mita Bullosh, who was both Indian and importantly, a British subject. His case looked like breaking the colour barrier with the precedent of a dark-skinned Indian allowed to vote but the government quickly passed a special law allowing the 2,300 Indians in Australia to vote while continuing to bar all others of colour. Indigenous Australians would not be allowed to vote federally until 1962, and only compelled to enrol in 1983.

Age has also been a barrier to participation, with those aged 18–20 only allowed to vote since 1973. The argument was that since 18-year-olds paid tax, could drive and were sent to kill and be killed in Vietnam, they should be allowed to vote.

A significant number of Australians are still not entitled to vote. Those younger than 18 cannot vote even though many drive cars, work fulltime, pay tax and can join the military and, potentially, kill people. Thousands of school children have taken to the streets to protest climate change, signifying they are knowledgeable about politics. They too are denied the vote. Some countries, such as Scotland, Austria, Brazil and Norway do, however, allow 16 and 17-year-olds the vote.

Those serving more than 3 years in prison are also denied the vote. Also barred are those of 'unsound mind' (incapable of understanding the nature and significance of voting). Between 1993 and 2018, 43,000 people, mostly elderly or dying, were removed from the Electoral Roll. Down Syndrome Australia chief executive, Ellen Skladzien noted there were occasions when people involved in her organisation were also removed, without their knowledge. Yet voters who are drunk or high on drugs can vote, undermining the logic of barring those "incapable of understanding the nature and significance of voting."

Homeless people can vote by being listed on the Electoral Roll as having no fixed address and being registered at their last abode or where a family member is enrolled. If they do not have family, they are able to register where they were born. But in 2015, less than 10 per cent of homeless people, who could benefit from electing governments determined to create clearer economic pathways, voted in the Victorian election.

In New Zealand, anyone who lives permanently in the country can vote. Australia had something similar until 1984 when Prime Minister Bob Hawke decided that only citizens could vote. In a quirky twist, anyone not a citizen but already on the Electoral Roll could continue to vote, thereby grandfathering the change. Under these rules, the 567,000 Kiwis who have moved to Australia since 1984 and live here permanently can't vote on legislation that directly affects them. Whatever the argument for or against Kiwis having the vote, we periodically enfranchise or disenfranchise significant swathes of people.

The socio-demographics of those allowed to vote has changed considerably over the past 150 years. People without property or a job, those on welfare, women, individuals under 21 years of age, Indigenous Australians and people of non-white ethnicity were viewed as lacking the interest or ability to make rational political decisions for themselves or the broader society and denied the right to vote until relatively recently.

This book similarly questions whether some people have the capacity to participate in our democracy. These questions, however, are not based on an individual's wealth, gender, ethnicity or age. They are based on whether a person has the motivation to become well-enough informed to participate in a rational and meaningful way in politics. Those who are not interested in politics generally abstain in voluntary voting systems. But in Australia, these questions are especially important as politically apathetic people are compelled to vote for policies and representatives that affect us all.

Our First Election

Democracy was not on the convicts' minds when they waded ashore at Sydney Cove in 1788. White Australia was a penal colony where many residents lugged ball and chain around while others cowered at the thought of the whip. However, the first Australian election was held in 1843, with locals electing 24 members of the 36 seat Legislative Council. The Governor of NSW, Lieutenant-Colonel Sir George Gipps, selected the other 12 members, although it was all a bit pointless as the council's powers were limited to advising Sir George.

The early colonial elections were a true Australian experience. Nominations for political office were generally made outside pubs, which may have caused concern for any responsible electoral official. Even though only 20 per cent of the locals were eligible to vote, those who couldn't vote also turned out to hear the candidates. Democracy was taking off, with candidates plying everyone with free grog to try and win their vote. Even at this early stage of democracy, candidates were aware they needed to treat potential constituencies differently. Dinner with the candidate in a flash restaurant was offered to rich voters. Middle-class voters dined at the local inn while the lower class feasted on roasted bullock and barrels of ale in the marketplace.

The voter wrote the name of their chosen candidate on a ballot paper and handed it to the electoral official, who asked them to show the ballot to the crowd.

The candidate knew immediately if his investment had paid off. If the election was close, drunks were rounded up and steered toward the ballot box.

The very first Australian election would set the scene for many of those to follow, with fear campaigns prevalent and a fear of other races at the forefront. The unfortunately named William Hustler's campaign slogan was "Vote for Hustler and No Coolies."

Maurice O'Connell, whose father was Irish, was the clear favourite for the seat of Sydney but a fear campaign was initiated arguing O'Connell was a closeted Catholic. This irritated a mob of 400 drunken Irishmen who armed themselves with fence palings and attacked William Wentworth's campaign tent. Wentworth's men retaliated with harpoons, killing two men.

This all led to Sir George reporting to London that "the election in general went off very well."[19] Wentworth went on to win the seat and advocated extending the vote to anyone who owned 200 cattle or 1,000 sheep. Wentworth is acknowledged as the father of Australian representative democracy and a portrait of him still hangs in the NSW parliament.

Federation? What Federation?

Australia became a federation in 1901, though federation had never been a sure thing. We could easily have become six independent countries and if we travelled between, say Queensland and NSW, we could be showing passports and declaring our duty free.

The Premier of NSW Henry Parkes proposed the idea of federating in 1867 but the Duke of Buckingham, the British Secretary of State for the Colonies, rejected the idea out of hand. Our British overloads thought federating and running the show ourselves was a very poor idea. Federation became a more serious idea in 1883 with rising nationalism and a worry over German influence in New Guinea and French influence in the New Hebrides. The debate was kicked along by anti-Chinese sentiment and a concern that indentured Pacific Islanders would want to stay in Queensland.

New Zealand was interested in joining the federation initially but New Zealanders had serious concerns over how Australia treated its Indigenous population, especially since New Zealand had signed the Treaty of Waitangi with Māori in 1840. The Kiwis even set up a Royal Commission in 1900 to consider joining our federation, concluding that they would go their own way as "New Zealanders were of superior stock to their counterparts across the Tasman."[20]

Political interest in the 1898 federation referendum was, however, so low that many were unaware that federation was happening.[21] To entice voters to participate in the 1898 referendum on the constitution, the Victorian Premier Sir George Turner promised a "gay picture card" as a memento to voters. It didn't work, with a Parliamentary Library study estimating that the turnout was less than eight per cent of voters. In a foretaste of politicians' penchant for broken promises, the gay picture cards were never delivered. The follow up referendum in 1899 saw just 13.8 per cent vote.[15] The turnout rate that embedded the Australian Constitution was embarrassingly low.

In 1903, the federal government was concerned over these low participation rates and was anxious for people to be involved in the new parliament. Police were sent from house to house registering citizens for the Electoral Roll. As some were missed, lists were displayed for citizens to see if they had been registered, but "few bothered to check."[22:322]

Even with this level of government management, only one in two enrolled voters turned out for the 1903 federal election. A rule requiring polling places to be more than 100 yards from the nearest pub may have been partly to blame. The lack of participation prompted a law change in 1911 making enrolment compulsory, with fines for not enrolling.

Compulsory enrolment saw the turnout rate shoot up to 74 per cent for the 1913 election. But participation dropped again in 1922 with just 59 per cent of enrolled voters trudging to the polling booth.[Annexure 2] Politicians fell over themselves to explain and fix the system. Labor Senator Albert Gardiner railed that "something should be done to compel people who are indifferent...to go to the polls."[23:9] Curiously, Senator Gardiner also thought "the opinions of the negligent and apathetic section of the electors are not worth obtaining."[23:9]

In 1924, Tasmanian Nationalist Senator Herbert Payne introduced the Compulsory Voting Bill, stating that "apathy and indolence...are to be found in all directions" and that compulsion would provide "a wonderful improvement in the political knowledge of the people."[24:20] Payne summed the bill up as a moral issue, with the aim being "to compel those who enjoy all the privileges of living in Australia and all the advantages of Australian law to take a keener interest in the welfare of their country."[25:32]

There was little discussion on the proposal and it passed the Lower House in just 52 minutes and the Upper House in 86 minutes. One of the biggest changes to our democratic system was considered for about an hour in each chamber. Since

1924, the Commonwealth electoral legislation has stated that "it shall be the duty of every elector to vote" at each election, which is what we now refer to as compulsory voting. Compulsory voting, however, is a misnomer because our ballots are secret, and no one can see if we have voted or not. What *is* compulsory is attendance at a polling booth.

Australia was the first country to introduce compulsory voting and only 21 other countries have followed suit. Most of these countries have dubious democratic credentials and many don't take compulsory voting seriously. Honduras, Costa Rica, Dominican Republic, Mexico, Panama and Greece have compulsory voting but apply no penalties for people who don't vote so the compulsory element is taken as a bit of a joke. Only 44 per cent of eligible voters cast a ballot in the 2015 Greek election; a better effort was made by Hondurans with 51 per cent voting in 2017. Even when fines are applied, more than half of the population don't bother in Thailand and Lebanon. In Egypt, only 28 per cent voted in a recent poll, which may have had something to do with the election being farcical as President Abdel Fattah El-Sisi received 97 per cent of the vote.

Other countries do achieve high turnouts because of compulsion. Argentina, Belgium, Bolivia, Brazil, Ecuador, Luxembourg, Nauru, Peru, Singapore and Uruguay all get over 80 per cent turnout, and even Paraguay and the Congo get about 60 per cent. North Korea had a 99.99 per cent turnout for its compulsory national elections in 2019. The state-controlled media reported voting occurred "amid patriotic enthusiasm of all the people". The high turnout may be explained by draconian penalties if citizens do not vote, enthusiastically, for the one candidate on the ballot.

The penalty for not voting in Australia is 20 dollars. In Singapore, the voter's name is taken off the Electoral Roll, which must seem more like a reward than a punishment for someone not wanting to vote. In Bolivia, non-voters are barred from making bank transactions for three months after the election, while in Brazil, a non-voter may have their passport cancelled. In Luxembourg, there are empty threats of fines and jail—no one has ever been prosecuted for not voting.

Compulsory voting is not practiced in other Australian institutions such as trade unions, company meetings or even within political parties themselves. Yet the government took the opposite approach to that adopted practically everywhere else and forced people to vote. Perhaps they believed they "could do anything— even make apathetic men and women into citizens."[22]

There is no doubt that compulsion has increased turnout substantially. The election after the introduction of compulsory voting in 1925 saw 91 per cent of enrolled citizens vote and turnout has since averaged about 95 per cent since. This is seen positively by those in favour of compulsory voting, who argue that compulsion forces people to vote for politicians they feel will do the best job. But as we'll see, many people don't know who they're voting for and don't care who wins government.

Another argument for compulsory voting is that it creates citizens who are politically engaged. This book will show that this claim is completely false, with many only voting to avoid a fine, which is neither political engagement nor ethical. Making people vote may also verge on authoritarianism as the right to not vote is a basic freedom. Some argue that the majority have selected a government, therefore legitimising that government for all voters, but if many don't even know who they vote for, how can this argument stack up?

A further reason offered for compulsion is that in voluntary elections around the world it is the poor and marginalised who do not vote. In Australia, no political party can afford to ignore the poor and marginalised under compulsory voting because the poor vote. This is a solid argument in favour of compulsion but falters if these voters don't base their voting choices on accurate information. Studies continually find that many voters would vote differently if fully informed.[26–31] Indeed, studies show that a whopping 25 per cent would vote differently if they had some basic information on which to base a rational vote rather than unknowingly voting against their own interests.[29,32,33]

The final argument in favour of compulsion is that it forces to the polls those who are uninterested and have no skin in the game of politics. It is these moderate, uninterested voters who balance out the crazies from either side of politics, thereby creating a sensible centre. The argument that uninterested voters are generally moderate and maintain the ballast in our democracy, ensuring we do not tip too far to the left or right, is wrong. Every study ever done in any country has shown that many uninterested voters would be happy for democracy to be replaced by an autocratic strongman who can sort things out or "drain the swamp."[10:34–39]

It is also the case that countries that we often identify with, such as Britain, Canada, New Zealand and Ireland, do not compel their citizens to vote and are no less moderate than us. The Kiwis elected arguably the most moderate government in the world and they don't compel their citizens to vote. There is no evidence that voters who know little about politics are the saviours of our democracy.

Ian McAllister, Distinguished Professor of Political Science at ANU, argues that compelling people to vote ensures "that the least knowledgeable, who would be most likely not to vote in a voluntary system, are compelled to attend the polls."[33:266] Founder of the Australian Democrats Don Chipp was blunter, saying "compulsory voting ensured that the morons in society would stir themselves to travel to the polling booth."[23] These are the voters who decide political outcomes.

Chapter Three
Are We Interested in Politics?

'95 Per Cent Vote'—Yeah, Right

Compulsory voting makes us appear engaged and interested in politics. How often has it been boasted that 95 per cent of Australians vote? The percentage is important as voter turnout is used as a measure of engagement in the democratic process. We feel superior to the US because only 58 per cent voted in the 2016 presidential election, although this increased to 66 per cent for the highly partisan 2020 election.

How about Britain, the birthplace of the Western parliamentary system? In 2019, with the backdrop of Brexit and divisive Labour and Conservative leaders, Britain only achieved a 67 per cent turnout rate. Canada's 2019 election was even lower, with only 64 per cent taking part. A 95 per cent participation rate therefore makes Australia look pretty good.

But are Australians interested enough in politics to vote without being forced? One way to judge interest levels is to look at how many enrol to vote. Both enrolling and voting are compulsory, but only voting is enforced, simply because it's easier to check that people have voted than it is to check they have enrolled.

About 500,000 people, or three per cent of eligible Australians didn't enrol for the 2019 election, significantly better than the six per cent average between 1987 and 2019.[Annexure 3]

A great deal of our money and time has been spent by Australian Electoral Commission (AEC) officials trying to get people onto the Electoral Roll. The AEC has historically sent letters to people, rung them up, and paid celebrities to do television advertisements asking people to enrol. The AEC also attends music festivals and schoolies. Mail-outs and phone calls in 2007 cost between 6 and 7 million dollars, on top of a 29 million dollar national advertising campaign imploring people to enrol.

NSW took a different approach in 2009 and Victoria followed suit a year later by directly enrolling people for state elections based on information from lists like those from the Motor Registry Office. If someone registered their car at 2 Jones Street, Wagga Wagga, the NSW Electoral Office sent them a letter to say they were enrolled to vote in the next NSW election. The same individual would then receive a polite letter from the AEC, asking them to fill in the form supplied so they would be able to vote at the next federal election. However, 80 per cent threw the letter in the bin.

In 2012, the AEC got tired of sending forms out and not receiving replies so it followed NSW and Victoria and started enrolling individuals through such trusted sources as vehicle registration, higher education authorities and Centrelink. This meant that 95 per cent of Australians aged 18 and over were on the Electoral Roll in 2016. ABC election analyst Antony Green said this increase may have contributed to the lower voter turnout in 2016, because "you end up enrolling people who tried to avoid voting for years."[40]

By 2019, this system had captured 97 per cent of those eligible to vote, leaving a stubborn three per cent still unenrolled. The AEC proudly proclaimed the 97 per cent enrolment rate in 2019 to be a "good policy outcome from the perspective of the health of the Australian democracy."[41] But it was only achieved by directly enrolling people who hadn't bothered to enrol themselves. It's likely that if these directly enrolled voters did vote, their vote would be random. It is hard to see how this is a good outcome for Australian democracy.

Informal Votes don't Count

Another way to measure political participation and interest is to look at how many people vote formally. When voters don't complete the ballot paper as required, the vote is not counted, and it is called an informal vote. Australia has one of the world's highest rates of informal voting, with an average 4.5 per cent of informal House of Representative votes.[Annexure 4] While informal votes are used in some countries as a form of political protest when elections are rigged or otherwise unfair, every study has found this is not the case in Australia.[42–44]

Instead, the AEC continuously finds that informal votes are "the functional equivalent of abstention".[45:5] Some people resent being dragged to the polling place, and they fill in the ballot as quickly as possible with no thought of whether it is a valid vote or not, just to avoid a fine and to get back to what is really important to them.

Others take the opportunity to make fun of the whole system, by writing jokes on the ballot while others write a kebab or coffee order. The most common, though, is the drawing of phallic symbols, with one voter drawing a penis around the Senate box of the Mature Australia Party. Another well-worn joke is to add a box and the name of a celebrity, such as Beyoncé. Cosmo Kramer from the 1990s comedy Seinfeld still gets significant support in Australian elections.

Let's add up all those who don't vote. Between 1987 and 2019, an average of six per cent didn't enrol to vote, about 5.9 per cent of enrolled voters didn't show up to the voting booth to vote on election day, and another 4.5 per cent voted informally. That's a total of 16.3 per cent on average of eligible citizens not registering a formal vote between 1987 and 2019.

But it has been worse, with 21.5 per cent of citizens not registering a formal vote in the 2010 federal election.[Annexure 5] That election was so close we had a hung parliament, with Labor and the Coalition winning 72 seats each. And yet 21.5 per cent of Australians, for whatever reason, didn't enrol, vote, or vote formally.

Voter turnout in elections is therefore "virtually irrelevant"[46:33] as a way to measure our real participation in Australian politics because we are forced to vote. The boast of a 95 per cent turnout rate hides the reality of political apathy. The real lack of political interest is ignored and the causes, effects and most importantly, possible solutions to political apathy are not spoken of at all. And it gets worse.

Apathetic Donkeys

While not registering a valid vote might seem like a cop-out, it's a good option if you're not interested and know little about politics. This is because these voters don't directly influence who gets elected and what laws are passed. We all live under those laws after all. Some people, however, don't vote informal or abstain; instead, they donkey vote.

The Liberal Party advertising guru Toby Ralph said that "undecided voters despise all politicians and they probably wouldn't vote if they didn't have to, so when they turn up it's an act of punishment."[47] One way to get the punishment over as quickly as possible is to donkey vote. A donkey voter writes 1 next to the person at the top of the ballot and then continues down the ballot, writing 2, 3, 4 and so on until the final name. It's a quick and easy way for uninterested voters to fill in the ballot paper to avoid a fine and it's a clear sign of voter ignorance, incompetence and uninterest.

The sorry saga of the No Land Tax Party illustrates the impact of donkey voting.[48] This party ran in every electorate at the 2013 NSW state election, and despite lacking any public profile prior to the election, achieved an average vote of 2.9 per cent when it was listed as number one on the ballot and 1.9 per cent when it was listed elsewhere. The No Land Tax Party benefited by one per cent of donkey votes when it was listed first on the ballot paper. This might not seem like much, but with Australian elections often decided by slim margins, even this small advantage becomes crucial for who governs and represents us.

And what were the donkey voters opting for in this case? As the name suggests, the No Land Tax Party opposed land tax on investment properties in NSW. Land tax is used by the state government to pay for hospitals, roads and schools, so if the tax is cut or abolished, either these services get reduced or other taxes would be needed to make up the shortfall.

The only people to benefit from cutting land tax were property investors and it was no surprise when the party leader Peter Jones admitted the party was funded by property developers. Donkey voters writing 1 on the ballot for the No Land Tax Party were opting for a policy that would see them pay more tax to fund essential services. They voted against their own interests.

In a parallel outcome, the No Land Tax Party promised it would pay workers 30 dollars per hour to hand out its how-to-vote cards at polling booths, with bonuses for any candidates elected.

About 3,600 people signed up but the No Land Tax Party failed to get anyone elected to parliament and fell into disarray. It was deregistered by the NSW Electoral Commission, taken to court and fined over 80,000 dollars for contravening workplace laws, with their leader berated by the judge for his arrogant attitude and lack of remorse. And the workers? They never got paid.

Another example of donkey voting is the Christian Democratic Party (CDP), which has contested federal elections since 1990 in a significant number of seats. Unlike the No Land Tax Party, the CDP does have a profile and relies on partisan, evangelical Christian support but as its vote is very low, any donkey vote for the CDP is visible.

The boost the CDP receives from being top of the ballot is close to what the No Land Tax Party received from donkey votes. The CDP achieves 3.3 per cent on average when they are listed at the top of the ballot, and 2.2 per cent when they are elsewhere, giving them a 1.1 per cent boost.[Annexure 6]

An interesting aside is the way the position of names on election ballots are decided. Essentially, the AEC draws names out of a hat and if you are lucky enough to get top of the ballot, or above that of your major opponent, then you benefit from donkey votes. For politicians who win with donkey vote support, it is like winning the lottery as they earn around 200,000 dollars a year in salary.

Would We Vote If Not Compelled?

National elections aren't the only time we are asked to vote, with polls ranging from federal and state elections through to local council elections and referenda such as the 2017 gay marriage plebiscite. Some are compulsory, others are voluntary; some require voters to travel to a polling booth while others allow postal voting. Comparing turnouts in the various polls gives us another indication of who might not vote if given the choice.

Victorian council elections are compulsory, though some councils require actual attendance at the polling booth with an average 66 per cent turnout rate, while other councils require a postal vote with around 74 per cent response. Victorians are less likely to vote if they have to go to a voting booth and less likely to vote in council than federal elections even though both are compulsory. The publicity surrounding federal elections may be a factor, with many Victorians blissfully unaware of council elections.

When elections are voluntary, many Australians show what they think of politics. Tasmania manages a 57 per cent turnout in voluntary local elections, while Western Australia can only muster 35 per cent on average. South Australia did even worse when their elections were voluntary, with just 27 per cent bothering to turn up. [Annexure 7]

Political apathy also affects who stands for politics. In 2019, 38 out of the 138 Western Australian council jurisdictions didn't hold a vote because not enough candidates stood. Michael McPhail was only 20 when he stood for the East Freemantle Council. He said:

> I was pretty young and naive when I put my hand up: I didn't really know what I was doing... It turned out the main contender had been there for 50 years and I won by two votes and his two kids forgot to vote for him, so it shows how fickle and random local democracy can be. [49]

In 1998, the first voluntary federal vote in 66 years elected representatives to the Constitutional Convention to discuss whether Australia should become a republic. Less than half the voters took part. A much better response was seen in the 2017 plebiscite on gay marriage. Many objected that the public was involved in the decision, seeing it as an issue for lawmakers to decide. But people got involved in the debate with an 80 per cent postal return rate. There are several possible reasons for the remarkably high response.

One may be that voters simply had to indicate 'yes' or 'no' in a postal ballot without a trip to the voting booth involved. The extraordinary amount of publicity on the issue may have also helped perhaps because it was highly emotive. Most people know someone who is gay, making the issue more personal than is the case for many political issues. And those opposed to gay marriage were also very motivated to participate in the plebiscite.

So voting was emotionally and personally driven. Those opposed were outraged that gays would have the same rights as heterosexuals. Some right-wing religious people equated gay marriage to that of parents marrying children, or siblings marrying each other. They argued that marriage equality equalled bestiality—a Sydney train was graffitied with swastikas and homophobic slurs. Some 'Yes' voters also went to extremes, spraying 'Bash bigots' on churches, while a priest was spat on and protesters held signs saying "Burn churches not queers."

The response rate to the plebiscite was a high point in Australian political participation but most of the evidence suggests that if we stopped compelling people to vote, many Australians wouldn't vote. Voting trends in Europe suggest something similar. When the Netherlands switched to voluntary voting in 1971, voting numbers immediately dropped 16 per cent. And when Italy ended compulsion in 1994, after 12 elections averaging 93 per cent participation, turnout steadily dropped, reaching just over 70 per cent by 2018.

Hands up Those Not Interested in Politics

One of the best ways to judge interest levels is to ask people—after all we can all accurately gauge our interest in rodeos, Star Wars or crochet. Politics is no different and interest levels can be worked out by asking.

The Australian Electoral Study has done this over the past 32 years, finding that 21 per cent of voters on average were not interested in politics. [Annexure 8] While politicians, issues, policies and attitudes have changed, this figure has remained remarkably constant. It shows a determination to not be interested, no matter what the issue, no matter who is in government and no matter how people might be affected.

Other surveys show even more dire results. A 1997 AGB McNair survey found 36 per cent of women and 27 per cent of men were 'not interested in politics'[50], while a 2013 Citizens Agenda survey found 36 per cent of voters were uninterested.[51] A Guardian poll in 2019 found that 15 per cent of voters followed politics, 15 per cent had no interest and the rest were 'casual consumers' of national affairs.[52]

Of course, everyone knows something about politics; we can't help but be exposed to politics in the media, especially around election time. Election campaigns are like royal weddings or the Melbourne Cup. It's hard to avoid news about the latest royal wedding, and most of us know the name of a horse running in the Cup. Election campaigns are similar in that everyone is going to pick up some information, whether true or not.

But it's one thing to know something is happening and have some basic information about it, such as Meghan Markle being a TV star and marrying her Prince Harry, and another to know the golden wattle was chosen to represent Australia and hand-embroidered into Meghan's veil as one of the 53 flowers from each of the Commonwealth countries (ok, we googled that).

In other words, while we may have rudimentary information because we are bombarded with it in the media, it is another thing to be interested enough to find out and understand the details of an issue. Harvard University political philosopher Joseph Schumpeter noted that most voters talk about politics in a way they "would readily recognise as infantile within the sphere of their real interests."[36:262]

And politicians know that many people don't care about election campaigns.[Annexure 9] That's why elections are never timed to coincide with events that are important. Asked when the 2016 federal election would be held, Prime Minister Malcolm Turnbull said, "The general rubric is before or after the footy finals." Nothing, not even the future of the country, gets in the way of the footy.

How about by-elections? These contests are often seen as a chance for voters to pass judgment on a sitting government. The 2011 Clarence by-election is an example. Interest should have been high in the northern NSW electorate as the government had only a narrow majority and scandal had forced the sitting Nationals MP, Steve Cansdell, to resign. He had been caught speeding and tried to pull a swiftie by getting someone to sign a statutory declaration claiming they were driving. Again, Cansdell was caught.

Cansdell's heavy foot gave the good burghers in Clarence the opportunity to show the government they were either unhappy with its performance or to vote for the government to potentially receive added benefits. But the turnout was just 85 per cent with the local rag reporting that "Saturday's Clarence by-election caught some voters off guard, with some only realising the election was on when they came to town to shop."

It quoted voter Shirley Walker, who said, "I actually forgot all about it this morning, then I had to come into town for something and saw them handing out how-to-vote pamphlets. I haven't given this election much thought really."[53]

The 2018 by-elections in Western Australia similarly failed to grab the interest of voters, with only 62 per cent turning out in Perth and ten per cent of these turned out to be informal ballots. The Fremantle election was similar, with 65 per cent turning out and seven per cent voted informally.

Of course, everyone looked around for someone to blame. Labor's candidate in Perth, Patrick Gorman, blamed the AEC for the low turnout saying it "should examine the way it communicated with voters in by-elections." The AEC didn't want to take the fall saying:

> Some of the strongest factors influencing turnout rates are outside of the AEC's control…Others who share the responsibility regarding awareness of participation in the process include the media, candidates and political parties.[54]

Everyone seemed to be copping the blame except the voters who didn't turn up and didn't give a flying toss about the election or who was going to represent them. The turnout shouldn't have surprised Labor as their own research showed that the 'disengaged blue collar' voters often ignored by-elections.[55]

Cooking, Dancing, Footy, then Government

We can assume that if Australians are at all interested in politics, they will be following it in the media. In fact, half of us don't read about politics in newspapers or listen to it on the radio. Television is more important as it's the main way many of us access political information. TV is seen as the most trustworthy and has the most profound effect on uninterested voters.[56] But while 80 per cent of Australians watch the news on TV, we prefer general news, music and entertainment to political analysis, which ranks last in the news people are interested in.[57:61 Annexure 10–12]

A 2013 Roy Morgan Poll also found that less than one in five Australian voters want to read, watch or hear any political analysis.[58] And a 2019 ABC national survey of 54,000 people found that in the western suburbs of Sydney, a demographically politically apathetic area, people want the ABC "to stop talking about Canberra…talk about things that are interesting." The survey found "big parts of the community not motivated by issues that politicians talk about all day long."[59]

Peter Manning, the former executive producer of ABC current affairs program *Four Corners* and later head of current affairs at the Seven Network, said the commercial current affairs programs *A Current Affair* and the now defunct *Today Tonight*:

> would(n't) touch an interview with a politician. They know their viewers are bored with them and don't believe them. So, exit politics. And that's in an election year that may decide the fate of the country.[60]

This is the reason we don't see many political stories or shows on commercial networks. People are not interested. Television executives would rather show people competing to lose weight or out-bitching each other in forced hook-ups in exotic locations. They are the rating winners.

You might think the leaders' debates would attract viewers. Many people base their votes on the personalities of politicians and personality can be laid bare when politicians are pitted against each other. Mark Latham was thrilled with his performance in the debate against John Howard in 2004, only to later learn that more people watched a singing competition on a rival station.[61:286] "Does politics matter that much in Australia? Not really" was Latham's conclusion.[62:346]

The 2007 federal election debate should have been prime viewing as there was a strong possibility the Howard government would be defeated. However, the leaders' debate was out-rated by the game show *National Bingo Night* and an episode of *Kath & Kim* on another station.[57:34] Politics was also behind celebrity in 2010, with the time of the election debate moved to avoid clashing with *MasterChef*.

Veteran journalist George Negus noted that the "order of priorities for Australians must be cooking, dancing, football and a very poor fourth: who runs the country."[63] Things haven't improved, with the 2019 leaders' debate scheduled between the British television programs *Bargain Hunt* and the *Vicar of Dibley* and beaten in the ratings by people playing with Lego in a show called *Lego Masters*. It is not just Australia that prefers reality television to politics. The final eviction in a Big Brother series in Britain received more votes than were cast in the general election.[63]

Many use online media but more than half of us don't pay any attention to politics on the internet.[Annexure 13] Among the top Australian Google searches in 2017 were three sporting events, two electronic devices, a toy, a weather event, a shopping site and a dead musician. Politics of a kind did at least feature, with 'North Korea' among the top searches—perhaps for tips from the Supreme Leader on hairstyles or suggestions on how to deal with annoying relatives.

But with social media revolutionising the way people interact, perhaps political discussion takes place here? Apparently not. 75 per cent of Australian voters do not talk about politics online and 15 per cent rarely discuss it.[Annexure 14] Ironically, politicians are very interested in people's social media interactions. 53 Australians downloaded an IQ quiz app in 2018, which then collected the personal information of 300,000 people connected to them via social media. The company Cambridge Analytica then sold the information, along with data from millions of others, to political interests.

Chapter Four
What do We Know About Politics?

Actually, Not Much!

If you are interested in a topic you probably know a fair bit about it. If you follow rugby, for example, you're likely to know who plays half-back for your team; if rugby isn't your cup of tea you may have never even heard the term. A rugby fan doesn't support a team thinking they are going to influence the outcome of a match—though side-line dads at kids' games often have other ideas. Most sport fans are content to take an interest in and barrack for their favourite team.

It's the same in politics. People who are interested are reasonably knowledgeable about politics and generally partisan about who they support. They enjoy finding out about candidates and the machinations of government, and they love deriding the other side. The chances of them influencing electoral outcomes are about the same as the sporting fan influencing the grand final: practically zero. But because of their interest, they develop political knowledge which is useful when voting. The more information we have, the better chance our decision at the ballot box will be a rational one.

In contrast, political ignorance is a good indication of apathy towards politics. People who know little about community affairs or about local, state and national government are usually those with little interest in these matters. Uninterested voters are, therefore, less likely to have rational and consistent attitudes towards political issues or parties.

Studies consistently show that politically uninterested voters are also less likely to support democracy, are less tolerant, more fearful and mistrusting of the political process.[10:34,35,37–39,64] In other countries, these people stay away from the polling booth, so their lack of knowledge has no effect on election outcomes. But in Australia, those who know next to nothing about politics must vote.

And the lack of political knowledge among voters runs deep. Studies conducted in the 1960s concluded many within the Australian electorate are "almost completely unable to judge the rationality of government actions, knowing little of the particular policies and what has led to them."[65]

Researchers found few people had any idea of policy differences between the parties. For most Australians, politics was "simply a vacancy, an unused space" as "Australians do not participate with any degree of vigour in almost any form of political behaviour; in fact, the political apathy of most respondents was the picture, which emerged most clearly."[66:109]

A 1970s study in Brisbane similarly found that knowledge of politics was "minimal"[67:328] while another study concluded that "most electors have a very limited knowledge…in some respects they are almost incredibly ignorant."[68:432]

Indeed, every study on political interest in Australia has reported similar findings. The AES found that in 2013, 46 per cent didn't know who their federal representative was, 45 per cent didn't know which party they were from,[Annexure 15] and 42 per cent didn't know which party finished second at the 2013 election. Only two parties can win elections in Australia, Labor or the Coalition.

If nearly half of us didn't know who finished second, it suggests that nearly half of us didn't know who won,[Annexure 16] or don't know that only two parties can win. In 2015, paramedics stopped asking patients if they knew who the prime minister was to gauge the patients "competency, alertness and capacity to make informed decisions." If they did ask, they often had to provide clues such as "it's not the bloke with the big ears."[69]

A 2009 Neilson News poll found that 95 per cent could not name the Deputy Prime Minister.[70] Admittedly, Warren Truss *was* forgettable. This poll did highlight what people *were* interested in, with 60 per cent able to name two songs by Lady Gaga and 50 per cent knowing that Erin McNaught was a Miss Universe contestant.[71]

A later Lonegan poll found that Truss's successor Michael McCormack fared the same—95 per cent had no idea who he was when he became deputy prime minister in 2018. He deserves to be better known. When editor of Wagga Wagga's *Daily Advertiser,* McCormack wrote that:

a week never goes by anymore that homosexuals and their sordid behaviour don't become further entrenched in society... Unfortunately gays are here and, if the disease their unnatural acts helped spread doesn't wipe out humanity, they're here to stay.[72]

His views on gays didn't stop him from obtaining the small business ministership and overseeing the move for the census to be held online, an abject failure that led to McCormack's promotion to deputy prime minister.

State politics is no different. Liberal leader Barry O'Farrell lost nearly half of his bodyweight in order to appeal to NSW voters and went on to rout Labor in 2011. Yet only 18 months later a Galaxy poll found 38 per cent of NSW voters didn't know the Premier's name, including a third of those who voted for his party.[73]

This trend continued for the 2015 NSW election with two-thirds of voters unable to name the NSW opposition leader and a third unable to name the Premier. Nine per cent thought it was slim, trim Barry, even though he'd resigned after being caught lying to the Independent Commission Against Corruption (ICAC).[74] The concerning thing was that this poll was taken just 12 days before the election.

Lonergan research also found that even though Victoria was due to go to the polls in less than 10 weeks, almost half of Victorians didn't know who the Premier was, with 68 per cent unable to identify the opposition leader. It was a similar story in Queensland: 71 per cent couldn't identify opposition leader Annastacia Palaszczuk, yet she was elected just weeks later. The poll's author, Chris Lonergan, concluded, "We are certainly not a nation of informed voters."[70]

It's not just the politicians we don't have a clue about. Surveys show "the majority know relatively little about politics and possess minimal factual knowledge about the operation of the political system."[75:56] This is reflected in people's self-assessment of their political knowledge, with just 20 per cent believing they are equipped to participate in politics.[Annexure 17]

But it's not true that most people are incapable of participating. Nearly all of us could understand political issues if we had the motivation to do so. Therein lies the problem. With more than a quarter of voters not caring who wins elections,[Annexure 18] why would they bother finding out who they should vote for?

How about referendums? These should be more straightforward as there is only one question asked. Yet, two thirds of voters believe referendums are too complicated. If they think referendums are too complicated, then it's clear the myriad of issues thrown at them in general elections and in day-to-day politics are way out of their league.

The 1999 referendum on whether Australia should become a republic failed because voters didn't fully understand the issue. One in two voters didn't know that the queen appointed the governor-general, or that the governor-general has the power to sack a government. If voters don't understand the issues, then it is natural to opt for the status quo, especially if the dominant message they are receiving is to avoid change. No wonder the republic referendum failed, as have 36 of the 44 referendums since federation.

Given the close relationship between interest and knowledge, it's not surprising that those who are uninterested in politics know the least about it. Just 37 per cent of voters who say they are uninterested in politics can name their local MP and in 2016, almost 9 out of 10 uninterested voters didn't know about proportional representation in the Senate.

Chapter Five
Voter Shortcuts

Is this lack of political knowledge a problem? One school of thought is that voters don't actually need much political knowledge as they can use several information short-cuts to help them make rational political choices. One shortcut is voting for someone based on ideology, another is voting for a party because they support a specific policy while a third is basing your vote on the person you most like.

Bogans Versus Hippies

Ideology sounds dry and boring to most people, although common stereotypes such as 'red-neck bogan' and 'hippie leftist' are attempts to capture positions on the ideological spectrum, even if they aren't exactly accurate. Some adapt the caricature to suit a narrative of their making. When the Greens started winning inner-city electorates, the Murdoch press switched its portrayal of left-wing people from that of dole-seeking bludgers, smoking dope and living in communes to one of latte-sipping elites out of touch with hard-working families. There was little irony in how the left was transformed from bums to elites overnight.

The terms 'left-wing' and 'right-wing' originated in France in 1789 when the French peasants were revolting. They were unhappy at taxes, which were so high they couldn't afford to buy bread. With Queen Marie Antoinette's suggested alternative of cake not going down well, meetings were arranged at the palace of Versailles to sort things out.

The peasants' representatives (it was really bourgeoisie representatives because no one trusted the peasants to elect proper representatives), nobles and the clergy gathered to debate the issues. The nobles and clergy grouped themselves together to the right of the King and supported the King's entrenched privileges and powers. They couldn't understand the peasants' grievances and argued that peasants needed to trust conservative practice and listen to the wise instruction of the King. After all, he was anointed by God.

The peasants' representatives grouped themselves to the left of the King and made the case for change. They argued the aristocracy and church had taken the peasants for granted, making decisions that only benefited those in power. They believed wealth should be more evenly distributed and the aristocracy and clergy should pay for themselves.

Baron de Gauville said, "We began to recognise each other: Those who were loyal to religion and the King took up positions to the right of the chair so as to avoid the shouts, oaths, and indecencies that enjoyed free rein in the opposing camp."[76] It seems that the left, even at this early point, were painted as vulgar.

At this stage, the terms 'left' and 'right' were simply seating arrangements. French newspapers later began referring to the 'progressive left' and 'traditionalist right' in the French assembly and by the 1850s the terms left and right had entered the French vernacular as shorthand for opposing political ideologies. The next step was that political parties began self-identifying as being on the left or right.

Why would some rely on ideology to help them vote? The argument goes that politics is complicated and it takes time and effort to work out what is going on. It's therefore simpler to take a shortcut by working out your personal ideology and then find a party with similar ideology and lock them in as the party to support.

The problem here is that the voter must actually have an ideology. Doing this in the old days seemed more straight forward. Political positions were closely tied to political cleavages such as class and religion. It was pretty much a given in the 1950s that if you were poor or Catholic you supported Labor and if you were better off or Protestant you supported the Liberals. For those living in rural areas, it was the Country Party. These social identifications provided a powerful incentive for people to be politically interested, support a party and vote.

But these gulfs have become blurred and the bonds between individuals and political parties have weakened. Ideological divides are more muddled now. An example are the 'Howard battlers', the poor, lower class western Sydney people supporting the Liberals. Or the well-off, educated inner city types voting Labor or the Greens. The political world seems to have turned on its head since grandma's time.

Still, those interested in politics find it relatively easy to place themselves and parties on an ideological scale. Not so for the uninterested. The AES has asked respondents since 1996: "In politics, people sometimes talk about the 'left' and the 'right. Where do you place yourself on a scale from 0 to 10, where 0 means the 'left' and 10 means the 'right'?" About 15 per cent of respondents, on average, didn't answer the question. Research indicates this is likely because respondents didn't understand the question.[77]

For those who did answer, 39 per cent selected, on average, the middle (5), which was by far the most commonly selected.[Annexure 19] The respondents in this group might view themselves in the middle and hold moderate views, or they didn't understand the terms and chose the middle so as not to appear foolish. Support for this interpretation comes from a study across 8 countries which found that a lack of political interest "generates the highest predicted probability to be in the middle of the scale."[78:190]

Hanson the Leftie

If a voter can place themselves on the left-right scale, the next step is to locate a political party that matches their position. Parties are generally on one side or the other of the scale and research shows the general perception of party positions closely matches expert views. The Greens are way to the left and with no possibility of gaining power they can advocate idealistic ideas from the side-lines. Labor was created by working people and is still dominated by trade unions. This makes them historically left-wing, a position they have generally stuck to.

The ideological term 'liberal' is defined as "willing to respect or accept behaviour or opinions different from one's own; open to new ideas." If the Liberal Party acted as its name suggests, it would be on the left of politics. Instead, it is on the right, advocating conservative social policies and values. It is also right-wing economically, with strong support from business.

The Nationals are the interesting ones. They are socially conservative, with a heavy preponderance towards God, guns, white people and traditional values. Economically though, things are less clear-cut. When it comes to country areas and farmers, they're all for government subsidies and state support for primary industries. This is why the Nationals are sometimes called "agrarian socialists". On most matters though, Nationals are generally considered to be way to the right.

The only significant party further to the right than the Nationals is One Nation. These guys are so far to the right there's a danger of putting your neck out when you turn to view them. One Nation is heavily focused on how people look. Initially, Pauline Hanson was terrified Asians would swamp the country. These days, it's

Muslims populating her nightmares. One Nation is almost a caricature, with strongly xenophobic views towards non-white ethnicities, and a big love of nationalism, God (just the Christian one, thank you!) and guns.

It's clear where our political parties stand ideologically, but not all Aussie voters have a grip on this. In response to the AES question asking respondents to identify political parties on the left-right scale, about a third of people who identify as uninterested in politics thought that Labor, the Liberals, the Nationals, the Greens and One Nation were all centrist parties.[Annexure 20]

These results may be influenced by the notion that people don't want to identify themselves as extreme, but it's more likely a significant number of voters don't understand the idea of ideology.

Some voters can't even pick which side the major parties are on. Despite it being the main party of the left, 22 per cent view Labor as a right-wing party, while 17 per cent on average view the Liberals and Nationals as left-wing. A quarter of voters viewed the Liberals as a left-wing party in 2007, even though the Howard government had epitomised hard-right policies since 1996: leaping into the war in Iraq, demonising refugees, introducing right-wing labour laws such as Work Choices, and refusing to ratify the Kyoto Protocol.[Annexure 21]

As many voters can't place the major parties on the correct ideological side, it's no surprise they have no clue where the minor parties sit. Fifteen per cent believe the Greens are right-wing and 32 per cent think One Nation is left-wing. In fact, 15 per cent are convinced One Nation is an extreme left-wing party. Many voters, especially the apathetic, won't be able to take a shortcut and vote according to political ideology.

Kyoto Protocol? I'll Have the Sushi

For a lot of voters, ideology doesn't get a look in. A Nepali friend said he liked the Nepalese communist politician Prachanda. Then he revealed he was also a fan of the Indian Prime Minister Narendra Modi, an ultra-nationalist Hindu right-winger. Ideologically, you could not imagine two more different characters and yet our friend supported both. The reason for his support was both men had managed to lower the price of onions. Their ideology was irrelevant—their actions directly benefited our friend and his family.

He was making use of another voting shortcut: using one issue to guide voting. In this scenario, voters only need to know about the issue they care about, work out where the political parties stand on this issue and vote accordingly. For this method to work however, the voter must be interested in an issue, hold an opinion about it, and understand which party or candidate holds the same view.

There are issues on which Labor and the Coalition strongly disagree. One is climate change. The Howard government refused to ratify the Kyoto Protocol, and did little to mitigate carbon emissions. Jessica Rudd, daughter of former Labor PM Kevin Rudd, revealed in 2020 that, "when we moved into the Lodge in 2007, the sole remaining disc in the DVD player was *The Great Global Warming Swindle.*" Tony Abbott, leader of the Liberal Party from 2009 to 2015 and prime minister for three of those years, said, "climate science is crap" and Scott Morrison even brought a lump of coal into parliament claiming there was nothing to be afraid of.

Labor, conversely, accepted the science of global warming, ratified the Kyoto Protocol when Rudd defeated Howard, and instituted measures to tackle carbon emissions. The climate change issue escalated after the 2010 election, when Labor joined with the Greens and Independents to introduce a carbon tax.

The Coalition used the carbon tax to scare voters, with the issue dominating political discourse over the next three years. Regaining power in 2013, the Coalition scrapped the carbon tax and abolished the Climate Commission, an independent body established in 2011 by the Gillard government to communicate "reliable and authoritative information" about climate change in Australia.

The difference between the parties couldn't have been clearer on an issue which has dominated headlines for years. Yet, 56 per cent of voters at the 2016 election didn't know the difference between the major parties on global warming.[Annexure 22] *Daily Telegraph* readers probably represent a large chunk of these as 38 per cent thought the Kyoto Protocol was the treaty that ended World War II while another 14 per cent thought it was a Japanese banquet.[79:264]

Ironically, the 2019 ABC survey found that climate change was the leading 'worry' among respondents; 72 per cent were worried about climate change, leaving all other issues in its wake, and yet Australia voted a party into power that does not believe in climate change science and does nothing to help mitigate its effect. Even Malcolm Turnbull agreed saying in December 2019, "the Liberal party has just proved itself incapable of dealing with the reduction of greenhouse gas emissions in any sort of systemic way."[80]

Industrial relations is another major ideological divide. The very basis of the Labor Party lies in industrial relations and it has remained intimately attached to unions for over 100 years. Former union leaders Bob Hawke, Simon Crean and

Bill Shorten have led the party and trade union officials make up nearly half of all Labor parliamentarians.

About half of the delegates at Labor conferences are union officials and affiliated unions donate huge sums of money to the party and are intricately involved in policy decisions. In contrast, the Coalition has long-standing ties to business. The differences between Labor and the Coalition regarding industrial relations should be easy to spot for any voter vaguely interested in politics.

Industrial relations became particularly prominent at the 2007 federal election after Howard introduced Work Choices in 2006, making it easier for smaller companies to sack workers. Work Choices also restricted a workforce's ability to legally go on strike and significantly restricted trade union activity. The passing and implementation of Work Choices was strongly opposed by Labor and the unions. They argued the laws stripped away basic employee rights and were fundamentally unfair. Trade unions ran television advertisements attacking the new laws and Labor vowed to abolish Work Choices, which it subsequently did.

While industrial relations hogged the spotlight in 2007, every election has seen major differences in industrial relations policy between the major parties. This issue affects many workers, especially those in lower socio-economic groups as they are more likely to have poorer workplace conditions. Yet, in 2016, 39 per cent could not pick differences between Labor and the Coalition on industrial relations.[Annexure 23] That's nearly 4 out of 10 voters who didn't know the most fundamental difference between the major parties.

The 2004 Iraq War provides the starkest example of differences in party policy, with the Coalition government only too willing to follow the US into war, while Labor opposed this. Howard claimed his decision was "right, it is legal, it is directed towards the protection of the Australian national interest" while Labor leader Simon Crean said joining the war was "unnecessary, reckless and against Australia's national interests." And yet, 28 per cent of voters didn't know Labor and the Coalition had different policies on the war.[Annexure 24] Climate change, industrial relations and the Iraq war are just three examples; there is a similar lack of awareness of party positions across every issue you can imagine.

It is uninterested voters who are the least able to differentiate between the policies of the major parties,[Annexure 25–27] so they wouldn't know which party was closest to their own view—if they had one. Because many voters don't know or understand the policies on offer by parties, it's a stretch for a government to claim they have a mandate for any subsequent decisions made. Any government spruiking the idea that their policies represent "the will of the people" is talking rubbish.

Budgie Smugglers, Strip Clubs, and Gastric Bypasses

Many apathetic voters take another shortcut and base their vote on the personality of a politician, especially the leader. This is the second most common way of deciding how to vote. Only family tradition—people voting the same way as their parents—provides a stronger influence.[81:416] We all have some interest in political personalities, although we base our impressions on different things. Apathetic voters can't choose a personality to support based on what a politician says and does, as they don't have the necessary information. Instead, they might be swayed by how the politician looks—a single action, a clothing style or perhaps the footy team the politician supports.

Tony Abbott's budgie smugglers drew people's attention. A friend who competed in triathlons voted for Abbott because he was fit, healthy and did triathlons. She knew little about his policies or ideology, she simply saw a fit, sporty guy as being good for the nation.

Low socio-economic voters identify with Pauline Hanson. The 1996 *60 Minutes* interview in which she replied "please explain" when the interviewer used the term xenophobia, made her look stupid in the eyes of many but played nicely with lower socio-economic, uninterested voters who saw commonality. The punters liked Kevin Rudd and the love only seemed to grow when he was thrown out of power by Gillard. Turnbull was painted as an upper crust snob, and Bill Shorten was portrayed as the most boring guy you could possibly encounter.

It is very human to base impressions of political personalities on looks and snippets of information. For those who are apathetic about politics it becomes the predominant way to judge politicians, with voting treated more like a popularity contest. Choose someone you like and let them get on with it. While this seems a risky way of deciding who to vote for, one political theory backs it up. The *Trustee Theory of Representation* goes back to the scion of conservative thought, British politician Edmund Burke, who was the representative for Bristol in 1774.

Burke argued that a voter's only role was to choose a representative of superior judgment and virtue. Essentially, this was someone the voter thought of as better than them, a kind of natural aristocracy. Once the voter chose a representative, they should leave the representative to get on with it and make any decision they thought was correct. Burke thought this worked well for both the voter and the representative. The representative had free reign, while the voter could get back to things that would have occupied a typical voter in 1744, such as father and son spending quality time hunting foxes. Unfortunately for Burke, the electors of Bristol didn't agree and tossed him out at the next election.

While things didn't go so well for Burke, the tradition of finding someone you like and voting for them is alive and well. It may sound a little far-fetched but research shows that politicians who are physically attractive garner around one per cent extra vote.[82] Turns out we all think symmetrical faces are more attractive and we prefer men who have strong features and women with fine features.

Psychologists refer to the beauty effect as 'thin slicing': we make snap judgements based on a small amount of information. When we know very little about a person, we tend to base this judgment on how good looking they are. This means that voters with minimal knowledge of politics rely heavily on how someone looks.[82]

Politicians like Natasha Stott Despoja or Tania Plibersek undoubtedly benefited from this as did Julie Bishop, while Anthony Albanese and Peter Dutton may well struggle. Julia Gillard may have struggled as well as she told the story of campaigning at a shopping centre while standing next to a poster displaying her photo:

> This old guy comes out of the supermarket, looks at the photo, looks at me, looks at the photo, then turns back to me and says, "Taken on a good day, was it love?" I said, "And you'd be bloody Robert Redford, would you mate?"[82]

With uninterested voters lacking basic political information, the way a politician looks and sounds becomes as significant as what they say. Perception matters more than reality. Politicians set about making themselves look as good as possible in the mass media. So we find them on commercial television shows such as *Sunrise* or popular FM radio shows like *The Kyle and Jacki O Show*. People who tune in to such shows find politics presented in a personable, humorous way, with one viewer stating he watched "cos I'm not really into politics at all, but it aims at a level you can understand."[83:186]

Women's magazines are another target, with Labor campaign strategist Bruce Hawker saying they "have been an important part of any serious politician's strategy, whether they are male or female, for a long time."[84] Presumably, Hawker defines "serious" as those politicians seeking to become better known to the apathetic section of society.[85]

Television provides the greatest exposure and politicians do silly things on light entertainment television shows to personalise themselves. Using his weight to advantage, Joe Hockey gave an impression of Shrek, complete with green pointy ears. Clearly on a roll, he then flounced around on primetime TV to Abba's *Dancing Queen*, complete with crown, tutu and magic wand. This was before he went to extremes with gastric bypass surgery to appeal to even more voters.

Cheryl Kernot danced the cha-cha and Peter Costello did the Macarena. Natasha Stott-Despoja seemed to be forever appearing on light entertainment shows, probably because she was young, attractive and charismatic. Max Walsh, the veteran Canberra journalist, wrote that Stott-Despoja had "that quality Paul Keating identified as necessary for a leader—the ability to throw to vaudeville."[86:159]

Rudd regularly appeared on music-oriented FM radio shows as well as *Sunrise*. When criticised for not appearing on more serious political shows, Rudd's response was, "Guess what? There's a whole bunch of people out there…who don't watch *Insiders* but do listen to FM radio. And my job as the alternative prime minister is to communicate with the entire country."[83:179] Rudd knew the audience for shows like these were more likely to be politically uninterested and easily influenced. Gillard went as far as employing comedian Corrine Grant to help inject some humour into her speeches.

In 2016, Bill Shorten appeared on Kyle and Jackie O, with listeners discovering he had never had sex with a washing machine or worn woman's underwear. If apathetic voters found this amusing, they might see Shorten as a likeable person and base their vote on his ability to be funny on radio. Shows like this can be as important as anything else done throughout an election campaign. In another attempt to polish Shorten's image, the Labor Party spent 60,000 dollars on stylists and new wardrobes for the Labor leader and his wife leading up to the 2016 federal election.

When prime ministers and opposition leaders trudge into the most politically apathetic areas of the country, namely rural and outback Australia, they know they must look the part, so almost without exception don an Akubra hat. Never mind that they rarely venture out of the city; having an Akubra goes a long way to show the locals they are one of them.

Bob Hawke could pull it off because he always seemed at one with the people but whenever John Howard headed bush in his Akubra he looked out of place. Kevin Rudd didn't fare any better and Julia Gillard in an Akubra? She just looked silly.

Malcolm Turnbull came across as a merchant banker casting his eye over a hobby farm bought to minimise tax while Bill Shorten's Akubra looked brand new. A staffer should have thrown it under a Melbourne bus to give it that authentic feel. One politician that refused to wear the Akubra was Paul Keating—he must have thought it would clash with his Ermenegildo Zegna suits.

With his advertising background, Scott Morrison understands the importance of image, although things didn't always go so well for him. He orchestrated the advertising campaign to attract tourists to Australia that featured Lara Bingle's "So where the bloody hell are ya?" The campaign was an absolute disaster which Morrison defended until he was sacked by the Liberal Minister Fran Bailey because he had kept information from the board, breached procurement guidelines, and had given jobs to private companies without the paper work and appropriate value-for-money assessments.[87] After being sacked, Morrison worked out he was eminently qualified for politics.

As immigration minister, Morrison painted himself as the hard man clad in a dark suit who stopped the boats and sent refugees to Nauru. He falsely accused staff at the charity Save the Children of coaching refugees to harm themselves and had to pay compensation. He brandished coal as a prop in parliament, abstained from all the marriage equality votes, voted against the banking Royal Commission 26 times and turned into a stern miser on becoming Treasurer.

Every turn in Morrison's political career was brutal, with his nickname at one point being Rottweiler. Morrison even had his arm around Malcolm Turnbull while doing the numbers behind his back. On becoming prime minister though, Morrison reinvented himself as 'Scomo' the daggy dad who wears comfy polo shirts and baseball caps, using phrases like "fair dinkum", and eating meat pies while watching his beloved Cronulla Sharks do battle. This makes Morrison appear more relatable and understanding of the day-to-day life and struggles of the average Aussie. This was also a savvy way to differentiate himself from Malcolm Turnbull and recast the Liberal Party as a party for the everyday person rather than just the rich. Ms. Singh, a self-confessed 'quiet Australian' commented, "I'm probably more swayed by the fact that he has said, or someone has said, he's just a guy from western Sydney (Morrison was from the eastern suburbs) with a mortgage like everyone else," while Mr. Diwakar said, "I have great respect for him...he's a sharks supporter. He's a rugby league man. He's a churchgoer."[88]

In 2020, Morrison went even further with his everyman persona when a photo of him was 'found' dressed in a suit jacket and tie but with shorts and thongs on. This showed everyone that Scomo was really a man of the people and only dressed formally above the navel for TV appearances.

In their attempts to appeal to the ordinary people, things can sometimes go wrong for our politicians. Kim Beazley lost the ALP leadership in part because he expressed condolences over Karl Rove losing his partner. His mistake was confusing the American political strategist Karl Rove with the Australian entertainer Rove McManus, whose partner had just died.

Another way politicians make themselves more likeable is with personal background stories to make them seem just like the average voter. Pauline Hansen has been extraordinarily successful with this but she probably pulled it off because she owned a fish and chip shop, left school at 15 and became pregnant soon after. These are all things her supporters can identify with.

Malcolm Turnbull always struggled with the idea he was a rich toff but he made concerted efforts to point out he grew up without a mother. Rudd made hay out of a poor childhood with his share crop father dying when Rudd was 11 and his family having to leave the farm. The Coalition recognised that this story was powerful and therefore accused Rudd of lying about his childhood. Gillard emphasised her working-class roots and Abbott spent a lot of the 2016 election with his daughters by his side, which inevitably softened his persona with women.

Bill Shorten drew on his mother for inspiration, citing how she was the first in his family to go to university and only did it as a mature age student because she had to support her family. The Murdoch press knew it was a compelling story so during the 2019 election campaign they attacked Shorten for not saying that his mother went on to have a successful career as a barrister. Shorten's tearful response defending his mum on national television boosted his image as a caring kind of guy.

We all like someone we can personally identify with and respect someone who does it a bit tough. Politicians play on this by offering up airbrushed excerpts from their personal stories to appeal to uninterested voters who would otherwise take no notice.

In Tune with Voters

Music is also a way to connect with voters. If voters think you are hip and trendy and on board with the music they like, then it may get you some votes. Rudd's Chief of Staff Lachlan Harris said his offices sat down and chose a band (Rudd) liked. They settled on Powderfinger and then for the remaining three years of his prime ministership Rudd was briefed on their new songs. When Rudd went on light entertainment shows, he was also advised on what was in the top ten, who was winning the footy and who was twerking.[47]

But Malcolm Turnbull got off key with voters when he was unable to name his favourite AC/DC song during a radio interview. The story ran on every news outlet and realising the damage it could do, the prime minister's office went on the offensive by asking voters to name their favourite Australian songs. Perhaps they were expecting Redgum's *Only 19* or Midnight Oil's *Blue Sky Mining*. Instead, they received Joe Dolce's *Shaddap you face* and Skyhooks' *Why don't you all get fucked*. Turnbull struck more trouble during the Commonwealth Games by not knowing the lyrics to John Farnham's classic song *You're the Voice*.

Morrison appeared guilty of over-sharing in 2019 when he shared details with FM listeners of his first pash. He also released an 11-hour, 146 song tribute to all that he loved about the 1980s. It seems Scomo didn't really like Aussie music as it included just one Australian song, Wa Wa Nee's *Stimulation*, to which Morrison received a tweet: "I'm the guitarist in Wa Wa Nee. What an embarrassment to have any association with this disgraceful government."

So Morrison released his favourite 1980s Aussie playlist of 87 songs. That list also hit a sour note as Morrison included only one female artist, Martha Johnson, from *Martha and the Muffins*, who just happened to be Canadian. In all likelihood, an aide compiled the song list as quickly as they could to make Morrison look cool and musical.

Food, Sports and Fashion: Disaster or Success?

Food can also be a politician's undoing. Perhaps the most famous incident is US President Gerald Ford eating a tamale at a campaign stop in San Antonia, Texas, in 1976. Tamales are a popular Hispanic food wrapped in corn husks. To eat one, you remove the corn husk and eat the inside. Ford didn't know this and tried downing the whole thing, nearly choking in the process.

The blunder dominated the media for days and showed Hispanic voters how little Ford knew of their culture. Ford went on to lose the state of Texas and the presidency to the Democrat Jimmy Carter, with many putting the loss down to the humble tamale.

In 2014, Britain's Labour leader Ed Miliband had problems eating a bacon sandwich, with a photographer taking a particularly silly photo of Miliband appearing to choke on the sanger. The photo led the front page of *The Sun,* the most popular paper in the UK.

The Daily Mirror claimed the photo made him "look a fool" while *The Independent* wrote that "despite extensive stage managing and with a seemingly simple task at hand, the Labour leader still struggled in his bid to look normal and back in touch with the general public." It was argued that if Miliband couldn't eat a sandwich like a 'normal' person then he was unfit for office. It seems the voters agreed.

British Prime Minister David Cameron was caught eating a hot dog with a knife and fork, a story which dominated British and international news. Imagine the reaction if an Australian politician used a knife and fork to eat a meat pie. Oh wait, that's what Malcolm Turnbull did during a 2018 by-election in Tasmania. 'Pie-gate' dominated media around the country and even went international. It reinforced the common view that Turnbull had no hope of relating to ordinary Aussies.

Another comestible delight that's caused trouble for the luminaries of Australian politics is the sausage sizzle (we're not a nation of culinary giants). Turnbull got himself into more trouble when he refused to eat a sausage sandwich when visiting flood-ravaged Lismore in 2017, while Shorten made a fool of himself in 2016 by eating his sausage sandwich sideways. Yes, this all makes news.

These stories get worse. Kevin Rudd was caught on camera in Parliament House eating his own ear wax. He laughed it off as him just picking his teeth, but it had the potential to derail his 2007 election campaign. And perhaps the strangest was Tony Abbott eating a raw, unpeeled onion in 2015, confirming for many that Abbott was weird. Even two years after he was tossed out as prime minister, Abbott was being asked why he did it, and he finally admitted it wasn't one of his proudest moments.

And just to show how focused Morrison was on image, while visiting a carrot farm he was asked to eat a carrot, to which he replied "No." We must return to the 1980s for a positive image, with Bob Hawke endearing himself to average Aussies for his ability to drink a lot of beer. His most notable achievement prior to becoming prime minister was downing 2.5 litters of beer in 11 seconds, a feat immortalised by the *Guinness Book of Records.*

Sport also has the potential to endear politicians to the Australian public. The Queensland Premier took time out of his busy schedule to complain that XXXX wouldn't be served at a Gabba cricket match and Bob Hawke endeared himself to every dinky di Aussie when he declared after the America's Cup win in 1983 that "any boss who sacks anyone for not turning up today is a bum."

During the 2000 Olympics, John Howard turned up to any sport when Australia had a chance of winning a medal, while Kevin Rudd flew to Beijing to bask in the glory of the athletes there. Gillard wasn't nearly as astute, copping criticism for not attending the London Olympics and going on holiday instead. Even Abbott was uncharacteristically subdued at the time. It seems both sides knew that discussing politics during the Olympics was pointless.

Morrison and Albanese are only too happy to show their support for local league teams, Cronulla Sharks for Morrison, and the Rabbitohs for Albanese. Morrison was so keen to demonstrate this that he attended a match during the Covid-19 outbreak. Funnily enough, before moving to the rugby league Shire area, he was a rugby man.

While Turnbull usually failed miserably in portraying himself as a man of the people, he made no mistake when he described as a "shocking disappointment," the Australian cricketers' attempts to scuff up the ball with sandpaper during a Test against South Africa. To a dispassionate observer, a few scratches on a ball might be less concerning than politicians stealing taxpayer money or the promotion of policies that benefit a few but harm the country's interests. But the cricketing incident was politically important as every Australian had an opinion and it benefited Turnbull to echo the thoughts of most Australians on the issue. It showed politically apathetic Australians that he understood a significant cultural matter.

Sport can be a mine field for politicians who have little real interest in it. Paul Keating, who would much prefer to be at a Wagnerian opera, claimed to be a keen Aussie Rules Collingwood fan but his credibility took a hit when he hoped Collingwood would score a try or two. He wasn't much better with league, congratulating player Steve 'Blocker' Roach, who he said had "kicked a lot of tries."[89]

When Turnbull yet again mixed up his football codes, calling the Sydney Roosters rugby league team an Aussie Rules team, one voter stated he was "totally un-Australian" while another said, "This man wants to be Prime Minister and he doesn't know anything about our national sport."[90]

Former NSW Premier Bob Carr also knew the political value of sport but got himself in trouble when he predicted NSW would beat Victoria in a State of Origin rugby league game (State of Origin is between NSW and Queensland). Carr felt forced to attend the game to show apathetic voters that he was one of them. It didn't work; he was spotted in the crowd reading a Tolstoy novel.

Fashion can also be important, with female politicians receiving much more scrutiny than males. The excessive attention paid to Julia Gillard's appearance is a clear example. She was criticised for wearing bold colours and when she retreated to white for safety, the *Courier Mail* tallied at least six variations on the white jacket theme, including the 'photo-op' jacket, the 'big event' jacket, and the 'serious policy' jacket. Gillard pointed out that:

> Most women who spend a lot of time worrying about what they're wearing want other people to comment on it and to say how well dressed they are. I spend a lot of time having to worry about what I'm wearing so no one comments on it.[91]

It didn't work, with image consultant Imogen Lamport complaining, "I don't think Julia Gillard is that interested in clothes…If we are distracted by your appearance, we are not listening to what you say." Gillard tried redoing her hair and even turned to wearing glasses rather than contacts. But it's easier to have an opinion on what someone wears and how they look than what they say.

Gillard also suffered because she was unmarried and had no children. Displacing Rudd was portrayed as 'back-stabbing' and 'disloyal' while Turnbull's rolling of Abbott was championed as taking the reins. With opinion polls going heavily against Gillard before the 2013 election, Labor reinstated the more popular Rudd.

Polls immediately improved, especially in the more demographically uninterested areas. The Blaxland electorate in western Sydney, one of the most apathetic electorates in the country, improved more than any other seat, with an overnight jump of 11 per cent.[92]

Given apathetic voters' lack of political knowledge, it is unsurprising they base their vote on who they like the most. Character traits are, however, something most of us are ill-equipped to judge as we can only go on a small amount of information, which is highly filtered. Think about how we all liked Rolf Harris or how Mel Gibson suddenly went from a great Australian to drunken anti-Semite. Politicians are the same in that we really know very little about them.

The public liked Rudd while his colleagues despised him. Barnaby Joyce enjoyed enormous support as he came across as a salt-of-the-earth bloke who didn't mince words. He was the ultimate retail politician, good with handshakes, family values and snags on the barbie. Turns out 'family values' really were his forte after it was revealed the married father of four fathered a child with a woman 17 years his junior. And everyone loved Hawkie, the larrikin who also happened to be a chronic drunk and womaniser. Years later, Hawke acknowledged that his infidelity remained secret because he had "staff and security people and so on who were dedicated to me." Would the public have voted for a serial adulterer in the early 1980s if they had known?

The personalisation of politics is appealing, not only for voters but for parties and political leaders. The shortcut it provides saves the voter time and gives them someone to hold to account for any mistakes, rather than a more complex bureaucracy or political system. For political parties, it is easier to promote a personality than to explain policy. And leaders benefit when they are in power as their position implies a personal endorsement from the electorate that gives them more influence within the party.

The trouble with voting based on personality is that uninformed voters might choose someone because they like them, only to suffer from their mismanagement or corruption. For the broader public, a focus on personality instead of policy has the potential to trivialise democracy as people base their vote on ill-informed judgments about someone's personality.

The focus on personality hurts us in other ways too. Long-term nuanced policy gets waylaid in the battle to find a popular leader. We have seen plenty of this in the past 10 years. Governing has taken a back seat as parties bicker about the person most likely to appeal to voters. How much time and energy was wasted by the Labor and Liberal parties deciding to toss Gillard, Abbott and Turnbull out in favour of Rudd, Turnbull and Morrison? If personalities were not so important, the parties could have spent more time running the country.

Another concern is that traditional Westminster cabinet responsibility is undermined by prime ministers who claim they have a personal mandate from the people, resulting in power becoming centralised in their office. The popularity of the government then depends on the popularity of the prime minister, leading to prime ministers becoming more powerful and the governing model edges closer to the dictatorships we belittle.

This leads to voters and politics becoming more volatile, with increased chances of wild swings depending on whether we like someone or not. And as soon as a leader drops in popularity they are replaced—we saw this happen four times between 2010 and 2018.

There is one shortcut that may be beneficial even for apathetic voters. This is retrospective voting, which occurs when the government of the day has done such an obviously rubbish job that it is a no brainer to vote the bastards out. This is a major advantage of democracy over dictatorships and a central reason to protect our democracy at all costs.

Chapter Six
Who's Politically Apathetic and Why?

Every study on apathetic voters shows they are from lower socio-economic groups: younger, poorly educated, lower income earners, living in poorer areas. The same has been seen in all democracies, from the Athenian version through to the United States and Australia. Lower socio-economic status individuals often need more from government services such as public health, schooling and social support and it would seem to be in their interest to pay attention to, and support parties that aim to level out economic benefits and give them a leg up the socio-economic ladder. But they don't. Is this just part of the laid-back Aussie culture, with some groups way more laid-back than others?

A lot has been written about this hands-off approach to civic life in Australia. We are characterised as not having a civic culture[93:27] and being politically passive.[94:121] Australian culture is traditionally seen as happy-go-lucky, with open, egalitarian citizens untroubled by large problems or issues, living lives dominated by sport, and regarding politics as "someone else's business."[39]

We can see three main drivers of political apathy. One is the socio-economic factors affecting political involvement. The second is attitudes—how people see themselves in relation to the political system. And the third is systemic—the political rules, lack of competitiveness and education which prevent greater political interest emerging.

Young, Uneducated, Poor and Rural

Young people do not generally give a flying toss about politics.[Annexure 28] They care less who wins elections and are less politically knowledgeable than older people. Many do not enrol to vote, wouldn't vote if they didn't have to, and when they do vote, they often vote informally. The younger the person, the more likely they are uninterested in politics.

As most parents know, many young people are not interested in much except having a good time and being like their peers. Most of us went through this stage. Young people are also busy doing other things. They're leaving school, learning new jobs, beginning to drive, entering tertiary education, playing sport, starting relationships and they are highly mobile, moving from place to place. This means that politics is usually way off their radar.

Young people also lack the confidence to discuss or participate in politics because of their lack of knowledge, and voting is new for them. They need to learn how to complete the ballot, and they may not yet have worked out their own political preferences. Their peer group is in the same boat, voting for the first time, not knowing or caring much about politics and unable to provide guidance. Indeed, the bubble in which most young people exist means that many will ridicule the notion of voting.

The irony is that because so many young people are uninterested and politically unaligned, they are open to coercion and are potentially important in deciding election outcomes. They display the most volatility over who to vote for, and as part of this swinging voter group they provide ripe pickings for politicians deploying manipulative campaigns based on emotion, *if* politicians can get them to listen.

A friend related how his 18-year-old daughter voted for the first time, turning out to avoid a fine but unsure who to vote for. She'd dragged her 15-year-old brother along and when he saw the Sex Party listed on the ballot paper, he convinced her to vote for it. For a 15-year-old boy going through puberty, the Sex Party was no doubt an attractive and funny way to vote, and it didn't take much to get his politically apathetic sister to agree. Many young politically uninterested voters make political decisions on a mere whim.

Socio-economic status is closely linked to education levels and education is often seen as the biggest influence on voting attitudes.[Annexure 29] Less educated people often feel they know little about politics and can't hold an intelligent conversation on the subject. In contrast, educated people are more interested and knowledgeable about politics. This is partly because educated people occupy higher social positions and are often more involved in social and community groups, so feel they can influence government. Educated people are also more aware of the impact that government has on their lives. The more educated people are, the more interest they have in politics.

Education and income are closely related, as the lower the education, the less chance someone has of getting high-level work and income. It's not surprising that the lower the income, the lower the interest in politics.[Annexure 30] Just scraping enough money together is a bigger concern than political issues, even though greater political awareness could benefit low-income earners and may result in action aimed at protecting their interests.

Where we live has always had a significant influence on political interest levels.[Annexure 31] According to Aristotle, ancient Greek farmers weren't interested in the machinations of Athenian democracy, and early US studies found that people living in smaller communities were also less interested. It's similar in Australia, with country voters less interested than city dwellers. This is unsurprising as people in rural areas tend to be less educated, have lower incomes and are generally from lower socio-economic groups, all major indicators of a voter's political interest.

As we saw with young people, there's an irony here because despite the lack of interest, rural people have a big say in who gets elected and which policies are implemented. But the rural demographic is very different to other uninterested groups. While young people are targeted as swinging voters, they tend to cast their votes all over the place, but this changes as they grow older. The 18-year-old who voted for the Sex Party is likely to start taking politics more seriously before turning 25 and choose a party that she will generally support throughout her lifetime.

Rural people are politically important as they are highly concentrated in certain electorates. This gives them political power which arises from the relative homogeneity of thought in country areas, and this can become more extreme without the moderating range of opinions found in cities. The sheer diversity of people in cities, varying in education and income levels, types of employment and cultural, religious and sexual orientation, tends to produce more moderate views overall. People adapt their views when exposed to other ideas and the more extreme opinions tend to cancel each other out.

This moderating influence is less obvious in country areas where people are less likely to interact with as large and diverse a range of people, especially when rural populations are static. Established views then risk becoming entrenched. In his book *The Big Sort*, American author, journalist and social commentator Bill Bishop describes how the increasing political polarisation in the US is the result of people choosing to live in like-minded communities. Bishop found that people feel comfortable surrounded by people like themselves.[93a] No surprises there.

The problem, however, is that if we only interact with people who think like us, we may struggle to understand why people outside our bubble have different views. In these circumstances, if politics is spoken about at all it is to reinforce shared views with like-minded friends.

In an unguarded moment, Barack Obama described people in rural US as clinging "to guns or religion or antipathy to people who aren't like them…as a way to explain their frustrations." It is similar in Australia. This lack of diversity in country areas explains why one deeply conservative party, along with a few extremist politicians, dominate rural politics in this country.

When rural people aren't voting for extremist politicians like Hanson, Katter, Palmer and their ilk, they tend to vote for the Nationals. With the Nationals in a Coalition with the Liberals, country voters have a disproportionate influence on Australian politics. Twice as many people vote for the Greens as for the Nationals, yet in 2019 the Greens had just one House of Representatives seat and Nationals had ten. The Greens have little, if any, influence over national policy. In contrast, when the Coalition wins government, the leader of the Nationals becomes deputy prime minister and the party holds several significant ministries. More importantly, the Nationals dictate a fair amount of policy within the Coalition.

And there's another irony here too, because even though country voters hold so much power over Australian democracy, they are particularly unhappy with the way it works. A common gripe is the disparity in wealth, infrastructure and opportunities between city and rural areas.

When rural people living in what Barnaby Joyce calls "little shithole towns at the arse end of the earth" compare themselves to city people, they realise they are disadvantaged. This difference in wealth is increasing due to urbanisation, globalisation and climate change. In these circumstances, it is easy for country people to blame their disadvantage on others, migrants for example, who look and act differently.

Lower socio-economic uninterested voters as a group are unsatisfied with democracy and often feel they don't get as much from it as others. They often blame this on the democratic system itself which they fail to understand. The panacea is for a 'strongman' to take over and clean out the system. Trump tapped into this mood with his 'drain the swamp' rhetoric.

Right-wing parties such as One Nation similarly blame the system or 'elite' politicians for lower socio-economic people's disadvantage. This plays well to a section of society: predominately white, Christian, rural people who are inherently conservative. They can blame someone or something else for their disadvantage and want the system torn down.

Other Socio-Demographic Factors

Gender is another factor, with women showing less interest in politics than men. [Annexure 32] Women know less about politics, discuss it less and have lower political efficacy. A study undertaken by the AEC found that:

> Amongst the female groups there was this feeling that politics and government is completely irrelevant 'to me'... Theirs was really the genuine apathy based upon a complete indifference to matters which they did not perceive as having any direct relevance or bearing upon their own lives. [68:431]

Reasons suggested for women being less interested in politics usually fall into three categories: socialisation, situational and structural. The socialisation argument goes, that girls grow up thinking that women have differing political roles to men and women should leave politics to men. Women who adhere to this hierarchal structure tend to avoid politics, as they are socialised to have less taste for conflict and see politics as an aggressive, male domain.

The situational argument is that women undertake roles that insulate them from the political world, such as remaining at home with children, which restricts their exposure to politics. Without the exposure to politics that men get in the workplace, women may feel they do not understand the issues as well as men and are less qualified to discuss politics.

The final argument is structural: women tend to be overrepresented in groups that are uninterested in politics such as those with low education. Women's education has, however, leapt ahead in Australia. In 1999, eight per cent more men than women earned a degree, however, by 2017, seven per cent more women than men had completed a bachelor's qualification. Yet political interest has not caught up. This suggests that until there is further erosion in the socialisation forces creating gendered cultural roles, women will remain less politically interested than men.

We know little about the democratic participation of Indigenous Australians because there has been little research in the area. [95] It wasn't until 2013, for example, that the AES even identified Indigenous respondents. The data since then shows much less interest among Aboriginal and Torres Strait Islanders than the population as a whole.[Annexure 33] Less than 50 per cent of Aboriginal people are enrolled, and of those enrolled many do not vote on election day. Turnout is also lowest in areas with large Indigenous populations, such as the Northern Territory, where just 82 per cent vote in federal elections, compared to 95 per cent in the rest of the country.

Long-term suffering at the hands of white settlers and government is no doubt a major cause of Indigenous political apathy. One of the first white people in Australia was Lieutenant James Cook who wrote that Aboriginal people were "the most uncivilised savages perhaps in the world," and labelled them "rank cowards"[96] because they ran away from the white people—who just happened to be shooting at them with guns.

Religious people similarly regarded Indigenous people with disdain. The first missionary to come to Australia was the dour Wesleyan preacher William Walker, who concluded that "Aborigines were descended from Ham, the son of Noah whom God had cursed with blackness and condemned to be a servant of servants to his brothers."[96]

Things started badly and went rapidly downhill for Indigenous people, with disease, slavery and massacres following in the footsteps of the early explorers and missionaries. Subsequent governments did little to alleviate Indigenous suffering. Indigenous people only obtained the right to vote federally in 1962 and in all state elections in 1965. Land rights weren't recognised until 1975 and the concept of *terra nullius*, 'nobody's land', was only expunged after Mabo's legal win in 1992.

Indigenous Australians are also at the bottom of the socio-economic ladder. They are generally younger, with much lower education levels and many live in remote rural areas. They frequently change addresses and are over-represented in the prison system. These are all strong indicators of political apathy.

It's no surprise, therefore, that Indigenous people are uninterested in politics. With the remoteness of many communities, strong attachments to local areas often replace trust in federal governments, from which they feel alienated. Indigenous voters feel powerless to influence central government and believe their vote won't count as they contribute just a small percentage of overall voter numbers. This is a real concern as they are heavily reliant on government support, and governments have found it easy to deny them rights other Australians have had for years.

Yet, Indigenous Australians represent about three per cent of the total population and a quarter of Northern Territory's, so they could have a significant impact on Territory elections as well as House of Representative and Senate seats in the Northern Territory. If they were interested and organised as a political force, they could dominate the Northern Territory and give themselves political influence.

With about a quarter of Australians born overseas, it's also worth considering the effect of migration on voter interest levels. European migration increased after World War II and the fact that new citizens can vote immediately may encourage a sense of political responsibility. However, migrants who don't speak English well are less interested in politics.[Annexure 34]

Studies consistently find this and it is supported by high levels of informal voting in areas where people struggle to speak English, such as western Sydney. Some migrants may lack the confidence to participate in politics because their English is poor and they struggle to follow political discourse.

Another group with low interest levels, and ironically one which is central in the thinking of politicians, is politically unaligned voters. Many of us support one party, which is often the one our parents supported. In fact, family is the biggest influence on how people vote in Australia. And once we've voted for a party three times, we tend to vote the same way our whole life.[97]

If you're this kind of voter, you're not going to be targeted by political parties because it's too hard to change how you vote. Instead, it's the politically unaligned, swinging voters who are intensively targeted because federal elections are always decided by small overall swings. These swinging voters decide election outcomes.

It's no surprise that politically unaligned voters are not interested in politics.[Annexure 35] If you're interested in something, you'll generally have an opinion on the issues involved. It'd be a bit odd to head down to the footy if you don't support one side or the other. Politics is the same, those who are interested usually back one side or the other, while unaligned voters are open to change, *if* the political party can attract their attention. To attract their attention, parties must be outrageous and that is why fear tactics are always at the heart of political campaigns.

Politicians aren't exactly going out on a limb here. Research over many years has drawn similar conclusions about unaligned voters. One early study found swinging voters would change their views between one interview and another:

> The people who found it difficult to distinguish between the virtues of the two parties and who at the same time were not sufficiently

interested in the election to push their way through to a definite decision were more subject to the currents of campaign influence and hence more changeable.[98:71]

A 1990s survey found "swinging voters, in the past and on average, are characterised as apathetic."[24:136] Labor pollster Rod Cameron also noted that for swinging voters:

> Politics is dull, boring and irrelevant to their lifestyle...Politicians are held in low esteem. They are essentially the products of mass-market commercialism, gaining their political information from tabloid newspapers and the occasional news bulletin. They are authoritarian, racist; hard line about dole bludgers, refugees, etc.[99]

These are the voters politicians rationally target as they are they are most likely to be open to manipulation or downright lies.

Too hard, Can't Trust them, Got Better Things to do

People's attitudes also play a big role in political apathy. Half of all Australian voters say that politics is too hard to understand. Unsurprisingly, politically apathetic voters say they don't understand important political issues. If you don't care about politics, you're not going to read the papers to discover that Labor and the Liberals think differently about climate change, for instance.

People feel they can't influence politics and this also reduces interest levels. Studies show that people often believe "there is nothing you can do to change things."[100:5] A 2013 survey found people felt they lacked influence and had a generally negative attitude toward politicians and politics[101] and they also believed more powerful interests dominate policy decisions. When asked who benefits most from government, almost half answered that government was run mostly or entirely for big interests, with only 16 per cent seeing government as helping everyone. [Annexure 36] Many thought the wealthy and big business manipulated affairs to suit, shutting most people out. This leads to a feeling of 'why bother?'

Given recent events, perhaps this attitude is not surprising. Take the mining tax issue, for example. Between 2000 and 2010, mining profits increased by 80 billion dollars, but mining taxes increased only 9 billion dollars, representing a measly 11 per cent tax on their extra profit. When income rises for ordinary

Australians, they get taxed at a higher rate and the government uses the extra money to benefit everyone, for example, by building infrastructure such as hospitals, schools and telecommunications. Recognising the discrepancy, Labor tried to bring in a super tax on mining.

The mining companies had other ideas, waging a 22-million-dollar campaign to sink the tax. At the height of the campaign, the mining industry was playing TV ads 33 times a day, causing support for Labor to slump and contributing to Kevin Rudd losing his job.

Labor ended up offering "1.5 billion dollars of concessions because (the mining industry) punched hard and the fight came when the government was vulnerable."[102] For the mining industry, 22 million dollars is pocket change, but it'd be impossible for most individuals or volunteer groups to spend this amount trying to influence a government decision.

Because of such outcomes, many people feel unable to influence politics. But we have to remember that the literal meaning of democracy is *people power*. If we were fully engaged and interested in politics, we would change the system so business interests did not have such power to dominate. And why are we so willing to be influenced by manipulative political ads on television? Allowing big business to manipulate us so they pay less tax shows that we are either happy with the situation, or too apathetic to change it.

Those who are uninterested in politics are also much less likely to discuss politics,[Annexure 37] and as their interest and knowledge is low, politics becomes an increasingly taboo topic. Being forced to reveal how little you know about something can be embarrassing. There's also the potential for conflict if politics is brought up. Many of us will have experienced the awkward silences and sudden changes of topic when someone drops a political clanger into the conversation.

And those who find politics complicated and do not discuss it invariably think it's boring. A survey of year 12 English students found almost two-thirds found politics boring. When students were asked to express an interest in politics, the researchers were met with 'vehemently negative responses'. Most said that they never discussed politics or considered it personally important.[103]

Trustworthiness is another issue. Surveys regularly rate politicians below used car salesmen, real estate agents and priests in trustworthiness. Politics is held in disdain, which further reduces interest levels. The AES found honesty was regarded as important at all times, yet also found 4 in 5 people thought politicians tell lies if they feel the truth will hurt them politically.

The irony is that the less interested an individual is about politics, the less trusting they are. 28 per cent of interested people see politicians as generally trustworthy, compared to just eight per cent of uninterested people. Uninterested people generally pay no attention to what goes on politically and don't get involved in anything political. The irony is that the *less* people trust politicians, the *more* freedom they allow those politicians to make decisions on their behalf, without oversight, concern or interest.

Politicians often sow the seeds of distrust themselves. It's not just Trump and his lackeys using 'alternative facts'. There are many examples of Australian politicians reneging on promises made before elections, lying openly, or rorting the system:

> Modern politics follows a cycle of deceit and broken promises. Policies that would be damaging during an election campaign (such as tax increases) or just plain embarrassing (such as knights and dames) are concealed from the public, to be unveiled from the relative safety of government.[104:18]

Politicians even admit they lie. On ABC's *7:30 Report*, Tony Abbott said he didn't always tell the truth and that his comments should only be taken as truthful if they were 'carefully prepared and scripted remarks', as opposed to those in a 'standard conversation'. Abbott also argued that you couldn't trust politicians during the republican referendum:[105]

> People come to expect duplicity in public speech, and the expectation tarnishes all public officials...And when people are mistrustful of government, they are also cynical about their own capacities to act on public goods and purposes and will attend to narrow domains of self-interest they can control.[106:328]

Politicians' rorting entitlements further adds to distrust. Abbott, for example, had to pay back taxpayers' money he claimed for attending colleagues' weddings, while two other Liberal politicians must have thought they were getting married themselves, going by their claim for more than 100,000 dollars in expenses for another wedding.

Labor member Mark Dreyfus also paid back some taxpayer-supplied money he used to go to a ski resort. Late for a Liberal Party knees-up, Speaker of the House Bronwyn Bishop used a taxpayer-funded helicopter to get there, and it was only after a considerable fight that she finally resigned as Speaker on account of this.

The 2019 election was mired in scandal. Liberal members Michaela Cash and Michael Keenan refused to give formal witness statements to the police during an investigation into leaked raids on the Australian Workers Union. Read that again. Ministers elected by us refused to cooperate with a police investigation. At least Keenan had the good grace to 'retire' in 2019. It was also revealed that taxpayers had forked out 800,000 dollars in legal fees associated with the case.

Then there was the Helloworld travel company, run by the Liberal Party federal treasurer and donor Andrew Burnes, which received a 3-year, 1-billion-dollar contract from the Coalition government. Finance Minister Mathias Cormann received free flights after ringing Burnes directly only a couple of months before the tender was up for grabs.

And when Dad tells you things were different way back when, he was right. Peter McGauran quit the Howard government after it became known that National Party members, but not McGauran himself, had wrongfully claimed 1,500 dollars in expenses for a charter flight. Or when Mick Young resigned from the Hawke government after failing to declare a teddy bear to customs. And then there were the Liberals Michael Mackellar and John Moore who walked the plank for stuffing up the importation of a colour television.

The media plays up stories of a politician's rorting because it's an easy sell. It's pitched as entertainment, corruption or divisiveness, which increases cynicism and distrust of politics. Those who usually pay little attention to politics are more likely to encounter this type of political news for its entertainment value.

One problem is the federal government doesn't have an independent anti-corruption watchdog. Although the Senate passed a bill in 2019 implementing the Independent Commission Against Corruption, the Coalition refused to support it in the House of Representatives. It seems that the Coalition believes corruption doesn't exist in federal government.

Busy lives are another reason for a lack of political interest. Everyday life takes over and people get swamped: getting the kids to school, paying the mortgage, worries about work, organising holidays, deciding the latest in-game purchases. Politics is often viewed as a distant relevance for people with more pressing, interesting and gratifying things to do. Government business also seems to have no immediate impact on their lives and people only take an active interest in matters in which they have personal experience.

The *7.30 Report* spoke to a number of people who considered themselves 'quiet Australians'. Richard Gough said, "I think quiet Australians are people that are just too busy…we're busy with families, we're busy with kids." For many Australians, when they do consciously engage with government, the experience is also generally quite painful, cutting into their busy lifestyles. Filling in tax returns, applying for a passport, driver's license, or dole payments are all onerous.

We even criticise governments when we have to slow down at road works; it's as if they deliberately schedule them at the busiest times. And if something goes terribly wrong like the bushfires in 2019 or job losses because the government curtails funding for the car industry, then we see the government as interfering and a pain in the bum.

Former Deputy Prime Minister Barnaby Joyce went on quite the rant about this over Christmas 2019. Videoing himself feeding cows, he asks us if we ever wonder what politicians do on Christmas Eve. The video went downhill rapidly, with Joyce angry about government interference in people's lives, noting that there was a "higher authority that's beyond our comprehension and right up there in the sky… I just don't want the government any more in my life."[107] Given that Joyce was a major part of that government, a lot of people were no doubt supportive of his stance.

On a brighter note, political apathy could be due to satisfaction with the system. If this is the case, there is no need to take an active interest and we can focus on what makes us happy. When compared to people in other countries, Australians exude a general satisfaction with democratic performance[108] and in a stable and prosperous society there isn't much for people to get up in arms about. Political satisfaction may stem from Australia's history of new arrivals and multiculturalism.

Migrants from countries with dodgy democracies or dictatorial regimes might think that Australian democracy works well in comparison and see no need to get politically involved, or even to vote. More than two thirds of us are satisfied with the way our democracy has worked over the past 20 years.

The great irony is that apathetic people are much less likely to be satisfied.[Annexure 38-39] As we saw earlier, these are usually people from lower socio-economic groups, pointing to "a more deep-seated exclusion of citizens with the fewest social and economic resources, who feel they have no real political voice."[109:78] They may have decided that it is pointless to try and remedy an injustice. Instead of satisfaction, their silence may signify resignation.

The System's Broke

The political and voting system is another cause for apathy. One aspect is the complicated nature of the Australian electoral system, with different tiers of government and differing voting procedures for each level. People might vote incorrectly because they're confused by the different ways to vote for upper and lower houses, and for federal, state and local electoral systems. Even the number of candidates standing might cause problems.

For example, the federal election lower house ballot requires that all boxes must be filled in with sequential numbers, whereas before 2016, Senate voting required voters to choose between voting 'above the line', by placing only a (1) next to your desired party, or voting 'below the line' by sequentially numbering all candidates.

Below-the-line voting seemed difficult and time-consuming, so nearly everyone voted above the line. But doing this meant voters didn't know where their preference votes went, as political parties didn't publicise this. So since 2016, Senate voters have been required to number at least 6 boxes above the line or at least 12 below.

Different state and federal election rules also complicate things. NSW and Queensland were both optional preferential before 2016, so a voter could choose between placing a (1) next to their favoured candidate or voting for as many, or all, of the candidates in order of preference. Federal elections, however, require all boxes on the House of Representative ballot to be filled and preferences selected. No wonder politically uninterested voters find this confusing and we can see this with NSW and Queensland having the highest proportion of "number 1 only" informal votes for federal elections.

Voter confusion can also be an issue when there are many candidates listed on the ballot paper. The number of informal votes increases as the number of candidates increases. When between two and four candidates are listed, 3.6 per cent vote informally; this rises to almost seven per cent when there are between 11 and 13 candidates.[Annexure 40] But it wouldn't be difficult to number boxes from 1 to 13 for something we were interested in.

Theoretically at least, Australia's systems of preferential voting and proportional representation should encourage voting as it avoids the 'wasted-vote' syndrome of winner-take-all systems such as those used in US and Britain. Australian voters can gain satisfaction from voting for a candidate they know has no chance of winning. They choose them to show their policies have merit or as a protest, while still knowing that through the preference system, their vote will go to another candidate who does have a chance of winning. Of course, for people to vote this way they must understand how the system works and the sad fact is that many voters don't.

Some voters also see both major parties as being much the same and so for them it doesn't matter who is in power. Part of this is the battle for the middle ground, with both parties becoming more moderate as they attempt to capture this middle ground. Any change in government is therefore unlikely to encompass radical policy change.

Just when Labor and the Coalition began to converge is unclear, although suggestions include Bill Hayden's budget of 1975, or perhaps the Hawke and Keating era which turned Labor into a catch-all-party like the Liberals. Keating's "super tax cuts proved so popular that Howard promptly aped them, as he would do with most of the policies Keating announced that year."[110:228] Keating would later argue the Liberals:

> only got in by pretending they were us…they couldn't win on their Thatcherite policy. They tried various versions of it, in 84, 87, 90 and 93, and every time they came a gutser, so finally they said the only way to win is to trick our way into power, say we're them.[61:169]

Others have pointed out similarities between the parties, with the right-wing commentator Gerard Henderson saying, "Howard's greatest victory had been the creation of a Labor Party in his own image."[111] We can see this in the 2007 federal election where Rudd adopted a "me-too" policy, asserting that on "macroeconomics there was not a sliver of difference between the government and Labor." Howard joked that Rudd was indulging in 'echo-nomics' while Barnaby Joyce mused that that if Rudd got any closer to Howard, he would have to ask permission from Howard's wife Janette.

An early 1960s study found that up to two-thirds of respondents could not see a difference between the major parties and this was a reason for political apathy.[112:173] In another survey, the feeling was "there's not much difference between them…they're all tarred with the same brush and they're much of a muchness."[39:27] And AES data from the past 20 years shows over a third of voters are unsure or don't think it makes a difference who people vote for.[Annexure 41]

It is again the low socio-economic, uninterested voters who are less likely to perceive differences between the parties and, because "the poor cannot respond to policy choices they cannot see,"[113:143] their interest in politics drops even further. In contrast, interested voters who long ago picked a side believe it matters which political party is in power, with marginal differences between policies taking on great significance.

One view is that the approach of uninterested voters is completely rational, as it's pointless to inform yourself on political issues and to vote, given that the chance of your single vote changing political outcomes is about the same as your chance of winning Lotto. This isn't always true though. In our closest federal election, in 1919, the National party candidate for Ballarat Edwin Kirby received 13,569 votes and the Labor candidate Charles McGrath received 13,568 votes.

Unhappy at the result, McGrath went to the High Court claiming dodgy dealings. The High Court agreed and McGrath won a subsequent rematch in 1920. However, most elections are decisive, meaning the rational action is to stay uninformed and uninterested because "even the cost in shoe leather of walking to the polling booth…(means) it is a waste of time for the citizen to vote."[114:49]

But if we all took this approach, we may as well abandon democracy altogether. Democracy is based on the collective will of the people and requires informed, willing participation to work well. Forcing people who are uninterested and know little, if anything, about politics to vote weakens our democracy.

The lack of civics education is one final factor contributing to political apathy. Schools taught civics until the 1930s, with students learning about the structure of government and the electoral process. Since then, "generations of Australians have passed through schools with little exposure to civics education (resulting in) widespread ignorance of Australia's system of government, the political process and other civic issues."[115:3]

Three enquiries in the 1980s and 1990s highlighted a need to re-implement civics education as "it was clear that many young Australians were remarkably ignorant about political and government systems and their role as citizens with their democratic country."[116:5]

The 1995 report was strongly supported by then Prime Minister Paul Keating and government funding was provided to implement recommendations. No sooner had it begun when the Howard government, elected in 1996, changed the focus toward conservative cultural and historical values rather than civics. Murray Print, author of the reports, believes it suits politicians for kids to leave school with little knowledge of politics. And if their parents are uninterested, their political education may be almost non-existent, resulting in apathy being passed down through the generations.

In this part of the book, we considered demographic, socio-economic, attitudinal and institutional factors contributing to political apathy. We saw that uninterested voters are different political actors to interested voters in that uninterested voters are less likely to understand politics, less likely to discuss politics, less trusting of politicians and less satisfied with democracy and most of them don't care who wins government.

Most people, however, understand their own interests if they're motivated to do so. Many of the causes of political apathy that we described above could be seen as excuses for those who can't be bothered to become interested in politics. Attitudes may therefore be the most important reason for political apathy. None of this would matter if political apathy didn't affect political actions, decisions or outcomes. The disturbing reality is that it does.

Chapter Seven
Ignorant Voters Decide Who Governs

The most important effect of political apathy is that uninterested voters decide election outcomes. This argument is not new. Australian National University politics professor Finlay Crisp wrote that "forcing people who are not interested in voting to go to the polls means that the government will be chosen by the ignorant and the uninterested."[117:111]

Until now, though, no one has provided evidence of this effect. We have, and the results are startling. If apathetic voters had not voted, there would have been a different federal government after the 1987, 1993 and 2010 elections. The Coalition would have won all three elections if uninterested voters had not voted.[Annexure 42–43]

In 1987, uninterested voters gave Labor a 3.8 per cent boost on a two-party preferred basis, and Labor won 21 seats by a margin of 3.8 per cent or less. If these uninterested individuals had not voted, the Coalition would have won 83 seats to Labor's 65, therefore securing government.

Uninterested voters were also decisive in 1993 as they swayed the two-party preferred vote 2.5 per cent Labor's way, allowing Labor to win 17 seats. Without apathetic voters' support, the Coalition would have had a 19-seat majority. These large turnarounds illustrate the political impact of uninterested voters. In 2010, Labor benefited by 1.4 per cent on a two-party preferred basis, winning 6 seats with that margin or less. If uninterested voters had gone fishing instead of voting, the Coalition would have won comfortably, by 78 seats to 66.

Even when apathetic voters don't change the government, they still decide around eight electorates each election. This has a major influence on the relative strength of each party in parliament, as well as influencing political discourse, media coverage, and our perception of government.

Uninterested individuals tend to vote for Labor. Since 1987, they have, on average, moved the two-party preferred vote by 1.2 per cent in favour of Labor. This is not surprising because uninterested voters generally sit at the lower end of the socio-economic scale. The logical choice for them would be to support a party that takes a more progressive approach to levelling out economic benefits.

What *is* surprising is that with an average of almost 2.5 million uninterested votes cast each election, many of these voters support the Coalition. Even more surprising, in 1990 uninterested voters split their vote evenly between the Coalition and Labor, and in 2004 they favoured the Coalition.

What can we make of this? For many uninterested voters, voting is like a coin toss. The scary part is the influence this can have on political outcomes. Informed voters with clear positions support the two major parties in reasonably equal numbers, which largely cancels out their influence. But Australian national elections are often close-run things on a two-party preferred basis, so small shifts in marginal seats can have a disproportionately large impact. This leaves the uninterested, swinging voters in these seats with the power to determine election results. If more of them happen to vote for Labor, Labor wins and vice versa.

Another concern is that many uninterested individuals appear to be voting against their own self-interest. They view voting as a lottery with no prize draw, a chore to be undertaken and finished as soon as possible. They are not carefully considering which party might be the better choice for them, their family, community or country, and are instead ticking boxes to avoid being fined 20 dollars.

A Few Votes Either Way

We can clearly see the influence of uninterested voters in the Victorian seat of Corangamite in 2010.[Annexure 44] The federal election that year was a cliff-hanger, with neither major party achieving a majority, resulting in the first hung parliament since 1940. Crossbench MPs held the balance of power, so it came down to which way each one jumped. The unfortunately named Tony Crook, the National Party member from Western Australia, supported the Coalition, as did the conservative independent Bob Katter. The Greens' Adam Bandt and Tasmanian independent Andrew Wilkie supported Labor. The decision of who would govern was in the hands of independents Rob Oakeshott and Tony Windsor. A lot of pressure was applied to these two MPs as they were formerly members of the National Party, representing historically conservative country areas. However, both supported

Labor, resulting in a 76–74 margin, which allowed Labor to form minority government.

Every seat was pivotal. If the Coalition had won just one more seat, it would have formed government. Of all the seats in 2010, Corangamite was the most marginal. In this electorate, the Liberals won the primary vote by 5,112 votes, but when preference votes were added Labor took the seat by 771 votes. If just half of these 771 had voted Liberal, the Liberals would have won Corangamite, changing the election outcome. But Labor received 1,280 more votes from uninterested voters than the Coalition and won the electorate. If these uninterested individuals had not voted, the Liberals would have not only won Corangamite but also government.

Donkeys Decide Who Wins

Donkey votes change election results and political parties have long understood their importance. Candidate names used to be listed on ballot papers in alphabetical order. This changed for the Senate in 1940 but only changed for the House of Representatives in 1984. As early as 1922, Labor won four seats with suitably named candidates: Amour, Armstrong, Arthur and Ashley. If candidates didn't have names beginning with letters early in the alphabet, they had no hope of winning.

During the 1950s and 1960s, Australian elections were often determined by the Communist Party, which just happened to have as part of their coterie the Aarons family. The anti-Communist party, the Democratic Labour Party (DLP) also got in on the action and would choose their candidate according to who was the sitting member. When a Mr. Ashton was the sitting member in 1969, the DLP chose Mr. Antcliff and then chose Mr. Bader in the seat held by Mr. Botsman. Prior to the 1984 election, a whopping 25 per cent of parliamentarians had a surname starting with A, B or C.[82] Rather than the considered opinion of voters, the make-up of the Senate and the House of Representatives depended on the alphabet.

Donkey voting continues today. The Liberal Democratic Party (LDP) achieved just 2.3 per cent Senate vote at the 2010 election. Over the next 3 years, it did little, if any, campaigning and appeared to have no chance of gaining political office. Yet after it won the number one ballot position for the Senate in NSW 2013, it received 9.5 per cent of the primary vote. Party leader David Leyonhjelm, quipped, "Looks like I'm going to be the Senator for the donkeys."[118]

Australian National University researchers found that the leader of the Labor Party Kim Beazley only won his seat because of donkey votes in 1996.[119] And the Electoral Reform Society estimated that donkey votes determined who won the 2006 South Australian state election.[120]

The donkey vote is about one per cent, so in any electorate where the winning margin is below one per cent and the winner's name is above that of the runner-up on the ballot paper, we can assume the winner had the advantage of donkey votes and would not have been elected without them.

This means that about 5 federal electorates, on average, have been decided by donkey votes at each election since 1987.[Annexure 45] An example is the federal seat of Hawker in 1990 which was won by the Liberal candidate, Chris Gallus. Luckily for her, she was at the top of the ballot paper and won by 14 votes. Another example is the seat of Herbert in far north Queensland which elected Cathy O'Toole in 2016 by 37 votes. O'Toole scored a 174,000 dollars job because politically apathetic people donkey voted.

The 2010 election was exceptionally close and if the Liberal candidate for Greenway had been listed above the Labor candidate, who won by just 0.88 per cent, the Liberals would have won this electorate and also government. So, rather than informed, rational voters deciding who governed the country for the next 3 years, it was the random draw of positions on the Greenway ballot paper.

Who did I Just Vote for?

Voting in Australia usually involves not just selecting your preferred candidate, but also ranking the other candidates in order of preference. If your first choice is eliminated, then your following choices (second, third and so on) are counted until one candidate receives 50 per cent of the vote. The allocation of preferences is therefore important in determining who wins the seat.

About a quarter of us vote for a minor party and direct our preferences to a major party. These preference votes have a huge impact on election outcomes; they decided the winner in around seventy per cent of electorates at the 2019 election, for example.[Annexure 46] It's a fair argument that if a minor party voter cared about election outcomes, they would know which major party they end up supporting with their preference vote.

Shockingly, about 25 per cent of all voters in 2019 did not know who they preferenced in the House of Representatives elections and 21 per cent in the

Senate.[Annexure 47]. As you'd expect, voters who are politically uninterested are less likely to know who they preferenced.[Annexure 48]

There may have been some excuse in Senate elections before 2016 because of the complexity of the voting system and the unpredictability of political alliances. Until 2016, 95 per cent of voters for the Senate used 'above the line' voting. This is the system in which preferences get automatically allocated by parties based on complex pre-election preference deals. Voters usually had no idea about the details of these arrangements, and it led to candidates being elected on small primary votes. In 2004, for example, Labor Senate preferences saw Family First elected in Victoria on a 0.08 per cent primary vote. Few Labor voters would have known, let alone supported, Family First, which opposed many things Labor stood for.

At the 2016 election, South Australian Greens Senator Sarah Hanson-Young, who was campaigning to ban coal mining, was re-elected, using preferences from Palmer's United Party, the party formed by coal-mine owner Clive Palmer. As payback, Greens preferences helped Palmer's Senate candidate win in Tasmania. The Animal Justice Party preferenced One Nation, a party with no concern for either animals or the environment, while the Wikileaks Party placed the Nationals above the Greens.

Ricky Muir of the Australian Motorists Party, secured only 0.51 per cent of the primary vote at the 2013 federal election yet was elected because of preferences from 23 other parties. It was later revealed that Glen Druery, the so-called 'preference whisperer', who orchestrated the preference votes for Muir, had originally negotiated for these votes to go to Family First, which had employed him to organise the deal. But Family First weaselled out of paying Druery and so at the eleventh hour Druery switched the preferences to Muir. It wasn't voters who chose their Senator; it was an act of revenge by a disgruntled employee.

Further confusion can be caused by parties themselves. The Liberty and Democracy Party won a minuscule 0.19 per cent of the NSW Senate vote at the 2007 election. A few months later, it changed its name to the Liberal Democratic Party. The Liberal Party objected, claiming the new name would confuse voters, ironically so considering there is little 'liberal' about the Liberal Party. In 2013, the LDP was drawn to go first on the NSW Senate ballot paper and its vote increased to 9.5 per cent. The Liberals and Nationals combined won 47.3 per cent in the lower house, yet only 34.2 per cent in the Senate. The political and economic journalist Tim Colebatch said:

It is a reasonable inference that almost one in five people who voted for the Liberals or Nationals in the lower house mistakenly put a '1' in the box of the Liberal Democrats when it was the first thing they saw on the congested ballot paper.[121]

Liberal Party Director Brian Loughnane also said the NSW LDP's success was "almost entirely at the expense of the Liberal Party" with many Liberal voters confused and voting for the LDP by mistake.[122] In contrast, the Victorian LDP faxed their Senate voting ticket to the wrong number and ended up getting listed at the bottom of the senate ballot paper, winning only 363 votes.

Voters who were less interested and wanting to quickly complete the ballot paper were more likely to confuse the two parties. As this shows, compelling politically apathetic people to vote increases the proportion of random votes, which leads to less popular candidates being elected.

As an aside, the Daylight Saving party applied to change its name to the National Liberals and the Flux party wanted to change to the Liberals for Climate in 2021. They claimed that voters were smart enough to distinguish them from the Liberals and there was nothing strategic in the name change. Of course they did.

Or how about a Communist-Coalition alliance? In the 1961 House of Representatives election in the Queensland seat of Moreton, a significant number voted for the Communist Party, yet their preferences flowed to the Coalition, thereby electing James Killen for Moreton and the return of conservative government.[123] If these Communist preferences had not flowed to the Coalition,— Labor would have won government.

In another outcome, if Labor had won this election it is probable Australia led by the pacifist Arthur Calwell would not have become embroiled in the Vietnam War. A strong argument can be made that apathetic voters were responsible for getting us into the Vietnam War, the deaths of hundreds of Australians and a proportion of the millions of Vietnamese deaths.

And we've seen that Labor won an election cliff-hanger in Corangamite in 2010 by just 771 votes. Unbelievably, Labor picked up 777 preferences from Family First and Liberal Democrats in Corangamite and those votes carried Labor to victory. You would think such right-wing party voters would be more ideologically aligned with the Coalition. Yet the preference votes from Family First and the Liberal Democrats not only delivered a Labor representative in Corangamite, but also a Labor government in 2010.

Joke Parties

Some voters don't take the political process seriously, trivialising it by voting for joke parties. Politically uninterested voters make up a significant proportion of the support for such parties. In the 1989 ACT election, the Party Party Party received 0.7 per cent of the primary vote, while The Sun-Ripened Warm Tomato Party received 1.2 per cent, with its preferences electing a rival party. Similarly, the Deadly Serious Party stood candidates federally in the 1980s. Its platform included dispatching a flock of killer penguins to protect Australia's coastline from Argentine invasion and the appointment of silly people to all portfolios that mattered. It achieved 3.4 per cent in the seat of Canberra in 1983. Sadly, no sign of the killer penguin army—they would have looked dapper and we would have saved a bundle in uniform costs.

In the 2019 federal election, Alex Dyson ran as an independent in Wannon, the Victorian seat held for 28 years by former Prime Minister Malcolm Fraser. Dyson explained his policies "via the medium of interpretive dance" before tossing himself off a pier into the ocean. The video of his performance went viral on social media and gained him 10.4 per cent of the primary vote.

And there was also John His Grace, the Most Noble Duke of Avram, who headed what he claimed was a micro-nation called the Grand Duchy of Avram. The 'Duke' was elected to the Tasmanian parliament as a Liberal in 1986 and held the position of Shadow Minister for Construction.

Democracy is also a little crazy in other parts of the world. The Best Party achieved 34.7 per cent of the vote in Iceland. Its leader, Jon Gnarr Kristinsson, said "nobody needs to be frightened of the Best Party because it's the best," otherwise it would be called the Worst or the Bad Party. The Best Party swept the polls, promising to keep Iceland 'cuddly and clean' with free towels for swimming pools, a drug free parliament by 2020 and a reduction in Santas.

Jacob Haugaard, leader of Denmark's Union of Conscientiously Work Shy Elements Party, won a seat promising more tailwinds for cyclists, the right to impotency, the addition of Nutella to army field rations and more bread for park ducks. Apparently, these last two promises were delivered, making Haugaard a surprisingly honest and successful politician.

The Polish Beer Lovers Party won 16 seats in Poland's lower house and the perennial Official Monster Raving Looney Party has won numerous council seats in the UK since it was founded by Screaming Lord Sutch in the early 1980s. One guy even ran as a clown for the position of Federal Deputy in the 2010 Brazilian election. His campaign slogan was "What does the Federal deputy do? Fucked if I know but vote for me and I'll tell you." He received the second highest number of votes in the contest's history. Meanwhile, a misogynistic, racist, serial-lying reality star won the presidency in the United States in 2016.

The Joke's on Us

A good understanding of various political positions reduces the possibility that voters will support extremists. Democracy benefits when everyone is exposed to a range of political views. It is a sad fact that uninterested and unknowledgeable citizens are more likely to vote for extremist or idiot politicians who are unfit for office. This is especially important in Australia because of compulsory voting.

An obvious example is One Nation. Academic research has shown that voters who support One Nation are "unskilled workers and workers in either blue collar or the agricultural industry." They also change residential addresses frequently, do not own their homes, are Christian fundamentalists and are located in 'deeply rural' areas that are 'disadvantaged'.[124]

One Nation voters are overwhelmingly politically apathetic and generally know little, if anything about, politics. They are the least able to make rational and coherent political arguments and the least qualified to participate in politics. It's unsurprising they vote for candidates that are inappropriate for public office.

Let's take a quick look at some of the candidates One Nation has offered up for office. 48 hours after becoming a One Nation candidate, Stephanie Banister said Islam was a country, mixed up the Koran with a harem, said "Jews don't follow harem, they have their own religion which follows Jesus Christ," and noted that the National Disability Scheme was "working at the moment" though it wasn't due to start for another 3 years.

The One Nation Queensland leader Jim Savage defended Banister, saying she had not been given "appropriate preparation," but you'd think as she was seeking to represent a party dominated by a hatred for Muslims, she'd at least know a little about Islam.

Banister was not the only One Nation candidate or member to make bizarre statements. The former One Nation Senator Fraser Anning sought a 'final solution' to the 'problem of migration by Muslims'. The One Nation candidate for the WA seat of Bateman, Michelle Myers, thought Christians were being swayed to accept the push for gay marriage through mind control, previously used by the Soviets and Nazis, but this time employed by the LGBTQI community.

Party leader Pauline Hanson questioned whether the Port Arthur massacre was a government conspiracy, and claimed men are the victims of domestic violence and women make 'frivolous' abuse claims over criticism of their clothes. She has also said Islam was a disease we had to be vaccinated against and argued that humans weren't responsible for the extinction of dinosaurs and so we can't be responsible for climate change.

Pauline Hanson is never far from controversy, claiming that people locked down in a public housing tower during the Melbourne Covid lockdown were 'drug addicts' and 'alcoholics' who 'can't speak English'. She later made amends by sending them all a beer stubby holder adorned with the words "I've got the guts to say what you're thinking" and a note saying "no hard feelings."[125]

One Nation's leader in Queensland, Steve Dickson, ranted about the evils of sex education, falsely claiming:

> We are having little kids in grade four at school, young girls being taught by teachers how to masturbate, how to strap on dildos, how to do this sort of stuff-that is the real problem in this country.[126]

Around the same time, a sex shop owned by One Nation candidate Mark Thornton posted on Facebook, "Good sex should be in the grey area between tickle fight and domestic violence" and "A blowjob a week can lower a man's risk of heart disease. So, don't be shy girls, save a life!"[127]

In 2019, Dickson went to the US to solicit money from the National Rifle Association for One Nation. He was caught on camera saying Muslims were "breaking into people's homes with baseball bats and killing people." Dickson was also filmed sexually harassing a stripper, asking her to "slide your hand onto my cock." He was later taped saying, "white women fucked a whole lot better; they know what they're doing. Asian chicks don't."

Hansen defended Dickson as 'a family man'. Dickson resigned and issued a statement asking journalists to respect his family's privacy as he was 'no longer of *pubic* interest'. Dickson not only has a potty mouth, he also can't spell.

Mathew Stephen, the One Nation candidate for Longman, ran a "jobs for Australians first and foremost" campaign while being pursued by his unpaid employees. Rod Culleton, erstwhile Senator for One Nation, was an interesting person, especially to creditors and the police. Bankruptcy had him tossed out of the Senate: it seems Culleton was happy to take out loans but less willing to repay them.

In another episode, Culleton was charged by police over the theft of a key valued at $7.50. He nicked it off a tow truck driver attempting to repossess his truck. Culleton justified his behaviour by saying it was "no different to taking a scone off someone's plate."

Culleton's next key problem concerned bank representatives showing up at his property to politely ask that he start repaying some loans. Culleton blocked the bank employees' car with hay bales and then tried to take their car keys. He ended up in court again, shouting at the magistrate and throwing his glasses at her. Police had to remove him from the court.

As Culleton was a bankrupt at the time of his election, he was ineligible for office. The Commonwealth Department of Finance wrote to him saying "payments made to you and in relation to you since the election on 2 July 2016, are a debt to the Commonwealth." In other words, the public wants its money back. Culleton's answer: "I'm just going to hang in there like a flea in between the shoulders of a dog right where they can't scratch." The taxpayers are still trying to get their money back.

Culleton tried to make a political comeback in 2019 with The Great Australia Party, whose main policy was ironically for criminals to have their property confiscated as a deterrent. At the time, another Great Australia Party candidate, Wayne Glew, was battling to keep his property after refusing to pay his council 300,000 dollars in rates and legal costs. Mr. Glew lost his property and the Great Australia Party received just 398 votes at the election.

Gun lover Charlie Rappolt became a One Nation state parliamentarian for Queensland. In his maiden address to parliament, he said:

> Only One Nation has a reasonable policy on firearms, which could be hailed as really Australian a policy which is in accord with our historic freedoms. The policies adopted by Canberra and forced upon the states are right out of the Godless archives of Nazi Germany and communist Russia.[128]

Rappolt only lasted four months in parliament after revelations he had beaten up his partner when she took out a domestic violence order against him. Rappolt killed himself the following year, blaming psychotic manic depression.

Another problem One Nation seems to have down to a fine art is the internal conflict that invariably develops; they act like spoilt teenagers bickering and bitching when together. One was a tiff between One Nation staffer James Ashby and the former One Nation Senator Brian Burston.

The issue seems to have come about because Burston allegedly offered to "fuck a staff member to make her feel better." Burston denied this, alleging that it was actually Pauline Hanson who was sexually harassing him. According to Burston, it was "right back when we had our first One Nation AGM at Rooty Hill RSL that was the first time she hit on me." Hanson denied the allegation saying "I might be 64 but I'm not that desperate."

James Ashby defended Hanson's honour by bashing Burston in Parliament House and Burston retaliated by smearing blood on Hanson's Senate office door. Making matters even more bizarre, Burston's wife defended the initial sexual allegations, saying "My husband never says fuck." The problem was that Burston was explaining to News Corp that he got into the fight with Ashby because "I told him to fuck off."

Malcolm Roberts claimed that One Nation Senators have their specialisations. "I'm strong on climate, Pauline's strong on Islam [and] foreign ownership; Rod Culleton's very strong on the banks." It may all sound like the hillbillies are in town but a lot of people vote for them!

Hissy fits also result in people getting thrown out of the party. The highest profile was David Oldfield, who had increasingly usurped power in One Nation, leading to his summary expulsion in 2000. A bigger problem for Hanson was the disaffection of One Nation candidate Terry Sharples who spilt the beans that One Nation didn't have enough members to legally form a political party. This was particularly bad news for Hanson as it led to her spending time eating porridge in jail and contemplating the company she kept.

Given the quality of One Nation's candidates, it's not surprising many come a cropper before an election. One in seven One Nation candidates either resigned or were sacked before the 2017 Queensland election. And it's not just candidates that One Nation struggles to hold on to, it's also parliamentarians.

One Nation has had 33 members elected to different governing bodies since its establishment in 1997. These include three Senators who gained election after other One Nation Senators were sacked from the Senate. Of the 33 elected, 22 resigned from the party not long after being elected. Fraser Anning didn't even take his seat as a Senator before leaving to join Bob Katter for a few weeks, then leaving Katter to start his own party.

Two were disqualified from the Senate because they were foreigners (ironic considering this is the party that hates foreigners). Culleton, the one who struggled with keys, was sacked as a bankrupt but he would have been sacked anyway, because he too was a foreigner.

One Nation Western Australian MP Charles Smith quit the party and on the way out he called a One Nation colleague named Rod Caddies a "semi-literate goon...you really are the septic pustule on the anus of vulgar society." Caddies responded by saying Smith had 'anger issues' which was quite muted for One Nation tiffs and probably on the mark.

The One Nation leader Colin Tincknell weighed in by claiming he was "child-like in the way he acts." It is thought Tincknell was referring to Smith but he could have been talking about any One Nation member and no one would be surprised.

Not only are One Nation politicians of particularly poor quality, when they get into positions of power in government they harm the very people who voted for them. Remember, One Nation voters are the politically apathetic and poorly educated. They earn the least amount of money, have poor job security if they have a job and are most likely to be on government welfare. They are overwhelmingly poor and marginalised. You would think One Nation voters would want to level out economic benefits, provide educational pathways for their children and maintain a reasonable standard of government welfare.

Yet One Nation generally votes with the government to cut support to low income earners. They voted with the Coalition to cut 6 billion dollars from welfare as well as making dole recipients wait four weeks for financial support. During an interview on the *Sunrise* morning television program, Hanson said welfare recipients should "get a job and start taking responsibility for your own actions." One Nation also claimed, "the plan to extend the taxpayer-funded paid parental leave scheme is too generous and can encourage women to get pregnant to access government benefits."

And One Nation has said that welfare should be limited to one child. The misogynistic theme to its rhetoric was clear in the comment by Brendon Grylls, One Nation leader in Western Australia, who said that single women were "too lazy to attract and hold a mate."

And One Nation's policy on domestic violence sought to relax restrictions on fathers against whom the courts had issued protection orders. One Nation Senator

Malcolm Roberts chimed in to say that the family law system sometimes left men in custody disputes little option but to "hurt the other person."

In contrast, One Nation supports policies that benefit the wealthy. It supported the Coalition's company tax cut for businesses that earn over 50 million dollars. It also supported the Coalition in restoring the Australian Building and Construction Commission, which unions blamed for weaker health and safety standards on work sites. One Nation supported tougher governance standards for unions and Hansen has called for penalty rates to be abolished. One Nation also helped the Coalition government block the establishment of an anti-corruption commission.

One Nation presents itself as anti-establishment to appeal to voters who feel shut out of the economic system, yet it votes with the Coalition 88 per cent of the time. One Nation voters who think they are voting for an anti-establishment party are wrong. Their votes support the policies of a conservative, right-wing ideology which historically supports the wealthy.

The Queensland seat of Hinkler is the poorest electorate in Australia and yet 19 per cent voted One Nation in 2016. The Hunter in NSW is also a poor seat and 21.8 per cent voted for the One Nation candidate Stuart Bonds in 2019. Bonds' resume highlight: he was a heavily tattooed mechanic who married his wife on a reality TV show. He questioned who orchestrated the 9/11 attacks, whether the bin Laden assassination took place and said, "the only thing worse than a gay person is a woman."[129]

Bob Katter supporters are similar to One Nation's. Katter was a member of the corrupt Joh Bjelke-Petersen cabinet in Queensland for many years, revealing in 2003 that he liked Joh so much he had a picture of him on his wall. Katter respected Joh's penchant for freedom, noting that Joh said "we don't want police pulling people up all the time all over the place. That's not what we want in Queensland."[129] That was the end of random breath testing.

Katter left state politics soon after Joh because he was asked to provide a condom vending machine in Aboriginal communities by Mike Ahern, who had replaced Bjelke-Petersen. "Premier Ahern told me that if I did not agree by five o'clock in the afternoon, I would be sacked. I agreed and before I implemented it, I resigned from cabinet."[129]

Katter later ran as the Nationals' federal candidate for Kennedy in far north Queensland before becoming an independent and then starting his own party, Katter's Australia Party. He said, "every decision I make and position I espouse in this place is backed up by very extensive research." So with this research in mind,

Katter has said, "I would walk to Bourke backwards if the poof population of North Queensland is any more than 0.0001 per cent," and:

> NSW…has its gay Mardi Gras and skites about all the people that came out from San Francisco, the city of a million people and 20,000 AIDS cases, presumably to bring their pestilence and plague with them.[129]

Katter also threw eggs at the Beatles when they toured Australia because "someone had to stand up and draw the line in the sand against Beatlemania."[129] Katter is also a member of the Proud Boys, a leading group in the 2021 US insurrection who have been classified as a neo-fascist terrorist organisation in Canada and New Zealand.

Katter represents a low socio-economic electorate, yet his voting record includes voting against restricting donations to political parties, against the availability of abortion drugs and against increasing funding for legal aid and stem cell research. He has also been an opponent of tougher gun control laws, saying, "there is something inherently disturbing with a society where the only people that have guns are the people in uniforms."[110]

The Liberal Democrats, the party that changed its name to fool Liberal voters, has policies that include privatising the ABC and the SBS, and selling public schools, public transportation and hospitals. Like Barnaby Joyce, they want the government to get out of our lives. This goes as far as removing all sin taxes against alcohol and cigarettes and allowing cigarettes to be smoked anywhere and anytime.

The rationale for this is that it impinges on the personal freedom of smokers, and the 87 per cent who do not smoke can find their own way to the hospital cancer ward which is, of course, privately owned. It may have helped that the tobacco company Phillip Morris donated 55,000 dollars to the Liberal Democrats. Another Liberal Democrat policy is to abolish Austudy, meaning that poor people would struggle to send their children to university. Their solution to crime is for the general public to carry guns.

In 2016, the Liberal Democrat Senator David Leyonhjelm, the 'Senator for donkeys' got into hot water for saying women's sport was not "interesting enough" to receive government funding and he further alienated himself from women when he told Greens Senator Sarah Hanson-Young during a debate about women's safety that she should "stop shagging men." Hanson-Young accused Leyonhjelm of "slut shaming" her, won 120,000 dollars in a defamation case against him and promised to donate the money to two women's groups.

Leyonhjelm is all for free speech but when the satirical television show *The Chaser's Election Desk* parked a Wicked campervan across the road from his house that had originally been painted with derogatory references to women but replaced with Leyonhjelm's name, he told the Chaser boys to "fuck off" and threatened to call the police.

The LDP also supports the right-wing Coalition and in August 2015 Leyonhjelm had the government over a barrel as they needed his vote on migration laws. Leyonhjelm had the opportunity to negotiate any number of things that may have benefited his lower socio-economic supporters. His most important priority, however, was to delay the ban on the importation of Adler lever action shotguns for a year in exchange for support. Just like One Nation and Katter, the Liberal Democrats regard arming poor people as a priority.

The Motoring Enthusiasts party was founded on 'road safety' yet Ricky Muir, who surprisingly won a Senate seat due to dodgy preference vote swaps, posted a video online of his 8-year-old daughter doing burnouts. A video of him spitting at the camera and throwing kangaroo poo at his mates didn't help. When it looked as if Muir would win the Senate seat, he went into hiding before doing an interview with Mike Willesee in which he stumbled and appeared flustered. He could not define what the balance of power was, even though he held it.

When Clive Palmer was elected to parliament for the seat of Fairfax, he declared that he would be a "full time politician" but couldn't commit to showing up to parliament every day. His first parliamentary contribution was to ask if his phone was being tapped, later nodding off in Question Time and saying that politics was no fun and he never expected to win. Indeed, Palmer only showed up to 7.7 per cent of the votes in parliament, the poorest record for any politician. A significant contribution from Palmer was to question whether it was a good idea to vaccinate children.

The leader of the Queensland Palmer United Party (PUP), Alex Douglas, sent an email leaked by a disgruntled former PUP candidate. In the email, Douglas derided bogans for "living empty lives. It is no longer satisfactory that they will just buy (and wear) Ugg boots, watch Big Brother, choke on a diet of grease…and rejoice in their ignorance."[130]

Many Palmer candidates in 2022 were anti-vaccine conspiracy theorists with some linking the jab to Aids or claiming that it caused miscarriages. It is unsurprising Palmer's party was anti-science considering Palmer himself advocated treating Covid with Ivermectin, a treatment firmly rejected by health professionals.

Ironically, research shows the higher the PUP vote, the lower the socio-economic status. Douglas noted that the Palmer party Senator-elect Jacqui Lambie was successful because she had an "ace up her sleeve," she came from "Boganland, and she was from a world we see daily and quietly hope will disappear."[130]

It is not just minor parties in Australia that have crazy members. Sri Lanka's health minister endorsed sorcery and magic potions as protection against Covid-19. He took a magic potion which turned out to be honey and nutmeg, claiming a lifetime inoculation against Covid-19. Naturally, he ended up in hospital…with Covid-19.

We have all witnessed how America has been overwhelmed by elected politicians believing that lasers are beamed down by aliens or that the Democrats are a secret cannibalistic paedophile ring based under a pizza shop. We follow closely behind the US in many areas, and with social media and the Murdoch empire peddling conspiracy stories, it is concerning to see the Coalition infected by members who increasingly promote whacky alternative narratives and conspiracy theories.

The elected Liberals Bernie Finn, George Christenson and Craig Kelly all tweeted support for Donald Trump's assertion that he had been robbed of votes. Christenson and Kelly also supported Trump's claim that hydroxychloroquine was an effective treatment for Covid-19, even though it had been debunked by health professionals across the world. Christenson asserted that masks and lockdowns don't work, likening Covid-19 restrictions to actions by Hitler and Pol Pot. He ranted "the truth is women are stupid… you're lucky god gave women no bloody brains." On one level, we can see these as a few politicians who fell through the crazy sieve. Yet when the Deputy Prime Minister Michael McCormack was asked to comment on the conspiracy theories, he said "facts are sometimes contentious and what you might think is right, somebody else might think is completely untrue."[131a] When the deputy prime minister starts spouting such rubbish, you know you've got a serious problem.

Another issue is that some parties and candidates deliberately set out to confuse voters. Perhaps the best example is the Health Australia Party which is anti-vaccine. The Shooters and Fisher Party, an extreme right-wing party focused on hunting, has run ads asking people to join to "protect our native flora and fauna."

The Labor NSW Racing Minister Kevin Greene knew that he and the Labor party were unpopular with voters so he had election signs made that closely resembled the Greens party. When asked about the similarity to Greens advertising, he shrugged and said "I am the one with the e."

One Nation, Bob Katter, the Liberal Democrats and others of this ilk illustrate a major consequence of political apathy in Australia. Parties and candidates of dubious quality gain political support and win seats in parliament. And when these parties have power they act directly against the needs of their constituents. If more Australian voters were interested and knowledgeable about politics, parties such as these would not be elected to parliament and those in lower socio-economic groups may have a better chance at life.

Swinging Voters are Kingmakers

We've seen how apathetic voters influence election outcomes and even decide who governs us. But these voters also dramatically influence the running of election campaigns and even the day-to-day operation of government. As we have seen, uninterested voters are likely to swing from one major party to the other at elections, with studies finding that swinging voters know little about politics. An internal Labor report said that:

> Contrary to popular myth (swinging voters) are not discerning, upper middle-class professionals who carefully reason their vote. They are basically ignorant and indifferent about politics. They vote on instinct for superficial, ill-informed and generally selfish reasons.[131b]

Liberal Party research supported these findings. So what? Does it matter if they can't decide who to vote for and make last-minute decisions based on shaky grounds? Part of the answer lies in the closeness of Australian election outcomes.

Federal politics is remarkably stable, making the choices of swinging voters highly significant as small swings greatly affect who governs. The average election swing between 1987 and 2019 was just 2.9 per cent.[Annexure 49] "It says something about the stability of democratic politics in Australia that 1 in 18 people changing their vote represents an unusually large shift,"[131] with elections of this magnitude often called landslides.

The smallest swing, in 1990, of 0.9 per cent represents 1 in 89 people changing their vote from one major party to the other. A very small number of voters changing parties from one election to another is potentially pivotal in deciding the outcome of individual electorates, as well as the election overall.

The 2010 election was so close that *if* 386 voters had voted Liberal instead of Labor in the electorate of Corangamite, the Coalition would have formed government. In 1993, *if* 2,131 voters in the most marginal electorates had changed their vote, the government would have been different. But it's not just one or two elections where uninformed, swinging voters have had such a potential impact.

In every single federal election between 1987 and 2019, *if* just 13,296 voters on average in the most marginal electorates had voted for the losing major party instead of the winning major party, the result would have been reversed. In other words, for the past 32 years, out of about 12 million votes per election, results have been decided by swinging voters numbering on average about the same as the population of Inverell, one of the towns Barnaby Joyce so colourfully described as "shitholes."[Annexure50]

Radical and Random Swings

So Australian elections only need a small change in marginal electorates to get a different outcome, and uninterested voters are more likely to be swinging voters. And they are also more likely to swing in a radical and at times random way, adding an unpredictable and volatile element to their already disproportionate influence. Six times in the past 10 elections, uninterested voters swung more radically than the actual swing.

In 1990, for example, uninterested voters swung seven per cent to the Coalition, while the general swing was just 0.9 per cent, and in 1993 there was a swing to Labor of 1.5 per cent, while uninterested voters swung 6.7 per cent to Labor. Uninterested voters also swing the opposite way from the overall trend, for example to the Coalition by 1.5 per cent in 2016, while the actual swing went 3.1 per cent to Labor. Only in two out of the last 10 elections did uninterested voters swing the same way but less radically than all voters.[Annexure 51.]

These radical and at times seemingly random swings suggest that uninterested voters are confused and disconnected. Swinging voters are generally described in academic literature as "inadequate, irresponsible and even stupid."[132:100] While academics see apathetic swinging voters as unstable, unpredictable, volatile and capricious, one group can't get enough of them—the politicians.

Chapter Eight
Broader Consequences of
Political Ignorance

Targeting Uninterested Voters

Most electorates are considered safe for one of the major parties, so during election campaigns, parties focus on the battleground seats that have the potential to swing and change hands. Even within these marginal electorates, most voters always support the same party and so it's the swinging, uninterested voter in marginal seats that political parties rationally target.

Liberal Minister and campaign strategist Nick Minchin noted:

> Election campaigns are concentrated in only 30 of the 148 House of Representative seats, and only the swinging voters within those seats. That amounts to about seven per cent of the total Australian voting population.[99:17]

In fact, the concentration is even greater: an average of 19 seats have changed hands since 1987 while the smallest was in 1987 when eight seats changed.[Annexure 52] As the swinging voter is most likely to be the uninformed voter, it is:

> the least informed members within the electorate who seem to hold the critical balance of power…[and] it is easy to take the stable vote for granted. What commands attention as the governor of party success at the polls, and hence administrations and polices, is the changing vote. And shifting or floating voters tend to be those whose information about politics is relatively impoverished.[133:136]

The startling reality is that politicians are most interested in voters who are least interested in politics. Scott Morrison acknowledged the Liberals specifically targeted voters they called the "quiet Australians" in the 2019 federal election campaign. According to Morrison, these people do not think about ideology and are neither left not right.

They are not the "angry mob on social media and in other media, shouting at each other and telling us all what we're supposed to do, think and say." They are simply ordinary Australians who want to go about their day to day business and be "kept safe," especially from boats of asylum seekers and "radical Islamic terrorists."

Crosby Textor Group are long term conservative political consultants credited with masterminding the political victories of John Howard, David Cameron, Boris Johnson and John Key. Jim Reed was Group Director of Cosby Textor and worked on 20 election campaigns, with a record of 16 wins, two hung parliaments and just two losses.

Reed noted that "quiet Australians" tend to live "outside the inner suburbs of our major cities…tend to have average, lower incomes, they have fewer job opportunities, and they have less access to infrastructure and services that we enjoy in the centre of our cities."[134] Unsurprisingly, these are the exact demographics of voters who lack interest in politics.

Morrison claimed that the quiet Australians idea came to him while holidaying on the beach and chatting to ordinary Aussies who didn't really want to talk about politics. It's a better bet the strategy came from a large group of advisers including Crosby Textor who helped shape Coalition election strategy for years, with a continuing focus on apathetic voters.

This strategy meant that all we saw during the 2019 campaign was Scomo kick a ball, Scomo toss some hay, Scomo play lawn bowls, Scomo hit a ball and Scomo throw paper planes in a pub. In contrast, Shorten's policy announcements would often go for an hour and he would invariably take 45 minutes to answer questions from the press. And importantly, Shorten did not do manufactured picture opportunities. One journalist noted that in contrast "Morrison is better every day…I mean he's shearing a fucking sheep."[134] Morrison outperformed Shorten in 2019 by being oriented towards events and issues that resonate with apathetic voters in marginal seats.

Election campaigns set out to target apathetic voters with information (positive, negative or even untruthful) which may seep through and influence their vote at the ballot box. Political debate therefore becomes focused on trivial issues, with parties trying to get apathetic voters to pick up 'snippets' that are positive toward one side or negative towards the other.[135:187]

Labor campaign strategist Rod Cameron said "election results depend increasingly on which party can best manipulate the votes of the politically apathetic. It is an open invitation to politicians to indulge in scaremongering."[99:18]. Manipulation is done in several ways, with the most prominent being the fear campaign. Karl Rove, George W. Bush's campaign strategist said, "The easiest way to get votes is to scare the shit out of stupid people."[136]

Fear campaigns have a long history in Australian politics. Some have failed, but overall they've been successful. Robert Menzies understood the power of fear as a:

> potent instrument of domestic policy. Indeed, a powerful case might be made for the view that the emotion of fear is the most significant of all the emotions on the field of politics...Suppose we are a group of politicians compiling a policy for a popular election. Shall we simply say, 'These things are right and good for Australia, therefore we shall advocate for them,' or shall we, if we are really shrewd men, in the popular sense of the word 'shrewd', ask ourselves what can we promise people in exchange for their votes, or wonder whether on some issue we can frighten the people into voting for us?[137]

Pig-iron Bob followed his own advice, scaring people first with the 'yellow peril', and then 'reds under your bed'. If yellow and red people didn't scare voters enough, there was always the fear of banks being nationalised, which helped Menzies secure victory in 1949.

Great Big Taxes

Campaigns based on the fear that the government is going to take our money are perennial favourites. Shock jock Alan Jones was an advisor to Malcolm Fraser and while having his portrait painted on the ABC TV program *Anh's Brush with Fame,* Jones told a story he thought was very funny:

> I shouldn't tell this story but we were behind and he (Fraser) found out that the polls were diabolical. We went straight to the advertising

102

agency [and] there was a great big screen that had all these houses and written right across them in red [was] taxed, taxed, taxed, taxed. So what's this, Malcolm said to the people. Well, basically, it's Labor taxing the family home. Malcolm said to one of his advisors, what do you think? And this person said, oh Prime Minister I don't think that is what the Labor Party is saying, it's not quite truthful. Alan, what do you think? Well, I said, well Prime Minister it's a bit late in the day to be worried about niceties, I'd be running with the campaign.[138]

The television campaign showed ordinary family homes with large writing dominating the screen saying Labor's 'wealth tax' and a dark, insidious voice saying, "Labor's new taxes, where else would they get the money for all their new promises." Jones added:

The ads were everywhere, taxing the family home going across Australia so I rung my old man the next morning. I said Dad, what are they saying? He said, pardon the language, he said, Jesus are these other lot going to tax the family home? I said why do you say that? He said I saw all these ads on TV, and the polls swung and Malcolm won the election. It's a touch dishonest don't you think? But you know, at the end of the day you're not telling people how to vote, they have to make their own mind up as to whether that is the truth or not.[138]

Labor got payback when the Coalition lost the 'unlosable election' in 1993. Labor Prime Minister Paul Keating exploited the "fears of the ill-informed…[with] opportunist opposition to the goods and services tax."[139] The irony is that Keating had championed his own GST of 12.5 per cent since 1985. During the campaign, Keating appealed directly to the uninterested, arguing, "If you don't understand it, don't vote for it."[140] If this argument was put to apathetic voters every time, they would never vote for anything.

The 1998 election was also dominated by Labor's opposition to the Coalition's GST. By this time, the public had warmed to the idea, with a majority supporting the proposal leading up to the election. But as Labor's fear campaign against the GST intensified, support faded, with opponents outnumbering adherents by almost two to one by election time.[141:388] The campaign helped Labor win the most votes on a two-party preferred basis, though they lost the election. Former Labor

Minister Greg Combet later admitted the scare campaign was dropped because it couldn't be sustained.

The GST seems to be a honey pot for Labor; they exploited it again in 2013 when Abbott refused to rule out a possible rise in the GST rate. Gillard warned Tasmanians they were going to have their portion of the GST revenue syphoned off to Western Australia and Rudd brandished a jar of Vegemite, warning that it would rise by a whopping 52 cents under Abbott.

We may laugh off the Vegemite story but this is pure retail politics aimed at lower socio-economic apathetic voters. They are not interested in macro or micro-economic policies. Anything innately complicated is a turn off. However, if they encounter Rudd brandishing a jar of Vegemite, then the idea that a politician like Abbott making them pay an extra 52 cents for Vegemite could be enough to influence their vote. This could be the sole piece of information they have about the election. In their mind, it's all they need.

Interest rates have also been used to scare voters into changing their vote. In the campaign for the 2004 election, Labor started ahead in the polls although it was shaping up to be a tight election. Then a Liberal Party ad came out showing interest rates had been 10.4 per cent under Whitlam, 17 per cent under Hawke, and 12 per cent under Keating. The ad conveniently omitted Howard's record as Treasurer in the early 1980s, when interest rates hit 13 per cent, claiming interest rates were always higher under Labor.

In fact, interest rates are set by the Reserve Bank and many conditions deciding interest rates are outside government control. A Reuters' poll of economists found they all agreed the 2004 election outcome would not make a difference to interest rates and former Reserve Bank Governor Bernie Fraser dismissed the Liberal scare campaign as "nonsense."[142:205]

The problem for Labor was that swinging voters weren't listening to economists or the former Governor of the Reserve Bank. Instead, they believed the Coalition's ads that interest rates would be higher under Labor and Labor lost the election. Unsurprisingly, 11 of the top 15 high-mortgage electorates exhibited a higher than average swing to the Liberals.

The seat of Holt, in the outer south-eastern suburbs of Melbourne, was the most mortgage-sensitive seat in the country and experienced a 6.1 per cent swing to the Liberals, three times the national average. Academics noted that "there seems little doubt that interest rates won the 2004 election for the Coalition."[143:268]

During the 2010 election, Labor's Emissions Trading Scheme (ETS) came under attack, with Abbott labelling it a "great big tax." Liberal Senator Judith Troeth admitted the campaign against the ETS was "obviously designed to scare."[144:166] Channelling Keating from a previous election, Barnaby Joyce stood up in parliament and said, "If you do not understand this tax then don't vote for it"[145] with Abbott parroting, "If you don't understand it you wouldn't ever vote for it."

By the 2013 election, the ETS had morphed into a carbon tax, which also became a focus for the Coalition. The Liberals' Joe Hockey called Labor Treasurer Wayne Swan "the scariest person in Australia" and Joyce confidently predicted that beef roasts would cost 100 dollars because cows would cost as much as a house.

Abbott claimed the carbon tax "is like a toxic wrecking ball that will destroy jobs" and that the South Australian steel town of Whyalla would be "wiped off the face of the map." The Liberals were successful with this scare campaign, with one Labor backbencher noting, "it's killing us."[146] Before the campaign, 88 per cent had favoured tackling climate change but by election day that figure had dropped to 40 per cent.[147]

The Coalition had been gnawing away at the climate change issue for some time. *Sydney Morning Herald* journalist Phillip Coorey noted, "it is safe to say that at least 80 per cent, even more, of Opposition questions over the last 18 months would have been on the carbon tax."[148] Political debate in parliament was hijacked in order to target uninterested voters and convince them the carbon tax was a bad idea. Meanwhile, a survey showed economists overwhelmingly favoured the tax.[144:170]

Management of the economy was considered the other major issue of the 2013 campaign. Abbott cited a "budget emergency" due to a "debt crisis" that would lead to "debt and deficit disaster" largely directed "at low-income, disadvantaged Australians". And what were the experts saying? Nobel Prize for Economics winner Joseph Stiglitz praised the Labor government, saying the economic stimulus provided after the Global Financial Crisis had saved 200,000 jobs and had actually reduced public debt.[149]

The overwhelming view of economists and the IMF was that the economy was sound.[150] The Gillard government had the lowest unemployment rate in the OECD, the highest growth, and one of the lowest debt-to-gross domestic product ratios. Treasurer Wayne Swan was named by banking magazine *Euromoney* as the world's Finance Minister of the Year for steering the economy through the global financial crisis, and Australia's economy was the fastest growing in the developed world. National accounts grew at 1.4 per cent, the fastest in four years, and the economy expanded 4.3 per cent, making it Australia's 20th consecutive year of growth. The international business advisory firm Dun and Bradstreet advised its clients that "Australia is one of the safest trade and foreign investment destinations globally."[151]

Despite the evidence, Labor lost the election, yet once achieving office the Coalition made no changes to the country's fiscal settings.[152] While 'outraged' that under Labor, government spending was 25.6 per cent of GDP, spending increased to 25.8 per cent under the Coalition soon after gaining office.[153]

The Coalition also increased the debt ceiling and within eight months of being elected, Treasurer Joe Hockey said the "Australian economy is not in trouble." 12 months later, with the economy in worse shape than when the Coalition took office, Hockey castigated those who talked the economy down as 'clowns'.[154]

Labor Hits Back

Labor ran its own well-targeted scare campaign in 2016 arguing the Coalition was scheming to privatise Medicare and 'Americanise it'. The so-called 'Mediscare' campaign had some basis in truth as the Coalition had proposed to outsource the payment system and the 2014 Coalition budget had dramatically cut health funding and GP co-payments.

The Coalition also has a history of privatising assets. It has never been a great friend of universal health care, having killed Labor's original health scheme, Medibank, when it took government in 1975. All of this, according to then Prime Minister Malcolm Turnbull, gave the Mediscare campaign "fertile ground in which that grotesque lie could be told." Tony Nutt, the Liberal Party federal director, said after the election:

> Isn't the broader lesson from this election that lying in Australian politics can win votes, seats and almost win an election…Are we really saying that taking an absolute lie, and shoving it down the throat of vulnerable people in their 70s and 80s who are scared to death that their Medicare might be pulled back is acceptable. Is there no standard? Is there no tactic unacceptable?[155]

The Coalition tried to neutralise the fear campaign by explicitly ruling out the sale of Medicare. Turnbull was indignant, claiming it is "a falsehood and...[Shorten] should stop misleading people."[156] Post-election polling found that almost 40 per cent of voters rated Medicare as the most important issue of the campaign.[157] While Labor lost, it gained 14 seats and came close to winning government.

Scary Different People

Besides hip pocket concerns, another perennial issue played upon is how other people are different to us and therefore, somehow, threatening. This perception seems irrational, given that Australia is a country of immigrants and a highly successful multi-cultural society. But xenophobia is endemic among politically apathetic Australians, which is why it has been used to scare the pants off them.

The Yellow Peril played on the fear of being swamped by Asians, more recently morphing into the Muslim Terror, otherwise known as the "Unlawful Boat People." John Howard's political career "was a sequence of probes to find the one issue with the power to incite the needed degree of resentment and fear in the Australian electorate."[158]

In 1988, Howard said, "if in the eyes of some in the community (Asian migration is) too great, it would be in our immediate-term interest and supportive of social cohesion if it were slowed down a little."[159:82] Anyone that wasn't white was a scary person. In 1999, Howard displayed maps showing that Indigenous Australians would make native title claims over most of Australia and in 2000 he allowed his Minister for Aboriginal Affairs to deny the existence of the Stolen Generation.

At the 2001 election, Howard tailored policy to attract One Nation voters after that party collapsed in the 1998 election. As we've shown, One Nation voters are poorly educated and overwhelmingly ignorant about politics. Demonisation of asylum-seekers with a concentration on border protection directly targeted their fears.

The Coalition's message was clear: vote for us and you won't have to worry about asylum-seekers moving in next door or taking your jobs.[160:244] The Liberals also distributed leaflets in marginal seats highlighting Howard's strong stance against refugees and noting they were interned in detention centres.

The arrival of the Tampa in August 2001 solidified Howard's campaign toward uninterested voters. The Norwegian ship had rescued 438 refugees from a sinking boat but Howard refused permission for them to disembark in Australia. Australian Special Forces boarded the Tampa and within days parliament had passed the Pacific Solution Bill whereby refugees were processed in Nauru rather than Australia.

Immigration Minister Peter Reith claimed that "whole villages of asylum-seekers were on the verge of arriving to spread tuberculosis." He started calling them queue jumpers that were "demanding luxuries denied to hard working Australians."

Reith instructed the Defense Department to avoid personalising or humanising images taken of asylum-seekers. Media images were engineered by the government to make refugees appear a threat, rather than a tragedy. It was a classic example of dog whistle politics, where a subliminal message, not apparent in the words used, is heard by sections of the community. Just to make it perfectly clear that refugees were undeserving of our sympathy, the Howard government falsely claimed they had thrown their children overboard.

Labor supported Howard's refugee policy. Labor MP Steve Gibbons argued it was "driven by those gutless western suburbs MPs who let rednecks determine Labor policy."[161] The last two days of an election campaign always sees a lot of swinging uninterested voters deciding who to vote for. Liberal Party advertising at this time focused exclusively on the Tampa issue. Full-page advertisements displayed pictures of Howard, fist clenched, declaring, "We will decide who comes to this country and the circumstances in which they come." Later academic analysis showed that the border security issue cost Labor power.[162:445].

Refugees were also tied to a fear of terrorism, particularly after the 9/11 attacks on the World Trade Centre in New York. In a *Courier Mail* article during the 2001 election campaign, Howard said, "Australia had no way to be certain terrorists, or people with terrorist links, were not among the asylum-seekers trying to enter the country by boat from Indonesia."[159]

The refugee issue was especially prominent in western Sydney, where migrants from the Middle East lived. Labor focus groups "went like this—boatpeople, illegal's, queue jumpers, street gangs, raping white girls."[163:152] Yet the chances of being killed or injured from terrorism in Australia were almost zero. Bees kill far more people in Australia than terrorism. No problem: politicians understand that most voters have little patience for facts and that myths or scare campaigns work best.

During the 2007 federal election campaign, the Liberals looked likely to lose government and seats such as Lindsay in western Sydney appeared set to return to Labor. So the Liberals created a scare campaign in Lindsay distributing leaflets purporting to be from the Australian Islamic Foundation thanking the Labor Party for its "support to forgive our Muslim brothers who have been unjustly sentenced to death for the Bali bombings"[164] as well as for Labor's support for a new mosque. The ruse was discovered and Howard immediately distanced himself from the leaflets, but his "final days in office were dominated by the dogs of racism and xenophobia he had whistled up in 2001 and which, on the eve of defeat, he was desperate to disown."[164]

Howard lost in 2007, but he had been a highly effective leader because he had learned "that in politics, people's fears are best heard and assuaged early, even when irrational or unjustified."[165:65] Howard played on and intensified these irrational fears, benefiting from them multiple times at the ballot box.

Abbott witnessed Howard's success with race and so he targeted lower socio-economic voters at the 2010 election with similar messages, especially in the western suburbs of Sydney. Major party policies shaped by:

> focus groups and opinion polls showed little sign of responsible and serious approach to the major issues of immigration, sustainable population and the impact of global warming. It is much easier to rail at the leaky boats and their desperate passengers.[166:276]

Race remained an issue after the 2010 election. "Stop the boats" became an Abbott mantra between 2010 and 2013, with one Liberal MP noting the issue of refugees "works incredibly well for us in outer metropolitan electorates."[167] Did Labor respond with an ethical, reasoned position? Nope. Instead, it excised the mainland from the nation's migration zone in 2012, something it had opposed in 2006. This was "an absurd proposal that Australia isn't part of Australia" and Labor was accused of "pandering to particular redneck views in our communities."[168]

Refugees already in Australia were also open to demonisation. Back in the seat of Lindsay, the Liberal candidate at the 2013 election, Fiona Scott, blamed traffic problems and hospital queues in the area on asylum-seekers who arrived by boat. And when one refugee was accused of a criminal offence, Shadow Immigration Minister Scott Morrison demanded that refugees be registered (they already were) and that if they changed address, the police and neighbours should be informed, just like paedophiles. Morrison also urged the shadow cabinet "to capitalise on the electorate's growing concerns about Muslim immigration."[167] The refugee issue delivered about one per cent to the Coalition vote in 2013.[81]

Concerns about Islamic terrorism were also highlighted by politicians in 2015, although their real worries were about something else. George Brandis, the attorney-general, labelled Islamic terrorism "the greatest national security challenge we are likely to face in our lifetimes" and Foreign Minister Julie Bishop called Islamic militantism a "greater threat to world order than Communism during the Cold War."

And yet just a month later, when Senators had the chance to grill the Australian Security Intelligence Organisation (ASIO), no Coalition Senator asked a single question on the issue. ASIO had allotted 3 hours for questioning yet were dismissed in under an hour, with one National Party Senator wishing to hurry proceedings because he was hungry. What were the burning issues that drew their attention? Nine questions were asked on the planned purchase of a kitchen device for the Governor-General and there were 29 questions on car parking in Parliament House.[169]

Race continued as a scare tactic in 2016 with Immigration Minister Peter Dutton claiming that refugees were lazy, illiterate and innumerate while also taking Australian jobs and languishing on the dole. How refugees could be lazy, illiterate and innumerate and, at the same time push dinki-di Aussies out of a job was unclear. No matter, apathetic votes are likely to hear that refugees are either bums and therefore, vote Liberal to keep refugees out, or that refugees are likely to take their job and have even more reason to vote Liberal.

In 2017, Prime Minister Malcolm Turnbull negotiated a deal with US President Barack Obama to send 1,250 refugees to the US on the understanding we would take "people…that they were very keen on getting out of the United States."[170] Turnbull later told Obama's successor, Donald Trump, that:

> We know exactly who they are. They have been on Nauru and Manus for over three years and the only reason we cannot let them into Australia is because of our commitment to not allow people to come by boat. Otherwise we would have let them in. If they had arrived by airplane and with a tourist visa then they would be here.[170]

In what seemed a very bad deal for us, Turnbull told Trump:

We are taking people from the previous administration that they were very keen to get out of the United States. We will take more. We will take anyone that you want us to take. The only people we do not take are people who come by boat. So, we would rather take a not very attractive guy that help you out (sic) than a Nobel Peace Prize winner that comes by boat.[170]

And we did take some nasty guys, including two Rwandans who were members of the Army for the Liberation of Rwanda, a terrorist organisation responsible for the genocide of thousands of people in 1994. They had been captured and confessed to murdering eight tourists in Uganda in 1999 but the case in the US collapsed when the judge determined their confessions may have been garnered by torture. They applied for asylum in the US but the judge rejected their claim because they were potentially violent and posed a danger. So we took them.

At the time of these revelations, parliament was beginning a rancorous debate over whether to allow sick refugees to come to Australia for medical treatment. The Coalition insisted the bill would allow criminals to come to Australia. Channelling Trump's rhetoric on Mexicans, Prime Minister Scott Morrison claimed, "they may be a paedophile, they may be a rapist, they may be a murderer."

Deputy Prime Minister Michael McCormack went further, by leaving out the 'may', and making it clear that 'spivs and rapists and murderers' were on their way even though all the refugees had been vetted and there was no suggestion from anyone other than partisan conservative politicians that these people were criminals. In contrast, when Morrison was asked about the Rwandans, he said he would not comment on people who had not been convicted of any crime.

Muslims and refugees are painted as dangerous yet the Coalition said nothing about extreme right-wing groups holding rallies around the country and refused to stop Liberal National Party MP George Christensen from speaking at one. Meanwhile, the ASIO Director Mike Burgess said that Neo-Nazi right-wing groups were emerging as one of Australia's most challenging security threats. And just to show how boat people and airplane people are treated differently, between 2007 and 2018, there were 44,581 applications to stay in Australia by boat arrivals compared to 110,910 by those who arrived by airplane. We never hear anything about airplane people being murderers or rapists or terrorists or a danger of any kind. Seems airplane people are a class above boat people.

Continuing with the scary foreigner theme, in 2018 Dutton claimed that "the Victorian public is really outraged by some of the goings on…the reality is people are scared to go out to restaurants of a night time because they're followed home by these (African) gangs, home invasion and cars are stolen."[171]

In fact, it was Aussies and troublesome New Zealanders who were overrepresented in Victorian crime statistics. Migrants were also the reason we were doing so well economically, according to the Reserve Bank. Migrants have "created one of the youngest countries among advanced economies, lowered the old age dependence ratio, increased fertility rates and driven economic growth." Recent migrants have achieved a lot while Aussies and Kiwis are running around causing mayhem and robbing people.

In 2022, transgender women were targeted to scare voters. Katherine Deves, hand-picked by Morrison to run in the seat of Waringah, was a well-known anti-transgender activist. She had stated that transgender children had been surgically mutilated and sterilised, and went as far as likening opposition to transgender women in sport to opposing Nazi death camps in World War II. This played well in providing a suitable distraction to Morrison's problems while potentially scaring a number of voters.

Normally in politics, the government and opposition aim to side with majority opinion in order to maximise votes. But when elections are determined by a small percentage of swinging, apathetic voters in marginal seats, as is the case in Australia; major parties are forced to placate the fears and prejudices of this group instead. And it is easier to attack than to inspire. All of us are affected by this because policy content is diluted, insulating "policy choices from public scrutiny, deliberation and contestation,"[114:119] and elevating trivial issues and lies to national prominence.

Ironically, it's uninterested voters who lose the most. Given many are from lower socio-economic groups, the serious concerns they should have about health, education and economic equality are hijacked by issues that have little influence on their lives. Sydney's western suburbs is a clear example. The area's infrastructure was largely ignored by politicians, with many areas without a sewerage system until the 1970s. The first hospital was only built in 1978 and a university only established in 1989. Yet it is the fear of differing races and religions which has been highlighted in order to win people's votes. In this way, a vote based on fear may elect a government that acts directly against the needs of these voters.

The Right Play Harder

We are more critical of the Coalition in this book and there are two reasons for this. The first is that the Coalition has won 7 of the past 9 elections and has held the reins of power more often than Labor and had more opportunity to manipulate us. It is only rational that we focus on those in power. It is also the case that the Coalition and the Right in general are better at playing political games and are prepared to play harder and dirtier than the Left.

The Right is prepared to vilify other races and falsely claim they are rapists and murderers. The Right is more willing to lie, as shown by Howard's claim that refugees had thrown their children overboard. The Right is also more prone to ridiculous hyperbole such as houses costing more than a beef roast because of the carbon tax or that Green activists are terrorists. And the Right will go as far as to blatantly say that science is wrong as we see with their refusal to accept climate science.

The Right is also happy to vilify personalities rather than argue rationally. An example is the Swedish climate activist Greta Thunberg. Conservative politicians and commentators vilified the 16-year-old schoolgirl for her looks, her clothes, her behaviour and her Asperger's. Trump said she had an "anger management problem."

The Daily Telegraph called her speech to the UN "crazy" and "absurd" saying she was in a state of "ridiculous distress" while News Corp commentator Andrew Bolt said, "I have never seen a girl so young and with so many mental disorders." This is how the Right treats a child who is simply reiterating what scientists and experts have been saying for years.

But the Right also go after experts. When academics produced a massive study of 8,343 workers showing Australian workers would be around 106 dollars per week worse off under Work Choices, Joe Hockey wrongly called the academics "trade union officials" who had "cooked up research."[172]

And when economists argued the carbon tax was the best policy to mitigate greenhouse gases, Tony Abbott said, "It may well be…that most Australian economists think that a carbon price or emissions trading scheme is the way to go." But "maybe that's a comment on the quality of our economists rather than the merits of the argument."

A more recent example is the way the Coalition acted during the global financial crisis (GFC) and the Covid-19 crisis. When Labor had power during the GFC, the Coalition continually harped on about the level of stimulus spending to support the Australian economy, highlighting spending on pink bats to insulate homes as well as building school halls.

Yet Australia was one of the few countries to come through the GFC relatively intact. In contrast, when Covid-19 rolled around and the Coalition was in power, they similarly stimulated the economy with around one trillion dollars spending. What did Labor do? They acted in the national interest and supported the Coalition.

If we need another example, we can look at how Morrison vilified the state Labor governments in Queensland, Western Australia and Victoria when they closed their borders because of Covid-19 concerns. No such vilification was directed at the Liberal states of Tasmania or South Australia that similarly closed their borders. Morrison came close to tears when telling the story of a Canberra nurse unable to attend her father's funeral in Queensland. A cynic would point to the fact that Morrison never shed a tear about numerous refugees who suffered under his watch and think it had more to do with the Queensland election being on the horizon.

Even when Labor get a free kick, they often fail to take advantage. The NSW Premier Gladys Berejiklian's secret boyfriend and colleague Daryl Maguire was subject to an ICAC investigation for using his political influence in personal business deals. Berejiklian was inundated with calls for her to resign but found support from the leader of Labor Anthony Albanese who empathised, saying "That's her business, as far as I'm concerned—consenting adults—that is no-one's business except hers."[173] We can readily imagine how the conservative political machine would have handled this had it been a Labor leader.

In an Orwellian twist, the Right also vilifies voters who are interested, knowledgeable and engaged in politics. They deride these people as 'woke'—the Merriam-Webster dictionary defines people who are woke as "aware of and actively attentive to important facts and issues." These are the people best positioned to vote and participate in politics.

Presenters on Rupert Murdoch's Sky television argued they are in a "daily fight" with "woke warriors," while our Deputy Prime Minister vilified "woke" voters who point out the danger of climate change. In contrast, the Coalition and the right pay homage to "quiet Australians" for not being interested in politics. This is *not* how a democracy should work.

The Left, while not perfect, does not vilify people for political gain or say as many obviously stupid things in order to manipulate voters. While the Right does all it can do to win, the Left give the impression they're in the corner discussing consensus decision making, holding hands and singing *Kumbaya*. This is why the Right wins elections in Australia and the Left does not.

And if you are wondering why the Greens feature very little in this book, it is because Green voters are Australia's most politically interested and knowledgeable,[3] which is why they aren't electorally successful. It is like the woman who called out to the US Presidential candidate Adlai Stevenson with "Governor, you have the vote of every thinking person" to which Stevenson replied, "That's not enough madam, we need a majority."

Economic Lies

Apathetic voters are manipulated by lies. The economy is always a major political issue and the Coalition constantly bombards us with the foundational lie that it is better at managing the economy. For impartiality on this, we can look to the International Monetary Fund (IMF), hardly a left-wing organisation; which found that the only Australian governments since World War II that were profligate—that is, profoundly wasted our money—were the Menzies government in the sixties and the Howard government. For all the conservative economic bluster about Whitlam ruining the economy or Rudd wasting money on pink batts, the IMF found that only the Coalition did this.

Leading up to the 2019 election, Morrison asserted, "We have a plan that has been keeping our economy strong." The Liberals even released an advertisement showing Morrison as the Star Wars character Obi Wan Kenobi with the caption, "The economy is strong with this one."

The problem was the economy wasn't strong and the Coalition's only plan was to bring in modest tax cuts, some of which would not kick in until 2024. Five years is a long time to wait for our personal balances to come right and to claim that taxpayers will pay less tax in five years is either empty bluster or foolish economics. As the Jedi master Yoda said, "Difficult to see. Always in motion is the future." And the future hit hard with bushfires in late 2019 and then the debilitating Coronavirus obliterating any budget or taxation promises.

A further dampener for the economy and the Coalition's management of it was that in 2019, the economy was growing at the slowest rate in a decade. We must go back to the September quarter of 2009, when the economy was being buffeted by the Global Financial Crisis, to find a lower rate. The economy Morrison was managing was only saved from falling into recession by population growth (remember those nasty refugees).

Household disposable income grew an average 3.2 per cent per annum in real terms since 1959, but only grew 0.9 per cent between 2016 and 2019. And just three weeks after the 2019 election, the Reserve Bank was forced to cut interest rates to the lowest level seen in this country in an effort to stimulate the economy. A further problem was wages stagnating since 2014, with the Reserve Bank Governor Phillip Lowe virtually begging the government to act more soundly regarding economic management.

And to make us all cry in our Weeties, within months of the Coalition returning to government in 2019, the IMF said that Australia was on track to have a weaker economy than Greece, which was experiencing several years of depression. The IMF echoed Lowe's plea for the government to manage the economy better.

Furthermore, the national debt was 175 billion dollars when the Coalition took office in 2016 and it doubled to 360 billion dollars by the time of the 2019 election. There was, however, no mention of a 'debt crisis'. And when the economy fell off a cliff in 2020 due to Covid-19 and the debt ballooned to 573 billion dollars in March 2020, the Treasurer Josh Frydenberg seemed unconcerned, saying we were looking good compared to other countries. When Sunrise TV host David Koch claimed, "We have relatively low government debt to the size of the economy," Morrison happily agreed.

This was in sharp contrast to his views on debt levels when Australia plummeted into the Global Financial Crisis in 2009 and Labor's stimulus package increased the national debt to 101 billion dollars. Morrison was highly critical at the time, claiming, "what we see now as we seek to climb out of recession" (Australia was not in recession) "is an economy saddled by debt."

Indeed, Morrison claimed in 2009 that Labor was mismanaging the economy arguing, "if you can't manage money, you can't run the country" while the Finance Minister Mathias Cormann mused that "No wonder Labor's budget is in such a mess. They can't add up. Can't get their own numbers right why trust them with ours?" And yet the Coalition made a 60 billion dollar accounting error in 2020 with their Job Keeper program, the biggest accounting error ever in Australian history.

A further problem was that just before the 2019 federal election, the government ignored the recommendations from Sport Australia on how to distribute about 100 million dollars in sports grants. Instead of following the agency's expert advice, the government funnelled the money into marginal electorates. Seeing an opportunity in the seat of Indi, previously held by retiring independent Cathy McGowan, the Coalition splurged 500,000 dollars there.

The ultra-marginal seat of Capricornia received 146,200 dollars and Pennant Hills also received 500,000 dollars, just six days before the 2019 election. A voter who has very little political information may hear that their local footy or netball club has received federal funding and this may be enough for them to vote for the government.

Morrison's reply, when the pork barrel was exposed, was that many worthy organisations miss out on funding and the Coalition "were a responsible government that manages public money carefully." If he meant managing public money to stay in power, he was closer to the mark. Labor did the same thing in 1993, helping them win government. It simply reinforces the impression we really don't care how our money is spent.

A further 150 million dollars funding was released on the eve of the 2019 election. Purported to be targeted at "regional and remote communities," the Coalition claimed the Female Facilities and Water Safety Stream would offer "support for women's participation in sporting activities in our regions and strengthening regional sustainability."

But 80 per cent of the money went to build new pools in just 11 Coalition-held seats, with the lion's share going to the ultra-marginal Liberal seat of Corangamite and the outer metropolitan Perth marginal seat of Pearce. Luke Howarth, Liberal MP for the marginal Brisbane seat of Petrie, announced 2 million dollars for a new school pool just a week out from the election. The pool was never built because the school didn't even want it. A further 10 million dollars was even allocated to the North Sydney swimming pool located under the Sydney Harbour Bridge, hardly a rural area.

Pork-barrel politics is one thing, but climate change presents a much more serious economic challenge. Cabinet documents unsealed in 2020 revealed that in 1989 the Queensland National government received an expert report warning that Queensland and Australia's economy would be adversely affected "if governments failed to act to reduce greenhouse emissions."[173a]

Conservative parties have fully known the detrimental effect of climate change on economic outcomes for over 30 years and yet they still refuse to accept the science of climate change. The Reserve Bank has noted that droughts need to be thought of as trends rather than cyclical events. This is supported by the Australian Bureau of Agricultural and Resource Economics and Sciences, which found that broad care farm profits have fallen by 22 per cent in the past 20 years while the cropping sector has reduced by 35 per cent. The same Bureau reported that climate change is costing each and every farm in Australia around $30,000 a year. Morrison's policy of providing "thoughts and prayers" for farmers just wasn't cutting it.

Professor Tom Kompas, chief investigator in the Centre of Excellence for Bio Security Risk Analysis at the University of Melbourne, found that there would be 1.2 trillion dollars in cumulative damage from 2020 to 2050 caused by climate change. And it was estimated that the bushfires of 2019/2020 could cost the Australian economy as much as 20 billion dollars, with smoke haze just in the cities costing an additional 500 million dollars. The Council of Small Business Organisations urged Coalition politicians who stymied preparations for the bushfire season by not acknowledging climate change to resign.

Morrison had earlier taken to the international stage at the United Nations General Assembly in 2019 to say that Australia is "taking real action on climate change and we are getting results." The reality was that emissions under the Coalition had risen for 4 out of the previous 5 years and were higher in 2019 than in 2013. In contrast, Labor had managed to get emissions to trend down between 2008 and 2013, but with the repeal of Labor's carbon tax, emissions were heading up.

Targeting uninterested voters, Deputy Prime Minister Michael McCormack said during the 2019 election campaign that Labor's proposed support for renewable energy would spell the end of night cricket and footy. In reality, a report showed that the traditional Boxing Day Cricket Test in Melbourne may need to be moved because of climate change.

When it was put to McCormack that 18 of the 19 hottest years on record had been in the past 18 years, he suggested that the Bureau of Meteorology had got its measurements wrong. And during the 2019 election campaign, the UN released a comprehensive, multi-year report revealing human society was under threat from the unprecedented extinction of the Earth's animals and plants. Morrison stepped up to say:

> We already introduced and passed legislation through the Senate actually dealing with that very issue in the last week of the parliament. We've been taking action on that.[174]

Morrison was having a senior moment or was lying because no such legislation existed and had certainly not passed that week. The following day Morrison called existing environmental laws "green tape," and complained that mining jobs were being held up because of native vegetation laws.

The Coalition also ran a campaign against Labor's policy in 2019 to increase the ownership of electric cars. The Coalition and Labor had virtually identical policies regarding electric cars and the Coalition essentially ran a fear campaign not only against Labor policy but against its own. Treasurer Josh Frydenberg had earlier likened Liberal policy of increasing electric vehicles to the introduction of the iPhone while McCormack tweeted that the installation of electric chargers throughout NSW "will not only support the local community but will attract more tourists."

Fast forward to the eve of the election and the Liberals were advertising that Labor was going to tax popular utes and was out of touch. A Facebook ad from the Liberals said, "Bill Shorten and Labor plan to introduce a Car Tax which would increase the cost of nearly all of Australia's new cars."

Morrison said Labor wanted to "end the weekend" for those who want to go four-wheel driving. Labor's only response was to remind voters that both major parties had very similar policies, claiming the government was "so addicted to scare campaigns, they're even scaring you with their own policies."

And Liberal tactics worked, with Therese Houghton from Toowoomba saying,

> I'm a quiet Australian, yes. The clincher came for me was when Shorten stood beside the electric car and started carrying on about electric cars…And it was just idiotic. I just went, 'Oh, my God' and I just thought, *I think you've lost it*. And that was the point I was convinced from that point, I like practical, down-to-earth, real solutions; things you can actually do and achieve, not all the la-la land stuff.[88]

It is fair game to point out the perceived flaws in your opponent's political ideas. It is, however, a travesty of our democracy that politicians can lie so frequently and get away with it. Even worse, politicians say things that are so obviously stupid and we elect them anyway.

Advertising Manipulation

Advertising is designed to get a sale and is often manipulative—just picture those wondrous creams that dissolve wrinkles overnight. Political advertising is full of similar baseless claims targeted directly at politically apathetic, uninformed, swinging voters. Campaign advertising is notorious for distorted information, partial truths or even lies, with issues presented as black and white to depict good and bad, complemented by uplifting or sinister soundtracks to fit the message. These ads aim to sway opinion through appeals to emotion rather than reason.

Clive Palmer spent about 60 million dollars on political ads during the 2019 election. One showed a dusty airport runway in WA and claimed China was attempting a 'clandestine takeover' of our country, supported by the Labor party. The ad was voiced by retired Royal Australian Air Force squadron leader Martin Brewster who was used, presumably, to give the claims legitimacy.

Brewster is Palmer's nephew and a former manager at the billionaire's Queensland nickel mine. The ad, an exercise in scaremongering, was universally condemned and Palmer failed to get any candidates elected but Palmer's preferences to the Liberals were significant.

Treasurer Josh Frydenberg faced a serious challenge from the former Liberal Simon Yates in his well-heeled Victorian seat of Kooyong. The Liberals falsely claimed that Yates was hypocritical about fossil fuels. Yates was understandably miffed the Liberals would tell porkies about him and had his lawyer write to the Liberal Party asking it stop the lies. The Liberals replied that Yates had misunderstood the rules of politics:

> Our primary concern, however, is the apparent misunderstanding of section 329 of the *Electoral Act*, which prohibits misleading and deceptive conduct in relation to casting a vote. Once again, we refer to the High Court authority. The scope of section 329 was carefully considered in the case of *Evans v Crichton-Browne (1981) HCA 14*. The High Court of Australia constrained the scope of that phrase to mean the actual voting process, not the broader process of deciding for whom to vote.[175]

In other words, the Liberals were blowing a big wet raspberry at Yates by pointing out it was lawful for anyone running for political office to lie as much as they want. Ad Standards, the body that self-regulates the advertising industry, noted that "currently, there is no legal requirement for the content of political advertising to be factually correct."[175]

It's a sad indictment of our democracy that we have a law that allows politicians to lie. It is sadder still when politicians lie to us, but the greatest travesty is when we believe them.

Another lie heavily advertised in 2019 was that Labor was going to introduce 'death taxes'. The Liberals started the lie and right-wing minor parties jumped on the bandwagon, with Pauline Hansen paying for ads that said, "IF YOU VOTE LABOR OR THE GREENS YOU'RE VOTING FOR A DEATH TAX." Clive Palmer saturated the market with death tax advertising.

The Liberals insisted they had no role in the lie although head office did pay for a series of Facebook ads 3 days prior to the election—when uninterested voters potentially start to look at politics—stating that Labor had a secret plan to introduce death taxes. Liberal MPs Peter Dutton, Ross Vasta, Ken O'Dowd, Warren Entsch and others all pushed the lie.

Labor MP Susan Templeman complained saying, "We really need truth in political advertising." She may have forgotten that Labor had repeatedly voted against Greens legislation that said political advertisements should be based on truth. Perhaps the strangest lie was Clive Palmer messaging pretty much the whole of Australia asking us to vote for him because he would ban the sending of annoying, unsolicited political texts. The Coalition advertising guru Toby Ralph noted "boring old truth and fact is boring and old. Who wants that? If you're going to change votes you need a strong, emotive misleading ad. I mean truth's a desperate and last resort in advertising."[176]

Major parties account for 90 per cent of political advertising during elections, with the majority concentrated in the final 2 weeks of the campaign.[177] This is because apathetic voters only decide how to vote just before the election or even as they are at the polling booth. Labor strategist Rod Cameron said political advertisements were targeted at the "lowest common denominator, that part of the electorate who would not vote if not for compulsory voting."[99:18] These are the swinging and undecided voters in marginal electorates.

Political parties spend large sums on these ads. The 2 major parties spent an estimated 28 million dollars between them in the lead-up to the 2019 election—and let's not forget Palmer's 60 million dollars. While Palmer didn't get anyone elected, his ads had a significant effect, especially in Queensland, of painting the

Labor party and Bill Shorten in a negative light, therefore benefiting the Coalition. The advertising works for the target audience.

Apathetic voters know little and can be swayed by these advertisements, even as interested voters see the same ads as silly or dishonest. 37 per cent of voters said advertising influenced their decision making in the 2006 South Australian council elections.[178:11] Labor leader Mark Latham reported one woman's view after the 2004 federal election, "The ads feed us, they let us know what's going on."[62:371]

Smaller parties understand the disadvantage such advertising creates for them. The Australian Democrats continually sponsored bills to impose honesty standards on political advertising, similar to the standards imposed on commercial advertising. The Greens similarly proposed a law that political ads must contain truths.

Unsurprisingly, both major federal parties objected. Perhaps neither should complain when the other side says nasty, untrue things about them. In contrast, the ACT, which is the best educated, most politically interested and knowledgeable electorate in Australia, passed a law in 2020 that political parties must tell truths when adverting.

Our Money—Their Lies

The spending doesn't stop after elections. When political parties get into power, they use our taxpayer money to advertise what a good job they are doing. Besides costing us money, the ads are often "full of dissembling, half-truths, fudging, questionable statistics and plain, straight lies."[179:183] Opposing parties, of course, complain about this until they get in and do the exact same thing. In 1995, opposition leader John Howard whinged about Labor advertisements, saying, "taxpayers will see through it. They don't want their money wasted on glossy advertising designed to make the Prime Minister feel good."[180]

Howard also complained about Labor's advertising for its Working Nation policy stating, "propaganda should be paid for by political parties." He claimed the ads were a "disgraceful sham."[110:351] 6 months before becoming prime minister he said, "in a desperate attempt to find an election life raft, the Prime Minister [Keating] is beginning an unprecedented propaganda blitz using taxpayers' money. This soiled government is to spend a massive 14 million dollars…as part of its pre-election panic."

Howard promised that if the Coalition won the election, he'd ask the Auditor-General to draw up new guidelines for the appropriate use of government advertising monies.[181]

Once in power, Howard did no such thing of course, instead spending 1.7 billion dollars of taxpayer money on political advertising. This included Work Choices advertising which cost 55 million dollars, boosting private healthcare at 19 million dollars, and a further 120 million dollars spent to advertise the GST. As *Sydney Morning Herald* journalist Peter Hartcher put it:

> This is a stunning amount. It's enough to accomplish real progress in our society…Howard has spent this vast amount telling us what a good job he's doing…To accept such a condition, we must be either mesmerised by the government's ads or wholly and ruinously apathetic.[180]

Opposition leader Kevin Rudd was just as disturbed about political advertising as Howard had been while in opposition. During Howard's final term, Rudd said, "make no mistake, the purpose of these advertisements was to re-elect the Howard government."[180] In May 2007, Rudd called such self-promotion "a sick cancer within our society, it's a cancer on democracy."

He offered a "guarantee that we will have a process in place that is run by the Auditor-General which will determine what is appropriate for use in government taxpayer funded television advertising campaigns." Asked if he would resign if he failed in implementing this policy, he said, "You have my absolute 100 per cent guarantee that that will occur."[90] However, when Rudd got into office, he suspended "his own flimsy guidelines for policing taxpayer-funded advertising in order to get 38.5 million dollars' worth of ads praising its tax reforms."[182]

Gillard kept up the dodgy tradition, spending 140 million dollars on advertising, about half of which went toward promoting Labor's carbon tax, with the Nationals leader Warren Truss branding it "political propaganda."[183] Once in power though, the Abbott and Turnbull governments spent 100 million dollars on political advertising, with government advertisements which proposed the deregulation of universities branded an "absolute disgrace" by the opposition leader Bill Shorten.[184]

The Coalition even spent 30 million dollars on ads in 2016 purported to be aimed at asylum-seekers, stating, "If you come here by boat without a visa YOU

WONT BE SETTLED IN AUSTRALIA." These ads were initially run only in English and only in domestic newspapers. Perhaps the government was banking on refugees reading online versions via satellite internet on their leaky boats. More likely it was a dog-whistle appeal to uninterested voters that Turnbull was tough on asylum-seekers. Turnbull also spent 8 million dollars of taxpayer money to advertise border protection issues during the 2016 election campaign.

The 2019 election was no better as the Coalition government spent 156 million dollars promoting itself in the year leading up to the election.

The Coalition also spent about 600,000 dollars a day in the final weeks of the election campaign, advertising everything from how the government was going to keep electricity prices down to how it was improving child care and tax cuts. Shorten mused that it would "be good if he (Morrison) surprised the nation and said no more TV ads by the government."

Morrison's reply was "that's the pot calling the kettle black as Labor did it when Rudd was PM." And Morrison was right, because Rudd had spent 3 million dollars doing the exact same thing.

Both Labor and the Coalition have wasted millions of our dollars advertising how great a job they are doing. The Coalition took it a step further in February 2019, just in time for the election, deciding that MPs could use their 137,000 dollars a year taxpayer funded budgets for radio and television advertising. Previously, this budget had been used for stationary, websites, supplies, flyers and print media. This was an important change as research shows that voters who don't care about politics are most heavily influenced by television advertising.

Political advertising calls into question whether Australian elections are free and fair, as voters are potentially influenced by deceptive messages. Apathetic voters are specifically affected as they don't draw on more accurate sources to balance misleading information, and this prevents them establishing informed positions.

The makeup of parliament is also influenced, with parties and candidates often elected because of advertising rather than merit. A major party with a large advertising budget that runs misleading advertising denies other parties, especially smaller and less well-financed ones, the chance to counter deceptive advertising. So not all parties are equally represented within our system. And the taxpayer funds used to advertise how wonderful our government is could be spent more effectively on services for the nation, such as health and education.

Alluring Catch Phrases

During election campaigns it's difficult for uninterested voters to avoid some form of exposure to political advertising and news. Even the most politically apathetic can spit out some information just prior to voting. The problem is the information is often a slogan or catch phrase that the major parties have constantly repeated throughout the campaign.

You might have wondered why politicians bother using such trite and seemingly meaningless buzzwords. But they are not designed for politically interested observers; they are constantly repeated by politicians in the hope that uninterested voters will encounter them at some point, latch on to them and support those politicians as more subtle analysis passes them by.

Slogans and catch phrases are part of every political campaign. Menzies' "forgotten people" was used to emphasise his links to ordinary people, despite his elitist background of a political family, attendance at a private school and studying law at university. Chifley's "light on the hill" referenced a biblical metaphor to appeal to Christian voters. The most famous is Whitlam's "It's time" which transformed itself to a popular song and catapulted Labor to government.

The Australian Democrats made a name for themselves with "keeping the bastards honest," and Howard's 2001 slogan "We will decide who comes to this country and the circumstances in which they come" was a very successful appeal to everyone who believed the country was in danger of being overrun by refugees.

Gillard used the phrase "moving forward" 24 times in 5 minutes when announcing the 2010 election, prompting former Keating speechwriter Don Watson to comment she "sounds like she is training a dog" and "treating voters like imbeciles."[185] Political journalist Laurie Oakes asked if Labor's slogan was procured from a company called "Slogans for Bogans."[186:144]

Tony Abbott constantly spoke in short sentences, useful for getting his message across to uninterested voters. He was also the master of slogans such as "stop the boats" and "big new tax".

"Jobs and Growth" became the mantra for the Coalition in 2016 with Treasurer Scott Morrison managing to say "jobs and growth" 13 times in a speech before the 2016 election. Moderating the Facebook election debate, journalist Joe Hildebrand pleaded, "Can we please make it a slogan-free zone, please no 'jobs and growth'...anything but that."

To no avail, within 12 seconds of the debate starting, Turnbull promised jobs and growth if re-elected. And Morrison premiered a new slogan, claiming Labor was all about "lies and taxes," setting the scene for the government to act more like an opposition party during the 2019 federal election.

There have been misses, with the most notable being the Liberals slogan of "The answer is Liberal" in 1990, to which then Labor leader Bob Hawke replied, "If the answer is Liberal, it must have been a bloody stupid question."

Just do Something!

Politicians also appeal to uninterested voters through action. Not real action of course, but publicity stunts designed to make them look like they are solving Australia's problems. This is seen as a better option than articulating complex policy. With apathetic voters unlikely to care much for policy detail or the subtleties of marginal improvements in macroeconomic conditions, appearing as a person of action is a straightforward way to appeal to them.

In 2003, to keep terrorism in the minds of uninterested voters as well as to look as though the government were doing things, the Howard government posted terrorism kits to all Australian households at a cost of 15 million dollars. Was the timing, one month before the US attacked Iraq with Australian troops sent to help, purely coincidental?

The kit included a fridge magnet with crisis contact numbers and tips on how to spot terrorists. Greens leader Bob Brown accused Howard of using fear as a political weapon: "the Prime Minister knows that keeping people fearful is...going to keep putting votes in his ballot box and...that's a very, very wrong ambition in politics."[187]

Kevin Rudd undertook a national tour of construction sites after the 2009 budget, which had an infrastructure theme. "His almost daily appearances in a hard hat on the evening news became something of a standing joke within government."[135:119] A Canberra journalist noted, "It's very obvious what the strategy is...get an image for the nightly news for people who don't follow politics—an image that makes the government look like it's frantically trying to help people through the economic crisis."[135:119]

Abbott took this further in opposition, turning up everywhere in a fluoro vest, painting himself as "an everyman, one of us, just another Joe who understands the problems and concerns of the everyday voter."[188] Shorten, Turnbull and Morrison also spent a large portion of their time campaigning in fluoro vests.

Policy may also be designed to highlight people's concerns and make it appear as though politicians are doing something. Labor focus groups in 2007 found the cost of living was a major concern so Labor created the impression that the Liberals were responsible for the rising cost of groceries and promised that under a new Labor government, prices would either fall or stop rising.

In fact, measures which have a real impact on reducing the cost of living, such as micro and macroeconomic reform, are complicated and abstract; so Labor unveiled Grocery Watch and Fuel Watch, which were designed to monitor grocery and fuel prices. Former Labor powerbroker Lindsay Tanner said these systems were introduced to appeal to voters who would otherwise pay no interest:

> To a hard-pressed person who doesn't follow public affairs very closely, it looks like the government is doing something…The fact that their impact on the cost of living would be extremely marginal at best was of little consequence: the appearance of doing something was everything.[135]

Both Grocery and Fuel Watch were scrapped soon after Rudd achieved power.

The Coalition hit back when it was revealed a Victorian pizza shop owner was going to increase the cost of pizzas because Gillard's carbon tax meant pizza boxes would cost an extra 2.5 per cent or 1 cent more per box. This became very big news leading up to the 2013 election with the Coalition's Climate Change Minister Greg Hunt saying this makes the pizza shop another carbon tax 'victim' because it has "no ability to pass on the increased charges to customers in a very competitive market."[189] The cost of pizza boxes would only increase a maximum of 1 cent but the scare played nicely to voters who ate pizza and knew little of politics.

While prices have gone up dramatically over the years, so have wages. Ben Phillips, from the National Centre for Social and Economic Modelling, found that the average household was more than 200 dollars a week better off in 2013 compared to the mid-1980s. Higher wages compensate for "higher, more visible prices such as electricity and petrol. In fact, right across the board our research shows Australian households, on average, are better off. We really are the lucky country."[190] Others agree. The OECD's Better Lives Index reports Australia has the "best living conditions among all the rich nations on earth."[191]

But telling voters to stop complaining because they already have it better is unlikely to win support. So political leaders act as if they are on the job and solving problems to appeal to the key uninterested voting bloc, even if they know that most individuals are already better off than before and that their more 'marketable' policies like grocery and fuel watch won't work.

Cost of living issues can attract the attention of uninterested voters because these voters generally earn the least. The Liberals, therefore, made the rising cost of electricity a major issue in 2019. Like groceries and fuel prices, the cost of electricity is something most people understand, and if a government can show itself to be doing something about it, this is potentially a powerful incentive to vote for them—just like our Nepali friend who based his political support on the price of onions.

The electricity issue tied in nicely to the Liberals' disdain of climate science and provided an avenue for calls to build more coal-fired power stations. Peter Dutton was apparently so concerned for the average Aussie struggling under the weight of electricity prices that he proposed axing the GST on electricity. More likely he saw it as an issue that could help him to the prime minister's office.

Electricity prices had increased but there were 12 other things that cost the average Aussie household more than electricity. We spent nearly twice as much eating out each week and nearly twice as much on beer and wine. Other items that emptied our pockets more than electricity were tobacco, fuel and overseas holidays. But telling people to cut spending on ciggies, grog and takeaways isn't politically palatable and may alienate the important uninterested voter.

The broader consequence of appearing as though you are doing things is that elected leaders squander time and taxpayer resources on events and policy designed to manipulate ignorant voters into voting against their own best interests. If uninterested voters devoted some time to better understand politics, they may be more able to protect these interests and avoid being manipulated by politicians.

Media Distortion

Many books have been written about the media's political influence. The media plays a prominent role because most Australians get their political information filtered through the media, with television the most prominent, although social media is dominant among younger age groups. Other than the ABC and SBS, the media is a business where owners are trying to make a buck out of their investment.

The news is, therefore, predominantly designed for a commercial purpose, catering to its audience with politics viewed as dull by most viewers and therefore a ratings killer by media owners.[57:78] Stories that don't suit simplistic solutions are dropped.

We can see the attitude clearly from one television news director who said, "what you news wankers don't seem to understand is we are not here to give our audience credible news at any cost. We are here to entertain and to make money for our owners."[135:155] Peter Manning, formerly of the ABC and the Seven Network, ran up against a similar attitude at channel seven when he tried to do a story explaining the introduction of the GST:

> Not only was the story rejected by every state producer as a threat to their ratings, but I began getting irate phone calls from state managers asking what I was doing. In my silly, ABC tinted view, it was important that Seven's largely working-class audience understood what the GST would do to and for them.[60]

On the other hand, stories about scandals boost circulation, and take priority over complex discussions on policy.[37] The former editor of the Sunday Age, Gay Alcorn said:

> As an editor, I always found scandals around politicians' expenses such as travelling to exotic places for meetings or spending hundreds on restaurant meals reliably dull. Usually, they're tabloid fodder, designed to foster outrage about those greedy bastards living it up on taxpayers dollars. Often the stories encourage cynicism about politics at a time when trust is already fragile.[192]

Even political programs regarded as serious often highlight entertainment rather than nuanced political reporting, meaning important political issues are barely discussed in the media. We can see this in the reduction in election campaign coverage, falling from an average of 4.5 minutes in 1980 to only 2 minutes in 2010.[135:85]

Some people get their political information from shows that are not predominately news-based, such as the morning TV show *Sunrise* or the satirical show *The Chaser*. One viewer summed up his reasons for preferring *The Chaser*, saying it's "a lot more tightly summarised…it takes a lot of concentration to sit through the *7.30 Report*, whereas (*The Chaser*) just sums it up pretty quickly so you can get it, and it's funny, and you actually want to pay attention."[83:205] *The Chaser* was entertaining, but its aim was just that: to entertain rather than inform.

Of course, the commercial media is happy to cover politics when stories have funny, disparaging or salacious elements. Rudd eating ear wax or visiting strip clubs are fun for the media. Gillard tripping and falling in India was a big hit. Howard falling while walking into a radio interview was potentially more serious as uninterested voters could have viewed just this clip and concluded the 67-year-old was too old for the job.

Howard also didn't do himself any favours trying to bowl a cricket ball in Pakistan and bouncing it around his ankles. The UN handed down a report by the Intergovernmental Science Policy Platform on Biodiversity and Ecosystem Services that pretty much said climate change would kill us all but a woman trying to crack an egg on Scott Morrison's head dominated political news that day.

When Rudd was challenging Gillard for the Prime Ministership in 2013, every television station covered the live action in Parliament House. The problem was a lot of Australians had settled down to watch the State of Origin Rugby League match and when 18 minutes of the pre-game analysis was replaced by the unfolding political drama many Australians expressed their annoyance. One viewer said "C'mon Nine, get to the fucken football, its half past 7, let the ABC cover the politics" while another said "is this a G up, its Origin time."

A major political news story was Johnny Depp smuggling his two dogs, Pistol and Boo, into the country on a private jet without proper permits or passing quarantine. Barnaby Joyce threatened to have the dogs destroyed unless "Pistol and Boo buggered off back to the United States." Depp was forced into a (two-faced) apology with the story dominating the news cycle for days and it even ran as the lead article for the BBC. Joyce later admitted that "By saying bugger off, I knew that gave it the surety of a run, though I didn't expect it would run around the world. And two dogs are apparently worth more than a heap of people under collapsed buildings in the 2016 Nepal earthquake."[193]

Sex Sells

Sex gets a good run in commercial media and when politicians and sex intersect then politics is suddenly newsworthy. The British journalist Malcolm Muggeridge said that "Who sleeps with whom is intrinsically more interesting than who votes for whom."[37] There is plenty of evidence of this in Australia.

One notable case was the wife of Hawke government Minister John Brown, Jan Murray, who let slip during a media interview with *60 Minutes* that the couple once made love on Brown's office desk and she left her panties in his ash tray. The program's producer assured Murray this was a private conversation and wouldn't be used in the program, but *60 Minutes* knew they would get better ratings with a sex story rather than dowdy politics and ran the story.

Sonia McMahon, wife of Prime Minister Billy McMahon, dominated world headlines when she wore a sexy dress split right up to her armpits to a White House dinner with President Nixon. She said later, "It certainly made an impact. Suddenly, the world knew where Australia was." Notoriety followed her home, with Billy McMahon commenting that people only wanted to see him so they "could have a squiz at Sonia."

The most famous sex story was Whitlam Minister Jim Cairns and his relationship with his chief of staff, Junie Morosi, in 1975. Speculation was rife that the couple were having an affair and a *Telegraph* photographer hid overnight in a tree outside a unit where Cairns, Morosi and their partners were staying. The photographer snapped a photo of Cairns and Morosi having breakfast on a balcony and the *Telegraph* ran the photo under the headline, "Breakfast with Junie."

It's hard to imagine the *Tele* going to so much trouble to get a story on a government policy decision. It didn't end so well for former Liberal leader Billy Snedden, who had a heart attack and died while having sex. The *Truth* newspaper ran the front-page headline, "Snedden dies on the job." Snedden had never before received so much press.

Over one million tuned in to hear the story of Barnaby Joyce, his affair and subsequent child with his media advisor. The interview was heavily promoted as "raw, unfiltered, and brutally honest" with "nothing off limits." The TV network knew viewers weren't interested in politics, they wanted to wallow in the personal details: how Joyce's wife reacted when she found out, why Joyce questioned the paternity of the child, how he was coping with nappy changing.

Serious political questions, such as excessive taxpayer-funded entitlements on travel with Joyce's mistress, or organising his sweetheart a job with his Senator mate Matt Canavan costing the taxpayer thousands, didn't get a look in. The only outcome was a sex ban between Ministers and staffers.

Political news from Western Australia rarely graces the eastern media. However, when it was revealed the Liberal opposition leader Troy Buswell had sniffed a chair that had been occupied by a female colleague, groaned and made "sexually satisfying noises," the story made headlines across the country.

Perhaps it is not the media's fault for highlighting sex stories. The media's obligation is to sell a product. If we were interested in nuanced political reporting, the mainstream media would cover it intricately as it would sell more newspapers and advertising space, and spike TV show ratings. But voters are not interested in politics and that is why the sport and entertainment sections of the *Telegraph* take up more space than politics and *Married at First Sight* dominates TV rather than the ABC's *7.30*.

The focus on silly, shallow and salacious political content results in cynicism towards politics and politicians. The media, therefore, has a major role in fostering political apathy, creating a downward spiral of decreasing interest. Voters, and especially uninterested voters, are less able to interpret political news in any meaningful way. They are more volatile in their decision-making and more open to shallow forms of persuasion, especially from occasional viewing of tabloid news.

Murdoch's Gift to the Nation

What and how the media chooses to report is highly influential on their customers' attitudes. And these attitudes affect policies and the regard for political parties and leaders. The media can also highlight certain issues which influence the political agenda, and ultimately people's opinions and voting choice. Rupert Murdoch's News Corp media company is especially influential in Australia because of its near monopoly of newspapers and its parochial coverage as it highlights news stories based on Murdoch's right-wing view of the world. Tony Abbott praised *The Australian* newspaper as Murdoch's "gift to the nation" but it's more a gift to the Coalition as Murdoch has done his upmost to deliver conservative rule.

On polling day in 2001, the *Telegraph* newspaper used pictures of a burning vessel to tell its readers that asylum-seekers were "the burning issue" of the election. Gillard was pilloried in 2010 for forming a minority government, with the *Telegraph* headline "The Big Steal" and the editorial demanding new elections. Murdoch's papers continued the attack throughout Labor's term with headlines such as "Carbon tax promise has Julia Gillard choking on her words." The article labelled Gillard as "ludicrously dishonest and dumb," not exactly the impartial reporting that might help readers make their own well-informed decision.

The 2013 election was a low ebb for the Murdoch papers with headlines imploring readers to "Kick this mob out". The ABC's Media Watch found that half of the *Daily Telegraph*'s 80 stories were slanted against Labor with none against the Coalition in the first week of the 2013 campaign. Over the next two weeks, only three stories favoured Labor.

You would think the Murdoch press would have been happy with a conservative government, but Turnbull wasn't conservative enough for them so it turned its guns on him, in large part advocating for an Abbott comeback. When it became obvious, even to the Murdoch press that the public wouldn't stand for Abbott returning, they started advocating for the arch conservative Peter Dutton.

Dutton makes jokes about "being on Cape York time" and that Pacific Island leaders would have "water lapping at their door" because of climate change. He boycotted the apology to Aboriginal people over the stolen generation but doesn't think he's racist for saying that Lebanese immigration was a mistake or that people in Melbourne were "scared to go out to restaurants" because of "African gang violence." And then there is his draconian treatment of refugees and his antipathy toward gay people. This is the man Murdoch viewed as the best and brightest to run our multicultural, super diverse country.

And so the Murdoch press set its sights on Turnbull. Headlines in the days leading up to the challenge included, "Political mistakes bring PM to moment of truth," "It's time for the Coalition to look for its next leader" and "Malcolm Turnbull has thrown up his hands as we sink in debt." National debt had dominated Murdoch papers while Labor was in power and we owed 175 billion dollars. It ignored debt when the Liberals got in, and the debt more than doubled to 360 billion dollars. But with the possibility of replacing Turnbull with someone more conservative, the issue was resurrected and Turnbull blamed.

In 2019, all the polls showed Labor was going to win and Shorten was so confident he became the first contemporary leader to decline a sit-down cup of tea with Rupert Murdoch. News Corp retaliated as the *Telegraph*'s first front page for the 2019 election campaign read "Tax Time Bomb," claiming Labor had a 387 billion dollar tax blowout and that "Bill Shorten would lead the highest taxing government in Australia's history".

The *Tele* warned a "raft of radical Labor policies on transgender issues would result in children undergoing unnecessary sex change procedures." Regarding Labor's support for bulk billing pathology tests, the *Tele* ran the headline "Blood Money" as well as a beat up on children protesting about climate change under the heading "Kiddie pawn."

Front page headlines on Labor's plan to tackle climate change included "Pay as you eat", "Labor's plan hits food costs" and "Carbon Bills Green Whack." The main line taken by News Corp was that prices would increase if Labor gained power and acted to stop climate change. Like Rudd's jar of Vegemite, this was retail politics aimed at apathetic voters who are economically disadvantaged. Seeing these headlines may have been all that was required to influence their vote.

Murdoch treats Labor and the Coalition very differently: when the Auditor General found that the Coalition had squandered 102 million dollars on the sports rorts affair, the story was buried on page ten in a minor article of the *Courier Mail*. In contrast, when there was an allegation the Queensland Labor government may have rorted 15 million dollars to pork-barrel seats it was a front page story, with News Corp calling for the minister to be sacked. It's not surprising that Murdoch's *Courier Mail* has endorsed the Liberal National party for the last 19 federal and state elections.

There is nothing wrong with a media organisation taking one side of politics. Indeed, most media outlets do this, with Fairfax and the *Guardian*, for example, generally on the left side of politics. The concern is that Murdoch's News Corp manufactures and distorts news for political purposes. Perhaps the best example is News Corp's portrayal of climate science. A report studied how climate science was reported in the *Telegraph*, *Courier Mail*, *Australian* and the *Herald Sun* between April 2019 and March 2020.

It reviewed 8,612 articles of news, opinion and editorials and found that 45 per cent expressed criticism of climate science, swelling to 65 per cent for opinion pieces. Indeed, Andrew Bolt, an acknowledged climate sceptic with no science background at all, alone accounted for 12 per cent of all climate coverage, totalling 405 opinion pieces. In contrast, just six per cent of articles featured *any* scientist at all.[194] This is how scientific issues are covered in Murdoch's media—without the actual science.

Not only does News Corp act against the rational interests of its audience, it also potentially kills and harms people. This is because lower socio-economic voters may be influenced to vote for parties more likely to constrain health services and more likely to go to war, evidenced by the Vietnam and Iraq conflicts which Labor and left-wing parties were fervently against.

Another stark example is Fox News commentators in the United States either ignoring or downplaying Covid-19 with the influential host Sean Hannity calling Covid-19 a "hoax." It didn't help that Australian Sky host Alan Jones claimed that Covid-19 safety measures were just "hysteria and alarmism…We now seem to be facing the health version of global warming" while broadcasting in splendid isolation of his home in rural Fitzroy Falls. Or when Trump suggested that people inject disinfectant as a way to fight Covid-19, Sky's Chris Kenny commented it was certainly "worth a look."

The Murdoch press also has the power to incite hatred. This may be Murdoch's most significant contribution to Australian life and culture. In 2018, Murdoch papers ran a total of 2,981 negative stories about Muslims. This is about 8 stories a day about Muslim terrorism, violence or the like. Columnist Miranda Divine devoted 16 per cent of her 185 opinion pieces to warn us of the dangers of Muslims, while Janet Albrechtsen wrote 27 per cent, Greg Sheridan 29 per cent and Andrew Bolt, who was found to be a racist by a court, had 38 per cent.[195]

Malcolm Turnbull and Kevin Rudd both pointed out that News Corp operates like a political party working closely with right-wing politicians who agree with

Murdoch. Kevin Rudd went further, describing Murdoch's influence on Australian politics as "the greatest cancer on the Australian democracy."

It is concerning for our democracy that Murdoch's Australian media has evolved into a version of America's Fox news and that a foreigner can own a virtual monopoly of newspapers that regularly lie and manipulate in order to gain electoral benefits.

Bushfire Manipulation

The bushfires that ravaged Australia in 2019 and 2020 illustrate the effects of the manipulation of the Australian public and their consequent suffering because of decisions made at the ballot box. Devastating bushfires kicked off much earlier than normal in September 2019 and culminated in massive, unprecedented blazes in December and January 2020.

Residents huddled on beaches in Eden and Malua Bay for safety. Around 1,000 Australians were evacuated from Mallacoota by the Navy, an unparalleled event in Australia. It was estimated that three billion animals perished in one of the "worst wildfire disasters in modern history."

The town of Eden lost its wood chip mill, Mt Selwyn lost its ski resort, apple orchards in Batlow and dairy farming in Bega were devastated and 17 million hectares destroyed. 33 people lost their lives, more than 3,000 homes were destroyed and 4.6 billion dollars of insurance was claimed for fire damage.

The air quality in Sydney, Canberra and Melbourne was the worst in the world, leading many to suffer breathing problems. The Australian Tennis Open delayed games and one player was taken to hospital with a coughing fit. Booms were needed in dams to protect Sydney's water supply from contaminated ash.

The havoc awaiting Australia because of climate change has long been known. The expert Climate Change Review undertaken by Professor Ross Garnaut in 2008 stated, "the weight of scientific evidence tells us that Australians are facing risks of damaging climate change." The report noted that:

> The risk can be substantially reduced by strong, effective and early action by all major economies. Australia will need to play its full proportionate part in global action. As one of the developed countries, its full part will be relatively large. [Without mitigating climate change, the projections] suggest that fire seasons will start earlier, end

slightly later, and generally be more intense… This effect increases over time but should be directly observable by 2020.[196]

A federal government plan to prepare for climate change national disasters was left to gather dust for one and a half years before the bushfires hit. The report by the National Disaster Risk Reduction Framework warned the changing climate was exposing Australia to natural disaster on "unimagined scales, in unprecedented combinations and in unexpected locations."[196]

By April 2019, 23 former fire and emergency leaders had been trying for months to warn the government that Australia was ill-prepared to deal with major fires but Prime Minister Morrison wouldn't speak with them, primarily because these experts were concerned about the impact of climate change. One of the group, Greg Mullins, a former NSW Fire and rescue chief, said earlier preparation of the kind the group wanted to suggest would have helped prevent deaths.

One of the ways politicians manipulate us is to follow the template of the National Rifle Association in the USA. The NRA told One Nation representatives their policy when a gun massacre occurred was to firstly say nothing. If the media persists then go on the "offence, offence, offence" by smearing opponents. 'Shame them' with statements such as "How dare you stand on the graves of those children to put forward your political agenda?"[197] This is how the NRA goes about manipulating the public and the tactics undertaken while bushfires raged across Australia were similar.

At first there was little said about the fires and certainly nothing about the effect of climate change. Morrison was in Hawaii sipping Mai Tais and saw little point in returning until he was shamed into it. Sarah Perkins-Kirkpatrick, a climate scientist with the University of NSW's Climate Change Research Centre, said she was "surprised, bewildered, concerned" that the emergency had prompted little discussion from political leaders:

> Here we are in the worst bushfire season we've ever seen, the biggest drought we've ever had, Sydney surrounded by smoke, and we've not heard boo out of a politician addressing climate change.[198]

Greens Senator Richard Di Natale said:

Every politician, lobbyist, pundit and journalist who has fought to block serious action on climate change bears responsibility for the increasing risk from a heating planet that is producing these deadly bushfires.[199]

When it was obvious experts and some media were not going away, conservatives started shaming those who spoke out supporting expert opinion. Deputy Prime Minister Michael McCormack attacked Di Natale saying:

Comments coming from a little Melbourne apartment from a little individual with a little mind should not be accepted or tolerated at this time...They don't need the ravings of some pure, enlightened and woke capital-city greenies.[200]

It may not have been the time to talk about climate change but it sure was time to call the Greens names. Greens MP Adam Bandt replied saying, "thoughts and prayers are not enough, we need science and action too" and likened the response to the bushfire crisis to that of conservative politicians in the US after a mass shooting.

Another way to confuse uninterested voters is to "flood the zone with shit," a term coined by Steve Bannon, the former political strategist for Donald Trump and former head of Breitbart News, which consistently promotes right-wing conspiracy theories and misleading stories. The purpose is to bombard people with so many contradictory claims, conspiracy theories and distortions that voters simply throw up their hands and say it's all too hard and thereby disengage.

And so conservatives set about flooding the zone with shit. Barnaby Joyce blamed environmentalists, saying they had stopped fire fighters from reducing fuel loads, while the Sky program hosted by Chris Smith implied that Greenies were starting fires to try and get their climate change message out. Tony Abbott said the world was "in the grip of a climate change cult."

The Liberal MP George Christenson claimed, "its man-made arson that, to me, almost borders on terrorism." Morrison initially refused to acknowledge a link with climate change, something the Australian Bureau of Meteorology has long known. He said the issue of fuel reduction burns was "commonly" raised with him before implying that people who blame climate change for the fire may be the same people who "don't share the same urgency of dealing with hazard reduction."

Appearing on a British television program, Liberal backbencher Craig Kelly defended the Morrison government. "I follow the science," he claimed, before saying, "if you look at our science, if you look at the long-term record rainfalls in Australia there is simply no trend."

Kelly eschewed any blame saying, "To try and make out—as some politicians have—to hijack this debate and exploit this tragedy, to push their ideological barrow that somehow or other the Australian government could have done something to reduce its climate emissions that would have reduced these bushfires is just complete nonsense." He also claimed that the fuel build-up and the drought were the main contributors to the bushfires.

The host, meteorologist Laura Tobin, pointed out that "you have the second highest carbon emission per person on earth and you're burying your head in the sand." Kelly later tweeted that Tobin was "an ignorant Pommy weather girl" with Tobin responding, "I'm a meteorologist: a degree in physics and meteorology, 4 years as an aviation forecaster for the RAF, 12 years as a broadcast meteorologist, attended a WMO (World Meteorological Organisation) climate course last year and up to date with all the science."[201]

The Australian ran a story that falsely claimed that 183 arsonists had been arrested in the "current bushfire season" which was subsequently tweeted by Donald Trump and other conservative groups. The figure of 183 was arrived at by including people who had contravened fire bans and used annual figures rather than those for the current fire season.

The misinformation was too much even for Rupert Murdoch's son, James, who declared that he felt "frustration with some of the News Corp and Fox coverage" of the climate crisis, particularly the "ongoing denial among the news outlets in Australia, given obvious evidence to the contrary."

While conservative politicians and commentators were flooding the zone with shit, experts such as the NSW's Fire Service said that arson did not play a role in the bushfires. Only one per cent of land burnt in NSW during the bushfire season was officially attributed to arsonists and this figure was less in Victoria. Philip Zylstra, an Adjunct Professor at the School of Molecular and Life Sciences at Curtin University, and a flammability expert, said that there was "twice the amount of prescribed burning compared to the decade before."

The Rural Fire Service (RFS) also contradicted claims that environmentalists had halted hazard reduction work. The Country Fire Authorities chief officer Steve Warrington said advocating hazard reduction as the panacea to bushfires "is just quite an emotional load of rubbish, to be honest." Professor David Bowman, the Director of the Fire Centre Research hub at the University of Tasmania, said, "It's ridiculous. To frame this as an issue of hazard reduction in national parks is just lazy political rhetoric."

Professor Ross Bradstock, the Director of the Centre for Environmental Risk Management of Bushfires at the University of Wollongong, said, "these are very tired and very old conspiracy theories that get a run after most major fires. They've been extensively dealt with in many inquiries."

A study of Queensland's historic 2018 bushfire season had found the extreme temperatures that coincided with the fires were four times more likely because of human-caused climate change. The peer-reviewed study, led by University of New South Wales climate scientist Dr Sophie Lewis, demonstrated the influence of extra greenhouse gases in the atmosphere on a single bushfire event. And as late as November 2019, Australia's National Environmental Science Program said that "Human-caused climate change has resulted in more dangerous weather conditions for bushfires in recent decades for many regions of Australia."

Yet despite the enormous amount of scientific evidence and expert opinion identifying the real cause, the tactic of obfuscating blame works. While experts do their best to challenge disinformation, invariably some uninterested voters are influenced by the lies.

The fires were so bad that Morrison was forced to return home from holidaying in Hawaii, but things went downhill from there. On a visit to Cobargo, which had just been devastated by the bushfires, Morrison encountered a woman who refused to shake his hand. He had to reach down and lift her hand to limply shake his. A crowd gathered and one woman said, "What about the people who are dead now, Mr. Prime Minister? What about the people with nowhere to live?" Another shouted, "You're an idiot mate" before Morrison and his offsiders beat a hasty retreat. One fire fighter approached the media with the message, "tell the Prime Minister to get fucked" while another screamed that Morrison should "stand down now."

Things didn't get any better when the Prime Minister visited Kangaroo Island. Morrison was captured on video saying, "thankfully we've had no loss of life" to which a person replied, "We've lost two." Morrison had shown a deft hand manufacturing his personality during the 2019 election, but faced with real life consequences of Coalition inaction on climate change, the facade was suddenly crumbling.

Morrison fell back on what he knows best: he released an advertisement of him in the bushfire areas beside firefighters, noting he had called out the military to help. The ad initially carried a donate to the Liberal party button, roundly panned as crass. The government then released full-page advertisements telling military reservists they were being called up. It may have been more economically sensible to send emails but it played better politically to advertise, especially in the Murdoch papers where full page advertisements ran just so the military could find the information.

In an attempt to rectify the government's image, Morrison grudgingly acknowledged that climate change was a factor in the bushfires. We even had the Science Minister, Karen Andrews, saying, "lets accept the climate has changed, the climate is changing and we need to look at what we're going to do about it." Everyone seemed shocked that Australia had a Science Minister; she had never said anything about climate change before.

However, the following week with the bushfires already in the rear vision mirror, Morrison was back arguing that "hazard reduction is as important as emission reduction and many would argue, I think, even more so because it has an even more direct practical impact on the safety of the person going into bushfire season."[201a]

The only other practical measure was to establish a Royal Commission into the bushfires which provided breathing room of around a year for the government. Any question on the bushfires allowed the response of "we are waiting for what the Royal Commission determines."

Unsurprisingly, "hazard reduction would form a key part of the inquiry, after Prime Minister Scott Morrison demanded an investigation into whether controlled burns and land clearing operations had been hampered across the country."[201a] Climate change wasn't even a reference item for the Royal Commission to look at.

Weeks after the bushfires, 270 scientists with expertise in climate, fire and meteorology signed an open letter calling on political leaders to take urgent action to reduce greenhouse emissions and engage constructively in international agreements. Australian National University scientist Nerilie Abram said the letter came about because of "despair" that scientists had been warning for decades that climate change would worsen Australia's fire risk.

The Bureau of Meteorology even told the Royal Commission that the bushfire season had "played out" just the way they had said it would as "climate drivers in the past few years lead to an extended dry period."

However, when Liberal Senator Jim Molan was asked what evidence he relied on to justify inaction, he boldly stated, "I'm not relying on evidence." The unfortunate reality is that uninterested voters will have forgotten about the bushfires by the next election and they will be more afraid of the cricket being cancelled because of Labor's climate change policies. There is, however, something innately wrong with our democracy when we elect a government that does not take expert advice and act to protect us.

Voting Against Your Own Interests

Uninterested voters are easily influenced by biased reporting and misinformation about key events and issues that affect them because they do not seek unbiased information. With a diet of celebrity gossip, pop culture and trivially biased political reporting, uninterested voters fail to recognise their own disadvantage and demand remedies.

Murdoch's opinions and interests are directly opposed to those of many of his readers. Wealth redistribution policies are logically more appealing to the poor. Yet the media that uninterested individuals are exposed to, such as News Corp, take little interest in health, education, poverty or social mobility. Instead, it focuses on issues that have little or no impact on their lives, such as refugees.

This means that the chance for serious political change is undermined as democracy requires voters to engage and understand issues. If the only news placed before most citizens is negative, personal and trivial, then serious reforms, especially ones that seek to address economic disparity, will be stymied. This is a major consequence of political apathy. As stated in the introduction, 25 per cent of voters may have voted differently if they had a better knowledge of the facts.

A good example is the 1999 republican referendum. 6 weeks before the referendum, 347 ordinary Australians were polled on how they intended to vote. Just prior to the vote, these 347 people assembled in Canberra for a weekend organised by the Australian National University in conjunction with the University of Texas to hear arguments from prominent Australians such as Don Chipp, Barry Jones and Bob Hawke.

Both sides of the republican debate were argued, and participants had ample time to debate the pros and cons of the republic with experts and each other. This gave participants a chance to understand how our democracy works and what the republic would mean for Australia. After the weekend, support for a republic among the 347 rose from 53 per cent to 73 per cent.[202]

Most Australians didn't have the benefit of these deliberations. The government funded an education campaign for the referendum, but "it appears to have had little success."[33:258] The Yes campaign focused on positive images of Australia, encouraging voters to vote for one of their own to be president. The No campaign railed against the "Chardonnay swilling elites" who had fomented a plot to change the politics of Australia.

Some No proponents asserted the republic would lead to Australia being thrown out of the Commonwealth and unable to compete in the Commonwealth Games, that we would have a new flag and they even floated the idea of a Weimar-like republic, with the spectre of Hitler hanging over it. The republic received strong support among educated, interested and knowledgeable voters and "indifference and hostility the further down the social spectrum one moved."

One academic study, by Professor Ian McAllister from the Australian National University, found that the least informed and interested people indicated they would not vote if not compelled. The study checked knowledge of the republican issue with four questions: those not wanting to vote could correctly answer only one question; those wanting to vote answered two.

Still not a great reflection on our democracy, but those who wanted to vote had a better knowledge of the issue. More importantly, the study found that if the voters who didn't want to vote hadn't voted, the referendum would have been successful and an Australian would be our head of state today.[33]

In another example, a 2007 conference on terrorism and attitudes to Muslims, more than 300 randomly selected citizens heard talks from Christian and Muslim religious leaders, psychologists, terror experts and immigration advocates, as well as survivors of terrorism. Participants also took part in discussion groups, exposing them to "extreme, progressive and conservative points of views…from both Muslim and non-Muslim perspectives."[203]

Before the conference, 49 per cent thought that incompatibility between western and Muslim values was a big contributor to terrorism. This fell to 22 per cent after the conference. Other opinions also changed. Initially, 44 per cent thought that Muslims coming to Australia was detrimental to national security; this dropped to 23 per cent after hearing both sides of the argument. And those who thought Muslims were a threat to the Australian way of life decreased from over a third to a fifth of attendees. A better understanding of the issues led people to change their minds.

Not only do apathetic voters miss the chance to be informed on issues, they also risk being harmed by the very politicians they vote for. When John Howard gained power in 1996, he cut the budget of the Aboriginal and Torres Strait Islander Commission and later closed the department. He cut the Office of the Status of Women by 38 per cent, Human Rights and Equal Opportunity Commission funding was slashed and grants for women's advocacy groups were halved. These agencies provided support for the most disadvantaged.

Paul Keating's Working Nation programs were also cut, which meant that many lower socio-economic individuals remained untrained, leading to skills shortages 10 years later. University fees were increased, meaning poorer people found it more difficult to attend university. Conversely, funding for private schools increased 92 per cent while public schools suffered from a six per cent funding cut.[204] Ironically, it was the 'Howard battlers', the lower socio-economic individuals who delivered the Howard government in 2004, who were the very section of society targeted for cuts.

The Abbott government's attacks on those who supported them are another example. Abbott's 2014 budget denied anyone under 25 unemployment benefits, stripped 80 billion dollars from health and education, and scrapped funding for homeless and housing groups. The Coalition also stripped more than 15 billion dollars from lower income families, in what ANU Political Science professor, John Warhurst, described as "one of the most vicious attacks on ordinary people that we have seen in recent Australian history."[150]

The poorest two per cent of households lost 7.1 per cent of total disposable income over four years, compared to the top 20 per cent whose disposable income increased by 0.2 per cent. Households in western Sydney lost around 1,066 dollars for the year compared to rich households in the eastern suburbs which gained 177 dollars.[205]

The Coalition also introduced a Medicare co-payment, meaning the cost of health would increase. Sydney University research showed it "would hit vulnerable groups the hardest and could deter them from seeking medical care", with pensioners paying an extra 200 dollars per year for medical services. All this was on the back of a two per cent swing by uninterested voters to the Coalition in 2013.

Targeting women, Tony Abbott had said, "I think it would be folly to expect that women will ever dominate or even approach equal representation in a large number of areas simply because their aptitudes, abilities and interests are different for physiological reasons."[206]

And in 2004, when a cervical cancer vaccination was discovered, Abbott said, "I won't be rushing out to get my daughters vaccinated [for cervical cancer], maybe that's because I'm a cruel, callow, callous, heartless bastard but, look, I won't be." The vaccination saw cases of human papilloma virus infection drop nearly 60 per cent by 2013.

Abbott as Health Minister in 2005 also banned the abortion drug RU486 against advice from the Australian Medical Association. The issue sparked controversy, ending with a parliamentary conscience vote to strip Abbott's power to block the drug. Medical experts at the Therapeutic Goods Administration were given power to take control of RU486.

Based on such a sterling record, upon winning government in 2013, Abbott appointed himself Minister for Women and when asked a year later what he had achieved for women, his only response was that he had repealed the carbon tax. This was important, he said because "women are particularly focused on the household budget and the repeal of the carbon tax means a 550 dollars a year benefit." Greens leader Christine Milne said Abbott may as well have said that "he's been able to give women more money to buy a new iron and stay at home and do the ironing more."

In March 2013, in one of its final acts, the Gillard government created the National Disability Insurance Scheme (NDIS) and used its last budget to commit 14.3 billion dollars to fund it. In 2014, just as the scheme was expanding nationally, the newly elected Abbott government imposed a staff limit for the NDIS of 3,000.

The Treasurer, Joe Hockey, said, "the days of borrow-and-spend must come to an end." The call centre and many other functions of the NDIS were outsourced to private contractors but it was plagued by IT problems, and funding for upgrades was not provided. This led to people with disabilities and service providers struggling to access the system.

A complete system meltdown in 2016 then left providers without payments for months. Things failed to get better for those most marginalised in our community. The Morrison government promise of a surplus in its pre-election budget in 2019 showed the conservatives were going to underspend 1.6 billion dollars on the NDIS. This meant that 92,000 disabled people would miss out on NDIS support and by January 2020 the result was that more than 1,200 citizens had died while waiting for an NDIS package. If any disabled people voted for the Coalition, they voted against their own interests.

The Labor opposition ran a complicated election campaign in 2019, wanting to do away with negative gearing for properties and halve the capital gains concessions when investors sold properties. Labor also wanted to stop share franking credits, where investors who pay no tax get a tax refund from the government through their franking credit.

It is doubtful poor voters knew what a franking credit was, let alone benefited from them. With the added tax revenue, Labor wanted to increase award pay rates for lower paid workers and reinstate penalty rates for weekend workers. This would have directly benefited casual and young workers. Labor also promised to better fund public schools and TAFE, fund cancer patients and restore indexation of Medicare, which the Coalition had cut.

Labor's policies were aimed at benefiting the poor and marginalised and the policies were released well before the election. The Coalition in contrast, had few policies, with the campaign focused on Morrison kicking balls or showing up in fluoro shirts saying, do not vote for Labor because it had "death taxes."

The conventional wisdom is Labor lost the election because it waged "class warfare" against richer Australians. John Howard, for example, argued that Labor had "overplayed its hand on the class warfare stuff." Howard may have been right that it was an election based on class; the crazy thing was that electorates that were dominated by poor and marginalised voters swung harder to the Coalition. In contrast, wealthy electorates that benefit from property and share investments swung towards Labor.

Indeed, the 10 seats with the largest swing to Labor had median incomes 40 per cent higher than the 10 seats with the biggest swing to the Coalition. Rich seats such as Higgins in Melbourne, which includes Toorak and South Yarra, swung to Labor; while poor seats such as Herbert the Queensland seat based around Townsville, swung to the Coalition.

That means richer voters, who own shares and property and are generally better educated and informed about politics, were willing to give up their financial benefits of franking credits and negative gearing so that more money could flow into the government's coffers to directly benefit the poor and marginalised. The poor and marginalised meanwhile, said stuff that, you guys keep your franking credits and negative gearing because we are happy to go without better health care and we will work Sundays without penalty rates so you can have cheaper cappuccinos!

On reflection, that doesn't sound like something the poor would say. A better explanation is the poor were manipulated by a dodgy fear campaign because they lacked basic information about politics. It's a curious conundrum when landlords backed Labor and renters backed the Coalition, especially when landlords voted to give renters free childcare and better wages while tenants voted for landlords to keep their generous tax concessions. It is curious considering the previous six years had seen the lowest wage rises since World War II, yet low wage earners voted against higher wages. Maybe we are more feudalistic than we thought.

And in 2020, the Coalition government was forced into a humiliating apology to welfare recipients who had been duped by the so called Robodebt. This was an automated system that wrongly targeted welfare recipients and asked them to return payments, threatening them with legal action. The controversial system was ruled unlawful in 2020 and around 373,000 Australians were repaid 1.2 billion dollars, though this only came about because the government settled just before a class court case was due to start.

The whole affair was a monumental stuff up at best or a sad betrayal of the most vulnerable Australians at worst. Morrison was the minister in charge at the time; unsurprisingly, no one was ever held to account. This is in stark contrast to the entire Dutch cabinet resigning after a government error saw 10,000 families forced to repay debts.

On top of this, the Coalition refused to increase an unemployment benefit called Newstart, which had not increased in real terms since 1994. The Nationals represent many electorates whose voters rely on Newstart and Barnaby Joyce was particularly empathetic with their plight. Joyce noted that he had a base wage of 211,000 dollars and found it difficult to make ends meet for his families. Joyce had to go as far as killing his own meat, fixing things around the house himself, not dining out and his only indulgence was a cup of coffee a month. It is still a mystery how he pays for his smoking addiction or his vast array of Akubras.

Attitudes changed dramatically when Covid-19 hit and the issue of survival on unemployment benefits suddenly became mainstream with millions affected. The Coalition roughly doubled the benefit to enable people to "meet the costs of their groceries and other bills." As the Covid-19 crisis diminished in 2021 and middle-class people began to resume work, Newstart, rebranded as Job Seeker, reverted to near previous levels. But the Coalition trumpeted the good news for the long term unemployed: they were increasing payments by a whopping $3.57 per day. Still significantly below the poverty line.

In 1936, the influential Yale University professor Harold Lasswell wrote, "politics is who gets what, when, and how."[207] The poor got it good and hard in 2019 with one of the first acts of the newly formed Morrison government to cut funding to Foodbank, one of the country's largest hunger-relief organisations. And the then Minister for Indigenous Affairs, Nigel Scullion, used money allocated to help Indigenous people to fund a fishing lobby group he used to chair.

Chapter Nine
Democracy Under Threat

Research used in this book shows that apathetic voters are less satisfied with democracy than interested voters. A major concern is that when political apathy is based on a sense of disenchantment, it can turn to anger,[37] and if apathetic individuals engage in politics out of anger, they may be influenced by charismatic, extremist figures who may harm or even terminate democracy.

Nazi Germany is, of course, an extreme example. The Nazis achieved just 2.6 per cent of the vote in 1928. Things changed with the Wall Street crash in 1929 and the Nazi vote increased to 18.1 per cent in 1930 and then 37 per cent in 1932, which allowed the Nazis to seize power. They were supported by the lower classes and farmers who had been most affected by World War I and the subsequent depression.

The German voter had a huge range of political options in the late 1920s and early 30s, with fervent activity across the political spectrum, yet Germany chose the National Socialists. While these voters cannot be held responsible for every atrocity committed by the Nazi regime, a great deal of Nazi behaviour was foreseeable by any well-informed person at the time and voters who supported the Nazis must be held partly to blame for the disasters that followed.

We are not arguing that Australia is on a similar precipice to Germany in the early 1930s. But there are worrying signs that democratic systems around the world are coming under pressure. In his 1992 book, *The End of History*, Francis Fukuyama, the Mosbacher Director of the Centre on Democracy, Development and the Rule of Law at Stanford University, argued that the spread of democracy across the world marked the endpoint in political evolution because democracy as a system of government had triumphed.[208]

The Cold War was ending and democracy was gaining ground in South and Central America. Countries such as Poland, Argentina and Angola were also evolving from dictatorships to democracies. Russia experimented with democracy and even China teetered toward democracy for a short time.

The trend has since reversed, with many countries moving away from democracy and toward more autocratic regimes. The Arab Spring failed to create the democratic systems it promised. Venezuela, Thailand, Nicaragua and Turkey, to mention a few, have opted for autocratic leaders over democracy. The 2018 report from Freedom House, the US government-funded independent watchdog organisation, titled Democracy in Crisis, showed that for the 12th year running, more democracies had regressed than improved.

The Global Financial Crisis exacerbated the trend, with large job losses hitting lower socio-economic groups. Blaming the status-quo for their hardship, unknowledgeable lower socio-economic voters readily turn to authoritarian figures who promise simple solutions. President Erdogan in Turkey is one such beneficiary, re-elected in 2018 despite his increasingly autocratic rule and attacks on journalists, the judiciary, teachers and anyone who opposes him. By re-electing him, Turkish voters effectively voted against democracy.

Fukuyama blamed politicians for "their failure to provide the substance of what people want from government: personal security, shared economic growth and the basic public services…that are needed to achieve individual opportunity."

However, it is the people who elect these politicians who are really to blame so ultimately it's our fault. And if people elect charismatic, authoritarian leaders such as Erdogan, who has imprisoned over 200,000 for political beliefs, it's a no-brainer we will end up with anti-democratic governments.

Democracies can fail for different reasons, but the process often follows a similar pattern. First, a crisis or perceived crisis occurs with a charismatic leader promising to save the people by solving the problem in a simple way. It helps if this leader can easily identify enemies who are seen as scary and can be blamed for the crisis. This is where fear campaigns come in handy. The charismatic leader then starts to nobble independent institutions that may hinder his or her actions. Finally, the rules of the game are changed so it becomes more difficult to dislodge the charismatic leader. It is at this stage that democracy succumbs to autocracy.

Hungary is an example of a country sliding toward autocratic rule. The country had developed into a reasonable democracy and even joined the European Union in 2004 but got into financial trouble when its citizens took foreign currency loans to buy a house. The Hungarian currency crashed and many Hungarians lost their homes. The opposition political party, Fidesz, led by Viktor Orban, blamed the government, promised an easy fix and won the 2010 election.

Hungarians were then spooked by thousands of Syrians fleeing their homeland and crossing into Hungary in 2015. Few Syrians stayed in Hungary but the Fidesz government found the Muslims a convenient, scary enemy. The government even built a fence to stop the flow of refugees but continued to play up the Muslim threat.

The government then organised a poll asking people if they agreed with a plan by the Hungarian-American billionaire and philanthropist George Soros to bring one million African and Middle Eastern immigrants to Hungary. A campaign poster showed Soros and Hungarian opposition leaders holding wire cutters, with the slogan "they would remove the fence altogether". There was no such plan by Soros but the campaign was designed to scare the socks off ignorant voters.

The government was duly re-elected with a massive majority. They have since bugged political opponents and when the independent newspaper *Népszabadság* uncovered scandals involving the Hungarian President, it was suspended and sold to a pro-government ally.

Other news organisations have similarly been bought by pro-government supporters and the state media now mirrors the party line, with the system overwhelmingly favouring the government. And when the Covid-19 pandemic arrived, the parliament voted to allow Orban to "rule by decree" and suspended parliament. Democracy is defined as the will of the people, and it appears the Hungarian voters have achieved their will: autocratic rule.

Ah, you say, these are developing countries that can't get their act together. There is still reason for concern. A Pew poll of 38 countries found that 24 per cent of people thought that military rule would be just fine and 26 per cent liked the idea of a "strong leader who can make decisions without interference from parliament or the courts."[209]

Some surveys show that a third of young Americans do not think it essential to live in a democracy. A survey by the Hansard Society, the United Kingdom's leading source of independent research and advice on parliamentary affairs in April 2019, showed that 54 per cent of respondents agreed that "Britain needs a strong ruler willing to break the rules" with only 23 per cent disagreeing.[210]

Britain's decision to leave the European Union was overwhelmingly supported by the demographic that is politically uninterested and lacking knowledge. Indeed, 'What is the EU?' and 'What is Brexit?' were among the most googled questions in the UK the day after Britain voted to leave the European Union. Uninterested and unknowledgeable voters engaged in politics to bring down the system that to their mind had so blatantly failed them, with little idea of how it actually worked. On the upside, voters were at least trying to inform themselves about politics. It's just a shame this happened *after* a vote of such significance.

We see concerning trends in other European countries too, with populist far-right parties winning greater support across 22 nations and tripling their vote in the past 20 years. They are propelled by rising inequality and disappearing jobs, fears over globalisation and immigration, along with a perception that elites rule their lives. The city of Dresden declared a 'Nazi emergency' in 2019, saying it had a serious problem with the far-right.

Right-wing authoritarian parties have gained political control in Poland as well as Hungary and have had electoral success in Scandinavia, the Netherlands and Germany. The spectre of an ultra-right French President in the form of Marine Le Pen was averted by the last-minute swing to the centrist Emanuel Macron in 2017.

Like Erdogan and Orban, Donald Trump was a beneficiary of disgruntled lower socio-economic voters who lack political knowledge and are unsatisfied with democracy. These voters supported Trump despite his anti-democratic behaviour. His bullying of those he saw as easy targets, including women, minorities, people with disabilities and migrants only seemed to make him more popular among his supporters.

The sycophantic cosying up to those Trump perceived as strong men— Philippines' Rodrigo Duterte, North Korea's fratricidal Kim Jong-un, and Russia's Vladimir Putin, suggested he was sympathetic to dictatorial brutality and disdainful of democratic processes. Trump's supporters admire such leaders because they are strongmen who they think will "get the job done."

By vilifying the press that shines a light on his shortcomings, Trump played to an audience that prefers Fox News and Breitbart's simplistic rhetoric and alternative "versions of the truth." Trump's attacks on government institutions that oppose him were part of a systematic devaluing of US democratic structures. Those who voted for Trump distrust such institutions anyway, seeing them as part of a grand conspiracy against God-fearing, conservative white folk.

The forces opposing Trump were drowned out by a nationalist-driven, US-first agenda. Trump went as far as to deny the political will of American citizens, falsely claiming that the 2020 election was rigged. He then went a step further by encouraging an insurrection to stay in power, in a direct challenge to US democracy.

Former US President Barak Obama captured the way political apathy can lead to destructive outcomes in a critique of Trump:

> When we turn away and stop paying attention and stop engaging and stop believing and look for the newest diversion, the electronic version of bread and circuses, then other voices fill the void. A politics of fear and resentment and retrenchment takes hold and demagogues promise simple fixes to complex problems. No promise to fight for the little guy even as they cater to the wealthiest and most powerful. No promise to clean up corruption, then plunder away. They start undermining norms that ensure accountability and try to change the rules to entrench their power further.[211]

Democracy is fragile and there is a concern that it may also be under threat in Australia. John Keane, the Director of Sydney Democracy Network, highlighted the possibility of 'democide', where a democracy self-implodes when a significant section of voters become disillusioned with the system and opt for more authoritarian leadership.

This concern is supported by a 2013 Lowy Institute poll which showed a majority of young Australians were ambivalent about democracy. A more recent study conducted in 2018 by the Australian National University's Centre for Social Research found that 33 per cent of Australians now rate having an "authoritarian style leader as being very good or fairly good."

The AES also noted in 2016 "that disillusionment had now reached a threshold where Australia was beginning to see the beginnings of corrosive popular disaffection with the political class of the type that had led to events including Donald Trump's Presidential victory and Brexit in the UK." And a third of domestic investigations by the Australian Security Intelligence Organisation (ASIO) were right-wing extremists using Covid-19 to recruit new members.

There are signs that Australian democratic freedoms are also coming under increasing pressure. Uninformed, apathetic voters are responsible for this as they support parties like One Nation, who continuously call for the ABC to mirror government policy.

When he was Prime Minister, Tony Abbott suggested the ABC should effectively act as a cheerleader for Australia and cover up the fact the government was illegally bugging the Indonesian President's conversations. Every dictator wants a compliant media to act as cheerleader. Conservative politicians also call for funding to be cut from the ABC.

The Coalition government has sided with Hanson to legislate the ABC to be "fair and balanced," which most people took as a push to make the ABC support the government and its right-wing policies. The Liberal Federal Council then voted in favour of privatising the public broadcaster. Conservative politicians regularly strong-arm the ABC to give it more positive coverage.

The ABC journalist and presenter Emma Alberici was 'hated' by the Liberals and the then ABC chairman, Justin Milne, wanted her sacked to protect ABC funding. The ABC board has been stacked with conservative cronies against the advice of independent recommendations. If this isn't enough, the Coalition ripped 546 million dollars out of the ABC budget between 2014 and 2018.

The media, including even News Corp, has called out the "culture of secrecy taking hold in Australia" whereby government decisions are covered up and Freedom of Information requests generally ignored or responses redacted. The media united to redact their front pages to highlight restraints on media organisations under draconian security legislation.

The government has blocked footage of live animal exports in case they are used to lobby against cruelty. They have also withheld information on controversial visa schemes allowing rich people to pay to reside in our country. This is especially ironic considering the Coalition's penchant for demonising refugees and 457 workers. All this shows that Australians are "being denied information on topics they absolutely had the right to know about."[212]

One Australian citizen, known only as "Witness J", was incarcerated without prosecution for the first time in our history, with the Liberal Attorney General saying "I am not aware of any similar cases." Even the *Telegraph* wrote:

> Our government is chilling a heap of freedoms, including attempting to silence whistle blowers and introducing very intrusive surveillance powers...History has taught us that when we wander down the path of government censorship that turns into a society that has dangerous hallmarks attached to it.[212]

Things took a decidedly nasty turn just 2 weeks after the Coalition won government in May 2019, with the police taking unprecedented action in raiding the ABC with a warrant allowing them to "add, copy, delete or alter" any material in ABC computers. The government appeared upset about an ABC report which alleged that Australian soldiers murdered innocent people in Afghanistan.

The alleged whistle-blower was a British SAS captain who was arrested and charged with releasing classified documents. His father was also a well-known whistle-blower who revealed the dangers of the drug thalidomide. After a four year investigation, Morrison was forced to admit in November 2020 that it looked as though 32 soldiers had killed 39 civilians. The report was duly sent off to a prosecutor, thus disappearing for several more years.

Prime Minister Scott Morrison was in England during the ABC raid, extolling the virtues of liberty, freedom and democracy at the anniversary of the 75th D-Day landings. When asked about the raid, Morrison refused to condemn the chilling attack on press freedom. The International Press Freedom Organisation, however, warned that "press freedom is under assault in Australia," hinting that Australia's position on the World Press Freedom Index would drop from its already lowly 21st position.

It is scary to note that Costa Rica, Uruguay and even Suriname are regarded as having a more open and free press than Australia. *The New York Times* went as far as to say that Australia "may well be the most secretive democracy."

It is unsurprising that the government waited until after the election to raid the ABC as it probably believed that voters had switched off after so much media focus on politics. And it probably thought the raids would be forgotten by the time the next election rolls around in 3 years. What is surprising is that we continue to elect politicians that try to restrict or manipulate our media and therefore undermine our democracy.

The Coalition has often stated that it is 'too busy' to implement a federal anti-corruption watchdog. It's true they have been busy: the Australian National Audit Office found the Coalition had used over 100 million dollars of our money to buy favours in marginal seats through the so-called sports rorts. The Minister for Energy and Emissions Reduction Angus Taylor was investigated by the police over the leak of forged documents used to attack the Sydney Lord Mayor.

The Deputy Prime Minister Michael McCormack used a VIP government jet to attend the Melbourne Cup with the gambling giant TAB and the government paid over 30 million dollars to a Liberal benefactor for land near the western

Sydney Airport which was only worth 3 million dollars. The Coalition also found time to slash the funding to the Audit Office which made these scandals public.

Opposition institutions are also under threat. The Liberal Government has proposed laws that require a citizen who donates just $4.80 per week to a not-for-profit political organisation to declare they are an 'allowable donor' and have a Justice of the Peace or police officer witness their declaration.

Failing to comply would result in 10 years' imprisonment or a fine of 210,000 dollars. This is clearly designed to destroy grassroots political groups that are primarily left-wing in nature, such as environmental and women's lobby groups. It doesn't stop the likes of billionaire Gina Rinehart writing huge cheques to their favourite politicians. The Coalition has also vilified the grassroots political organisation GetUp, arguing it is an arm of either Labor or the Greens. An examination by the AEC found that GetUp was indeed a grassroots organisation. The conservatives had attempted to shut it down simply because it was from the Left rather than the Right. This is not how a free democracy should work.

Vilification of the vulnerable and attacks on those that can't fight back is a classic tactic of politicians and governments looking to win support from uninformed voters. Look at Trump's slandering of migrants from desperately poor South American countries, Hungary's attacks on Syrian war refugees, Duterte's sanctioning of the murders of mentally ill drug addicts, or Bolsonaro's vilification of gay people.

Politically motivated fear campaigns focused on race and refugees in Australia are similar, stoking the paranoia of politically ignorant voters to win their support. Few Australians would be negatively impacted by refugees; in fact, the diverse ethnic groups coming to this country have overwhelmingly enhanced Australia as a nation.

No country can afford to allow unchecked immigration, but when Peter Dutton can say in one sentence that refugees were lazy, illiterate and innumerate while also taking Australian jobs and languishing on the dole, we see the depths to which political debate has fallen. These comments are aimed at the apathetic voter. On one level, we can argue that it is shameful for politicians to act in this way, but an alternative argument is that politicians are merely exploiting the apathetic voter to stay in power. Dutton wouldn't get away with comments like these if more voters were informed and interested.

Chapter Ten
Solutions

We have shown that a large number of voters couldn't care less about politics, yet this same group has dramatic effects on political outcomes in Australia. It's true of course that any large group of voters can potentially affect political outcomes in the same way.

If women were magically taken out of the voting pool for example, it would invariably change election results. So too would pensioners or perhaps men with beards. The difference is that these voters usually have rational reasons for their vote. Women may vote for female candidates in order to change social constructs and empower women, both reasonable and rational grounds for a vote.

Pensioners may vote for parties that promise to increase the pension and men with beards might vote for lower taxes for hairy blokes. These voters may also vote according to a myriad of other rational reasons such as economic management, health policy or environmental concerns. The point is that these are all rational reasons to cast a ballot.

In contrast, uninterested voters don't vote according to rational reasons, and so they are very different political actors compared to interested voters. Because they are apathetic about politics, they lack political information, and they often vote arbitrarily, meaning they're less likely to know who they voted for. But they are political actors nonetheless, and the irony is that this group has a large impact on our democracy despite their lack of interest.

It might be better for them to decide who to vote for by flipping a coin rather than by choosing a candidate, as coin flips are not subject to corruption, manipulation, or scare campaigns. While the coin toss proposal is unlikely to get much traction, there are a number of other possible actions that could be taken to minimise the effects of uninformed voting and to strengthen our democracy.

Ending Compulsory Voting

One obvious suggestion is to end compulsory voting. This would mean that uninterested voters wouldn't bother to drag themselves to the polling station to vote, therefore mitigating the effects of uninformed voting on election outcomes, and giving those who are politically interested and engaged a greater say in democratic outcomes.

The former Labor election strategist Rod Cameron says that election campaigns would also have a higher level of political debate and political advertising as politicians would talk genuine policy rather than orientating the campaign and slogans to apathetic voters. Ending compulsory voting would also highlight the true extent of political apathy. Compulsory voting masks the symptoms of public apathy and ignorance while ignoring its causes, and it still hasn't resolved the issue of widespread political apathy.

However, while voluntary voting may reduce the impact of uninformed voters on election outcomes, it will not remove it completely. This is because an uninformed electorate:

> poses a danger not only to the ignorant voters themselves but to the country as a whole. Thus, it is difficult to defend allowing the ignorant to vote on the grounds that they have a right to vote as they please, without reference to the impact on others.[31:182]

A radical suggestion is to limit the franchise. In this argument, everyone having an equal vote is hardly justifiable considering the 'wisest person has as much voting power as fools'[213] and while we have a right to vote, we have a greater right to good government.

The elected government governs not only for the individual voter but for all of us. The right to vote gives an individual power over others, however small that power may be. As their vote may affect our incomes, our job prospects, our health outcomes, the opportunities afforded to our children and even in some cases whether we live or die, it is fair to ask people to justify their vote.

In fact, we already limit the franchise by excluding individuals lacking the capacity to make rational decisions, nor do we allow politically aware, knowledgeable and capable 17-year-olds to vote. There is an arbitrary line drawn at age 18 and this is rarely questioned.

We're not arguing that the average citizen is *incapable* of developing political knowledge and understanding politics. Instead, we have shown that a significant number are simply *unmotivated* to bother trying. It may, therefore, be sensible to place barriers in front of them until they develop this motivation. We're suggesting that in order to vote, a citizen must first pass a knowledge test. After all, we demand competence from government, so why not demand competence from the people who elect that government?

On the face of it, this may seem quite a radical suggestion, but our society already makes people pass all sorts of tests to demonstrate competence to carry out even relatively minor tasks. Students have to pass tests at school to show potential employers or tertiary institutions they have the requisite ability. If someone wants to be a doctor, they have to pass tests, as do accountants, builders, baristas and even stop and go people at road works.

You even have to pass a test to become a bar worker. If it's important enough to be tested on your ability to serve a beer, then it's a fair argument to say citizens should pass a test if they want to hold coercive power over other citizens in a way that affects their lives.

Compare voting to driving. Nearly every citizen aged above 17 is potentially allowed to drive a car. However, they need to pass a knowledge and practical test to show they are capable of driving. Once we reach 75 years of age we need to have a medical review every year to show we are capable of driving and at 85 years we have to go back to square one and pass a practical driving test. This is because driving is dangerous and as a society we do not want people lacking the ability to act safely and rationally on the road.

Voting is no different. All citizens should be potentially allowed to vote and would simply need to understand some basic policy differences between the parties, the voting rules and how to fill in a ballot paper formally. This has the potential to actually broaden the franchise. Any citizen, no matter what age, could vote as long as they have the motivation and cognitive capacity to pass the test.

And consider the fact that in order to become an Australian, we make migrants pass a test that asks them specific questions about how our democracy works. If it is so important that someone wishing to become Australian has to understand our democracy, then surely the people already living here should at least understand the same things.

We recognise that deciding what goes into a knowledge test to permit someone to vote is fraught with problems. What do we need to know to be informed enough to make a rational vote? Ideally, a voter would have a good idea of what political parties are proposing, how our system of governance works and how our preferential system works so they can vote according to their wishes. Is this too tall an order to ask of citizens?

It may be a tough call to ask citizens to understand every party's policies, so to simplify things the test could check a voter's basic understanding of the platforms of the two major parties, or the platform of one major party and a minor party of their choice. The test could be administered two months prior to the election, with people who fail given the opportunity to re-sit the test two weeks before the election. A benefit of this timeframe would be that political parties would have released their policies, allowing the tests to be based on the latest information.

Indeed, we could require all major party policies to be released on a particular day prior to the test, negating the current practice of parties waiting for the opposing side to release a policy and then making theirs slightly more attractive. Or the other sleight of hand of releasing policies just a few days before the election so there is little time to adequately scrutinise them.

Instead, policies would be in the public domain and open for scrutiny at least two months prior to the election. If parties are planning to implement change, then it's fair to allow voters time to assess these planned changes.

The tests could be organised and administered by the Australian Electoral Commission and run out of state motor registry offices which already conduct tests for driving licenses. The test does not have to be onerous, potential voters could be given a computer tablet of multiple answer options that may only take a few minutes to complete. Some of the questions may look like this:

The way our democracy is structured.

Q Which of these statements about Australia's system of government is correct?

a) The Queen of Australia chooses people to form the Australian Parliament.
b) The government is elected by the people.
c) The Prime Minister chooses our Members of Parliament.

Q Which arm of government has the power to interpret and apply laws?

a. Legislative
b. Executive
c. Judicial

Q Which of these is a role of the Governor-general?

a. The appointment of state Premiers.
b. The signing of Bills passed by the Australian Parliament.
c. The appointment of the Head of State.

The above questions are, in fact, taken straight from the practice citizenship test for new Australian citizens. Other questions that may be asked include:

Preferential Voting

Q If my first choice on the ballot does not get elected, does my second choice count? Yes/No

Major Party Policies

Three or four questions on differences between major party policies or on a major party's policies and a minor party's policies.

The test would mean those who are politically apathetic, misinformed or ignorant about politics would be excluded from voting. In practice, however, the majority of apathetic voters would exclude themselves by not wanting to vote in the first place. With mainly interested and knowledgeable voters taking the test, it's expected that the vast majority would pass without any problems at all.

We are not arguing that excluding apathetic voters would be a panacea for all the ills of our democracy but it would help counter the undue influence of random swinging voters panicked by fear campaigns and deliberate lying by politicians. It would also reduce the impact of informal and donkey votes and overall would increase the electoral power of informed voters.

If so desired, we could incentivise people to take the knowledge test by paying them to vote. This financial incentive could motivate politically apathetic people to become interested in politics, which would directly tackle the original problem. A study on financial incentives during tests found that the payment of money and

24 hours to come up with the correct answers unsurprisingly produced a 24 per cent increase in correct answers.[31] If we compare it to another common civic duty, jury service, the payment makes even more sense.

We pay jurors, so why not voters? Some would say the idea of paying individuals to vote is abhorrent, as voters should be motivated instead by a sense of civic responsibility. Yet civic duty isn't enough of a motivation for many voters to work out basic differences between the major parties or the way proportional representation works. A financial incentive for voting may also be politically acceptable as voters are likely to welcome money from government and it would act to stimulate the economy.

It must be acknowledged, however, that knowledge tests have a negative and chequered history, as they have been used to exclude people of colour from voting in the United States. Racist southern states made citizens pass knowledge tests before allowing people to vote, and often used very different tests for white and black people, as a way to keep black people from voting.

Alabama required the prospective voter to read a passage of the constitution out aloud. A white voter may have been asked to read section 20: "That no person shall be imprisoned for debt." A black person, on the other hand, was likely asked to read section 260:

> The income arising from the sixteenth section trust fund, the surplus revenue fund, until it is called for by the United States government, and the funds enumerated in sections 257 and 258 of this Constitution, together with a special annual tax of thirty cents on each one hundred dollars of taxable property in this state, which the legislature shall levy, shall be applied to the support and maintenance of the public schools, and it shall be the duty of the legislature to increase the public school fund from time to time as the necessity therefor and the condition of the treasury and the resources of the state may justify, provided, that nothing herein contained shall be so construed as to authorise the legislature to levy in any one year a greater rate of state taxation for all purposes, including schools, than sixty-five cents on each one hundred dollars' worth of taxable property; and provided further, that nothing herein contained shall prevent the legislature from first providing for the payment of the bonded indebtedness of the state and interest thereon out of all the revenue of the state.[214]

A 1964 test in Louisiana required prospective voters to answer 30 questions in just 10 minutes with just one wrong answer deeming you unfit to vote. That works out to be just 20 seconds per question and the questions weren't just tough, they were outrageously stupid, to the point of being unanswerable. Below are some of the questions. Have a go and see if you would pass the test allowing you to vote in Louisiana, but keep in mind that only one wrong answer and you don't get to vote:

Question: Spell backwards forwards.

Question: In the third square below, write the second letter of the fourth word.

Question: Write right from left to the right as you see it spelled here.

Question: Write the word noise backwards and place a d over what would be the second letter should it have been written forward.[214]

As you can see, the questions were deliberately convoluted and hard to understand, and with only 20 seconds provided per answer, test takers had little chance of passing the test. Not one person from a 2014 Harvard University class who took the test managed to pass.

A video of the class trying to make sense of the questions is on YouTube; it's funny until you remember the racist rationale for the test. Another impediment to voting was the official who determined whether you passed or failed was always white.

This was, however, a racist culture abusing a knowledge test, rather than an intrinsic flaw in knowledge tests themselves. Any test could potentially be misused. If applied equally and fairly, there is no reason why a knowledge test would not deliver a more knowledgeable and interested group of citizens electing our government.[215]

Educate or Delegate

There are a number of other suggestions that if implemented would make our democracy stronger. The first is to teach politics in school which may result in kids leaving school as young adults ready to make rational political decisions. This makes sense as those leaving school at 18 are already eligible to vote.

One road hump is that politicians would be the ones largely deciding the subject matter and governments have historically used such courses to indoctrinate children toward their chosen ideology. Howard managed this in part with what was termed the 'culture wars' and Abbott changed school curricula to include an emphasis on western culture.

Another problem with this approach is that political education at school has received little political support. Major party politicians benefit from the apathy of the electorate, so there is little incentive to change things.

However, if schools concentrated on the electoral process and taught aspects such as the way the preferential system works, it may allow young adults to at least vote according to their wishes. Of course, it would be ideal if students were taught something about political ideology and the role of government in their lives as well. This may still not solve the problem of political apathy though.

Civics education is well entrenched in the United States school system and they suffer from similar rates of political apathy as we do. It may be the case that politics simply can't compete with much more interesting and important things in people's lives and teaching them civics at school would be a waste of time. At the very least though, we could teach students how to fill in a ballot paper correctly, which would be worthwhile.

Another strategy would be to delegate more political decisions to experts. We already rely on experts to make significant decisions without political interference. The Reserve Bank makes decisions on monetary policy without regard (at least in theory) to political ramifications or influence. Can we imagine the political machinations if a government had to decide whether to raise interest rates just prior to an election? We also outsource the setting of minimum wages to the Australian Industrial Relations Commission, thereby alleviating political pressure on government to increase minimum wages.

This outsourcing of potentially contentious decisions with political ramifications could be expanded. The obvious example is science-based issues where there is overwhelming evidence of what is needed to benefit Australian voters. Carbon pricing could be treated like interest rates with an arms-length group of scientific experts empowered to set carbon prices every three years. This would provide business with confidence, allowing companies to plan around targets and costs just as they do with interest rates. Ridiculous claims about 'clean coal' would disappear from the political agenda and be replaced with serious policy initiatives to tackle climate change. Science and rational policy that benefits us all would dominate at the expense of vested interests and political scare campaigns. The public could still have input into such issues through a process of public consultation, and important decisions such as the time frame for funding of climate change mitigation efforts could still be politically debated, but a science-based approach would provide a much more robust and rational framework for such debates.

Some might say an approach where experts guide decision making smacks of elitism, and would act as a further disincentive to become involved in political matters for the apathetic section of society. But let's reconsider the role of elites in society for a moment. The word 'elitist' has been hijacked by some pundits and politicians in a desperate attempt to cast a bad light on anything opposing their own stance. No doubt they do this because much of the evidence-based research produced by experts comes to the opposite conclusions to their own jaundiced views.

Rather than admit they're wrong, they attack the messenger by labelling them as an 'out of touch elitist'. This goes down well with a sizeable proportion of the population. The loss of manufacturing jobs, poorer employment conditions and lower job security in a number of countries, exacerbated by the Global Financial Crisis, is real and contributes to a sense of alienation felt by many lower socio-economic voters. Right-wing politicians spin a narrative around this, claiming that elites are controlling our lives, with government policy dictated by politically correct zealots who want to siphon off our hard-earned money to pet causes.

In fact, 'elite' simply refers to someone who is superior in terms of ability or qualities to the rest of a group or society. Many aspects of our lives are already dominated by elites. We take our car to be repaired by elites, otherwise known as mechanics, who know and understand cars much better than we do. We want a doctor to diagnose us rather than the average punter off the street.

And we certainly don't have a problem with elitism within sport. We see sporting elitism as part of our cultural identity to such a degree that if the Wallabies fly half has a bad game, we immediately call for someone better, or more elite, to replace them.

The possibility that experts could have more input into important decisions affecting the well-being of the Australian people should in fact be welcomed, as policy would be guided by robust, science-based evidence and rational, clear-headed thinking, rather than politicians pandering to vested interests and targeting the apathetic with simplistic messages to win their vote.

Dealing with Advertisements

We could also deal much more directly with the issue of deceptive political advertising as apathetic voters are manipulated by misleading advertisements from political parties. To counter this, we could make political advertisements subject to the same regulations governing commercial advertisements and legislate to force advertisements to be based on fact.

If the AEC found that political advertisements were not factually based, significant fines could be levied. The issue of deceptive political advertising has received much more attention recently in light of the proliferation of fake news and the manipulation of voter opinion in the US presidential campaign via advertising on social media platforms.

With major players like Facebook allowing lies, we may need to impose even harsher punishments than fines, charging the proponents of misleading ads with criminal offences and jailing them if found guilty. At present, parties regularly mislead and get away without punishment. As the will of the people is perverted through manipulative advertising, stronger disincentives may be required—we need to keep the bastards honest.

Or we could simply ban political advertising altogether. Britain bans political advertising on television and radio, with the exception of political broadcasts prior to an election.[216] As UK Culture Secretary Maria Miller explained:

> Political adverts are—and have always been—banned on British TV and radio. That ban has wide support and has helped sustain the balance of views which is at the heart of British broadcasting—and ensures the political views broadcast into our homes are not determined by those with the deepest pockets.[217]

Information about candidates and parties is in any case widely available online and through the media so there is no need for advertising designed to manipulate and deceive.

There are also other benefits of a ban on political advertising. The vast majority of political campaign funding is spent on advertising and a ban on political advertising would mean parties require fewer donations to run their campaigns. This may reduce the political leverage that powerful vested interests have over political parties, their policies and our democracy. In fact, Australia already bans political advertising on TV and radio from Wednesday midnight before a state or federal election to 'enable a time for sober reflection'.[218] As we already recognise the negative effects of political advertising before an election, there is a case for banning political advertising altogether.

Reigning in the Donkey Voters

Getting rid of the unwanted effect of donkey voting would also help. As we've shown, donkey votes, even when comprising just one per cent of votes each election, still decide the outcome of five electorates on average each election. That is five politicians who would not have a job if not for apathetic voters' donkey voting.

Remember, donkey votes occur because Candidate Bloggs wins the lottery by being placed above their major opponent on the ballot paper. This automatically means that Candidate Bloggs wins at least one per cent more of the vote than their major adversary. This problem has been overcome in Tasmanian state elections and Australian Capital Territory elections, which both use a system called Robson rotation.

In this system, ballot papers are printed in equal-sized batches with each batch having the candidates in differing spots on the ballot. Candidate Bloggs is top of the ballot for one voter, another spot for the next voter and another spot on the ballot for the third voter. Of course, this does nothing to stop our apathetic voter from donkey voting. It simply means that their donkey votes are reasonably evenly distributed to all candidates, therefore negating their impact.

Just Don't Vote

Of all of the suggestions above, the ones likely to have the most impact are those where uninterested people end up staying at home and not voting. This would certainly be better for Australian politics as it could function in a more rational way, but it would also probably be better for uninterested voters to abstain, and leave the decision in the hands of individuals who are interested and knowledgeable and do care about election outcomes.

Abstention is not relinquishing the right to rule. Indeed, it may lead to better decisions for both those who abstain and also for everyone else, as citizens have the right to vote but they also have the right to good government.

Consider this: you are out of town and in discussion with local colleagues and you make it known you wish to go to the best restaurant for dinner. You are a connoisseur of food but your knowledge of local restaurants is zero. A discussion ensues and although ignorant of the town you have the right and ability to make your thoughts known.

Yet, because you want to go to the best restaurant, you abstain from voting because the locals know best. Abstention is an indirect vote for collective wisdom.[213:96] If Australians with little knowledge of politics abstained from voting, we might end up with better political outcomes for everyone.

This book has questioned whether uninterested individuals have the motivation to be involved in politics. By any measure they don't. This suggests compulsory voting and the right to vote just because you are a citizen is unjust. We have a right to expect that any political power held over us should be exercised by competent people in a competent way. In Australia's voting system, citizens are denied this right, with the whim of apathetic voters determining electoral outcomes and driving political debate. To ensure a more robust Australian democracy, this must change.

Afterword

Since this book was sent to the publisher, there have been significant developments in Australian politics, with the most important being the May 2022 federal election. The two major parties again ran electoral campaigns targeting uninterested voters, in every respect the same as their previous campaigns. Yet the 2022 election produced startlingly different results to those of other recent elections, and is therefore deserving of an afterword.

First, let's take a short run through the traditional campaigns of the major parties. Just as in 2019, the Coalition presented very few policies to the electorate. Labor learnt from its 2019 mistake of policy overkill and mimicked the Coalition, with photo opportunities and sloganeering dominating the six week campaign of both parties. Morrison washed people's hair, rolled croissants and showed his welding skills. Albanese continually stated over and over that he and Labor had a "plan" which was essentially kissing babies and drinking coffee with people. No need to bore people with real policies or visions for Australia.

The campaign had its usual personality attacks. Morrison's personality was readily critiqued by those who knew him best. Liberal senator Concetta Fierranti-Wells described Morrison as a "bully who has no moral compass" while the Liberal Premier Gladys Berejiklian weighed in describing him as a "horrible, horrible person (who was) more concerned with politics than people".

Another unnamed cabinet minister described him as a "fraud" and a "complete psycho". The National leader Barnaby Joyce insinuated the culprit was female and called on them to out themselves, until a text surfaced of Barnaby critiquing Morrison as "a hypocrite and a liar from my observations... I have never trusted him, and I dislike how earnestly [he] rearranges the truth to a lie." French President Emmanuel Macron, angry over the lost Australian submarine contract, weighed in, accusing Morrison of lying, and Turnbull reinforced the message, saying Morrison had a "reputation for lying".

Labor's ads constantly attacked Morrison as unfit to be prime minister, highlighting his Hawaiian holiday during the bushfires and his excuse that he wasn't the guy to hold a hose. They showed Morrison repeatedly saying "that's not my job" whenever action was required.

Meanwhile, the Coalition painted Albanese as unqualified for the job because of his relatively low public profile. Never mind that Albanese had been in parliament for 26 years and had even been deputy prime minister. Indeed, it would be hard to envisage an opposition leader with greater experience. But the target audience of uninterested voters wouldn't have heard of Albanese and that was all that mattered. It didn't help, of course, when Albanese couldn't name the unemployment rate in the first few days of the campaign.

Albanese instead set out to paint himself as a man of the people—constantly reiterating his story of living in a council house and helping his mum who was on a disability pension. The rags to riches story was told over and over. It helped when Morrison in a moment of panic admitted that people really didn't like him, saying he was like a bulldozer and promising to be more empathetic if re-elected. Albanese's response of "bulldozers destroy things, I'm a builder" was perhaps the pivotal moment of the campaign.

The perennial campaign topics of music, food and sport all cropped up again. When Morrison forgot the words in a ukulele rendition of Dragon's April Sun in Cuba, Dragon's lead singer Mark Williams quipped "if his trip to Hawaii had not been cut short, he could have learnt the lyrics". Morrison's culinary angle involved him posting a photo of a chicken curry he had cooked. The trouble was, the chicken looked partly raw. Morrison averted "currygate" by arguing it was just the light bouncing off the chicken.

Morrison's sporting credentials took a literal nosedive when he crash tackled an 8 year old while playing soccer. Senior Liberal minister Stuart Roberts tried to blame the poor kid, saying it "was an error from both of them." You can see how the right plays harder than the left. The next day, when Morrison asked kids at a tennis court "Who wants a hit?", many of their parents were understandably reticent. Yes, this all dominated the 2022 election; in fact these are the highlights, with little if any policy or ideas on how to improve the lives of Australians.

Naturally, many of the favourite fear campaigns were resurrected instead. The Liberals again played the tax card, releasing ads saying Labor had a "sneaky climate tax" as well as a "death tax". One ad featured a poker machine with a line warning of more taxes under Labor. A popular ad featured a rusty old bucket with a hole in it leaking coins. The slogan over them all was "it won't be easy under Albanese"—its catchiness designed to appeal directly to the uninterested.

Inconveniently for the Coalition, the Reserve Bank increased interest rates in the middle of the campaign, so the Liberals had to change their tune from their 2004 interest rate scare tactic. Instead, Morrison blustered "it's not about what it means for politics, sometimes you guys [the media] always see things through a totally political lens. I don't". It'd be funny if it weren't so serious.

The Coalition also warned Labor's support for a $1 per hour pay increase for minimum wage workers would "destroy the economy". This was from a government that gave $40 billion dollars of taxpayers' money to rich businesses that increased their profits during Covid. It is odd how raising the minimum wage for poor people destroys the economy yet when we funnel taxpayers' money to rich people it helps the economy.

Labor had another crack at the Coalition's record on Medicare, warning of future cuts and even an end to Medicare altogether should the Coalition be re-elected. Facebook ads on the theme were viewed around six million times in the penultimate week of the campaign. E-vehicles featured again too, this time Morrison was promoting their benefits. When asked by a reporter "how can you honestly spruik electric vehicles' when you campaigned against them in the last election," Morrison replied "but I didn't, that is just a Labor lie." And in a last minute desperate attempt to keep their jobs, the Coalition sent a text message on election day to alert voters to a refugee boat which had just been intercepted.

This all ties in with the themes in the book, and election results in uninterested lower socio-economic electorates were again unsurprising. While the Coalition vote did decrease in lower socio-economic areas, they generally hung onto these seats. Bob Katter increased his vote, suggesting that apathetic voters might have been attracted by his policy of giving free guns to every high school kid over 13 years of age. Even Barnaby Joyce's vote only decreased by two percent in the low socio-economic seat of New England.

But the surprising outcome of the 2022 election is the rise of the teal independents. These are a collection of primarily professional women running in inner city high socio-economic electorates. Just to be perfectly clear, these electorates were not focused on in this book. They are the wealthiest, best educated and most politically interested and knowledgeable electorates in the country, with a long history of supporting Liberal party candidates.

So what changed? Firstly, these teal independents highlighted women's issues severely neglected by the Coalition, who were also reeling from myriad allegations of rape and abuse. Morrison had downplayed such concerns, at one point suggesting that women were lucky not to be shot while protesting sexual violence. It is easy to see how female candidates resonated with politically interested electorates. Women standing for election also provided female voters with a role model to support, in stark contrast to the stale pale Liberal males. These areas looked at the sitting Liberal members and didn't see people supporting liberal ideology. Instead, they saw right-wing extremist misogynists.

Corruption was another concern, with the Coalition failing in their promise to establish a corruption commission. The extraordinary interjection by 31 former judges just days out from the election demanding the establishment of an anti-corruption body highlighted this. They warned that Australians risked being exposed to the "corrupt exercise of power" if parliament did not act. Politically interested, knowledgeable voters in these electorates saw a government that had instead funnelled billions of dollars to their political donors and friends.

Educated voters also saw a government that refused to recognise the science of climate change, whereas it was obvious to anyone that Australia had been devastated by climate change-induced bushfires, drought and floods. The government these wealthy, educated voters had elected had then failed dismally to act in any meaningful way to support those in affected areas.

These teal candidates were also natural Liberal supporters and candidates. Allegra Spender, who won the seat of Wentworth, came from Liberal royalty with her father and grandfather both representing the Liberal party. Kate Chaney, who took the seat of Curtin from the Liberals, comes from a similar lineage, with her grandfather Fred a deputy leader of the Liberal party. And Dr Sophie Scamps, who routinely aligns herself with the policies of the NSW Coalition government, won the formerly safe Liberal seat of Mackellar. The Liberals also lost the high socio-economic seats of Ryan and Brisbane, held by the Liberals for the last four elections, to the Greens.

The losses of such inner-city blue ribbon Liberal seats is because the Liberals developed into an extreme right-wing party. Knowledgeable and interested voters in inner-city seats across the country recognised this and voted them out in favour of candidates that better represented their views. This is exactly how a democracy should work and it is a reassuring sign that the democratic system works when voters care enough to be interested.

This book has presented the Australian democracy as dominated by negative campaigning, fear campaigns and outright lies that manipulate voters to often vote against their own interests. We don't resile from this critique but recognise and indeed rejoice that the 2022 election was decided by interested, knowledgeable and indeed woke voters. This is how democracy should be!

There are also further green shoots of optimism emerging. At the time of writing this postscript, there have been massive demonstrations in Turkey against authoritarianism, French voters again rejected the neo-Nazi Marie Le Pen in the presidential race, and if Ukraine can repel the Russian invasion, it seems likely that democracy will be entrenched in that country. Indeed, Volodymyr Zelenskyy has become a cult hero for open, liberal democracy.

It is our fervent hope that democracy flourishes and can be further enhanced by the suggestions we make in this book. As Winston Churchill said, "democracy is the worst form of government—except for all the others that have been tried."

Annexures

Annexure 1: AES Response rates

Year	Response Rate (percentage)
1987	62.8
1990	58
1993	62.8
1996	61.8
1998	57.7
2001	55.4
2004	44.5
2007	40.2
2010	41.9
2013	33.9
2016	22.5
2019	42.1

Source: AES

Annexure 2: Voter turnout figures 1901–1925

Year	Senate	House of Representatives
1901	54.3	56.7
1903	46.9	50.3
1906	50.2	51.5
1910	62.2	62.8
1913	73.7	73.5
1914	72.6	73.5
1917	77.7	78.3
1919	71.3	71.6
1922	58	59.4
1925	91.3	91.4

Source: AEC (All figures are percentages).

Annexure 3: Number of enrolled citizens

Year	Estimated unenrolled Citizens	Enrolment rate (percentage)
2001	0.9 million	95
2004	1.2 million	92.8
2007	1.1 million	93.1
2010	1.4 million	90.9
2013	1.2 million	92.8
2016	816,000	95
2019	490,000	97.1

Source AEC Note: the AEC doesn't have figures prior to 2001.

Annexure 4: Informal voting in federal elections 1987–2019

Year	House of Representatives	Senate
1987	4.9	4.1
1990	3.2	3.4
1993	3.0	2.6
1996	3.2	3.5
1998	3.8	3.2
2001	4.8	3.9
2004	5.2	3.8
2007	4.0	2.5
2010	5.6	3.8
2013	5.9	3.0
2016	5.1	3.9
2019	5.1	3.9
Average	4.5	3.5

Source: AEC. All figures are percentages.

Annexure 5: Actual per cent of Australians who did not register a formal vote 1987–2019

	Estimated individuals not on roll	Enrolled individuals who failed to vote	Informal vote	Total percentage who did not register a formal vote	Actual turnout rate
1987	5.5	6.2	4.9	16.6	83.4
1990	5.5	4.7	3.2	13.4	86.6
1993	5.5	4.2	3	12.7	87.3
1996	5.5	4.3	3.2	13	87
1998	5.5	5	3.8	14.3	85.7
2001	5.5	5.1	4.8	15.4	84.6
2004	7.2	5.7	5.2	18.1	81.9
2007	6.9	5.2	4	16.1	83.9
2010	9.1	6.8	5.6	21.5	78.5
2013	7.2	5.4	5.9	18.5	81.5
2016	5.2	9	5.1	19.3	80.7
2019	2.9	8.9	5.1	17.2	82.8
Average	6	5.9	4.5	16.3	83.7

Source: AEC

Annexure 6: Donkey votes for Christian Democrat Party 1990–2019

Year	Top of ballot	Other position
1990	4.2 (1)	2 (14)
1993	4.8 (1)	1.8 (15)
1996	2.9 (4)	1.8 (19)
1998	2.9 (4)	1.7 (24)
2001	3.3 (3)	1.9 (24)
2004	3.6 (1)	2.8 (21)
2007	3.1 (2)	2.1 (42)
2010	2.8 (6)	2.6 (18)
2013	2.9 (10)	2 (38)
2016	5.1 (7)	3.7 (40)
2019	1.1 (8)	2 (32)
Average	3.3 (4)	2.2 (26)

Source: AEC 1990–2019. Figures are percentages except those in brackets which are the number of seats contested at the relevant election.

Annexure 7: Turnout rate for compulsory federal, and Victorian Council elections contrasted against voluntary SA, WA and Tasmanian election 1987–2019

Year	Lower House	Senate	Victoria	South Australia	Western Australia	Tasmania
1987	93.8	94.6		17.2		
1989				20.1		
1990	95.3	95.8				
1991				22.2		
1993	95.8	96.2		17.3		
1995				18.8		
1996	95.7	96.2				59.5
1997				34.4	46	
1998	95	95.3				
1999			74.1		41.2	55.7
2000			78.5	40.1		57.8
2001	94.9	95.2	72.2		38	
2002			75.2			57.9
2003				32.7	35	
2004	94.3	94.8	71.1			
2005			75.2		37.4	58.5
2006				31.6		
2007	94.8	95.2			34	57.4
2009			74.4		33.4	55.5
2010	93.2	93.8		32.9		
2011					31	54.3
2013	94.6	93.9	71		28	
2014				32		54.6
2015					27.5	
2016	91	91.9	72.2			
2018				33		58.7
2019	91.1	91.9				
Average	94.4	94.8	74	27.2	35.2	56.8

Sources: AEC, Tasmanian Electoral Commission, South Australian Electoral Commission, Western Australian Electoral Commission, Victorian Electoral Commission. All figures are percentages.

Annexure 8: Political interest

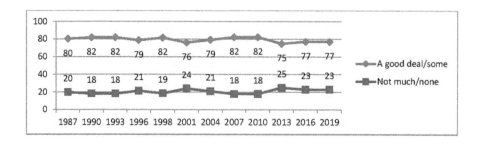

Sources: AES 1987–2019 "Generally speaking, how much interest do you usually have in politics?" All figures are in percentages.

Annexure 9: Interest in the election campaign

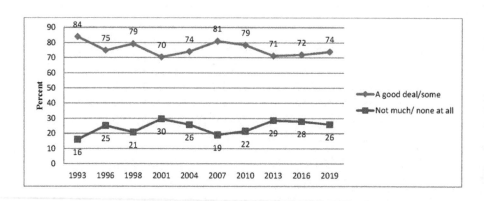

Sources: AES 1993–2019 "And how much interest would you say you took in the election campaign overall?" The question was not asked prior to 1993. All figures are in percentages.

Annexure 10: Followed election news in newspapers

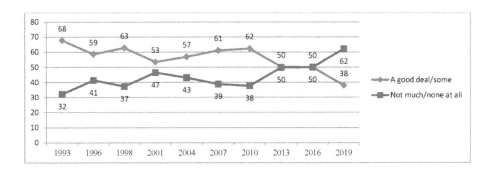

Sources: AES 1993–2019 "How much attention did you pay to reports about the election campaign in the newspapers?" Reponses were different prior to 1993 and have, therefore not been used. All figures are percentages.

Annexure 11: Followed election on the radio

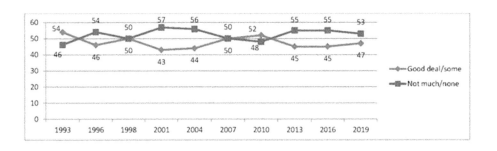

Sources: AES 1993–2019 "How much attention did you pay to reports about the election campaign in the radio?" The question was not asked prior to 1993.
All figures are percentages.

Annexure 12: Followed election news on TV

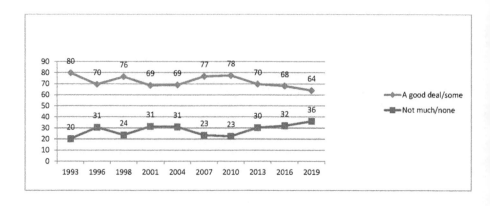

Sources: AES 1993–2019 "How much attention did you pay to reports about the election campaign in the television?" Reponses were different prior to 1993 and have, therefore not been used. All figures are percentages.

Annexure 13: Followed election on the internet

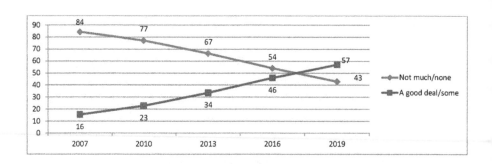

Sources: AES 2007–2019 "How much attention did you pay to reports about the election campaign in the internet?" The question was not asked prior to 2007. All figures are percentages.

Annexure 14: Discussed politics online

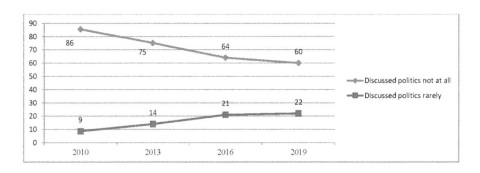

Sources: AES 2010–2019 "How often did you discuss politics online during the recent election?" The question was not asked prior to 2010. All figures are percentages.

Annexure 15: Can you name your representative or party?

Year	Unable to identify representative	Unable to identify Party
1993	30	23
1996	39	30
2013	46	45
Average	38	33

Sources: AES 1993, 1996, 2013: "Before the election, did you know the name of your local federal MP in the House of Representatives, and his or her political party?" These are the only years these questions have been asked in the AES. All figures are percentages.

Annexure 16: Quiz questions on political knowledge

Historical questions	Correct	Incorrect	Don't know
"Can you give the name of the federal treasurer before the 2004 federal election?"	87	2	11
"Which one of these persons was the federal Treasurer before the recent (2014) federal election?"	50	13	36
"Prior to the 2004 federal election, who was the most recent Australian Labor Party prime minister?"	82	13	5
"Can you say which political party has the second largest number of seats in the House of Representatives, following the 2004 federal election?"	67	14	20
"Which party came in second in seats in the House of Representatives (2013)?"	58	8	34

Sources: AES 2004, 2013. These are the only two years these questions have been asked in the AES. All figures are percentages.

Annexure 17: Qualified to participate in politics

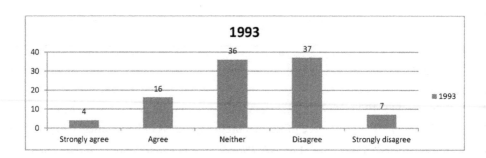

Source: AEC 1993: "I consider myself well-qualified to participate in politics?" The question was only asked in 1993. All figures are percentages.

Annexure 18: Care which party wins the election

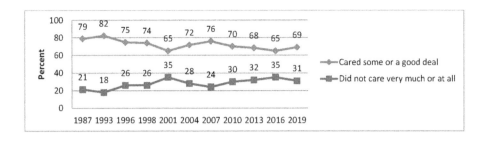

Sources: AES 1987–2019 "Would you say you cared a good deal which party won the Federal election or that you did not care very much which party won?" The question was not asked in 1990. All figures are percentages.

Annexure 19: Individuals self-placement on the left right ideological scale

Year	1996	1998	2001	2004	2007	2010	2013	2016	2019	Average
0 Left	2	3	2	2	2	2	4	3	3	3
1	1	1	1	2	1	2	3	3	3	2
2	4	2	4	4	4	5	7	9	7	5
3	6	8	9	9	9	9	10	12	9	9
4	9	11	8	10	10	10	9	11	8	10
5	42	40	42	38	39	39	36	33	36	38
6	11	11	9	9	9	9	8	8	8	9
7	9	11	10	10	9	9	10	9	8	9
8	2	9	9	9	9	6	7	7	8	7
9	5	2	2	3	2	2	2	2	2	3
10	5	4	4	5	6	6	5	4	3	5

Sources: AES: 1996–2019. "In politics, people sometimes talk about the 'left' and the 'right'. Where do you place yourself on a scale from 0 to 10, where 0 means the left and 10 means the right?" All figures are percentages.

Annexure 20: Individuals who placed the political parties in the middle (5) ideologically

Year	Labor	Liberal	Greens	Nationals	One Nation
1996	24	18	27	22	
1998	22	15	25	17	15
2001	25	21	23	21	16
2004	22	14	18	19	
2007	24	16	24	20	
2010	26	21	22	23	
2013	25	19	21	23	
2016	26	21	22	24	
2019	20	17	17	18	
Average	24	18	22	21	16

Sources: AES 1996–2016. "In politics, people sometimes talk about the 'left' and the 'right'. Where do you place (each party) on a scale from 0 to 10, where 0 means the left and 10 means the right?" This is a table of those who placed the political party as a (5) in the exact centre. All figures are percentages.

Annexure 21: Individuals who placed the parties on the wrong side of the left-right axis. It does not include respondents who placed the party in the middle

Year	Labor	Liberal	Green	Nationals	Democrats	One Nation
1996	24	15	17	17	22	
1998	26	17	17	21	26	31
2001	29	17	15	19	20	33
2004	23	12	13	17		
2007	15	24	15	17		
2010	20	16	12	20		
2013	22	16	20	11		
2016	18	16	11	17		
2019	15	14	10	17		
Average	21	16	14	17	23	32

Sources: AES 1996–2019 "In politics, people sometimes talk about the 'left' and the 'right'. Where do you place political parties on a scale from 0 to 10, where 0 means the left and 10 means the right?" All figures are percentages.

Annexure 22: Major party closest to own view on global warming

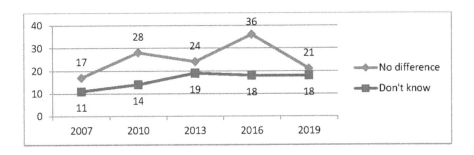

Sources: AES 2007–2019 "Whose policies, the Labor Party's or the Liberal-National Coalition's, would you say come closer to your views on (global warming)?" Graph shows those who answered don't know and no difference. The question was only asked since 2007. All figures are percentages.

Annexure 23: Major party closest to own view on industrial relations

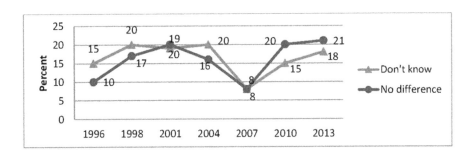

Sources: AES 1996–2013 "Whose policies, the Labor Party's or the Liberal-National Coalition's, would you say come closer to your views on (Industrial relations)?" Question not asked prior to 1996 or in 2016. All figures are percentages.

Annexure 24: Major party closest to own view on the war in Iraq

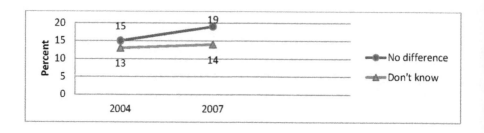

Sources: AES 2004–2007 "Whose policies, the Labor Party's or the Liberal-National Coalition's, would you say come closer to your views on (Iraq war)?" Question asked only for 2004 and 2007. All figures are percentages.

Annexure 25: Did not know there was a difference in major party global warming policy and interest in politics

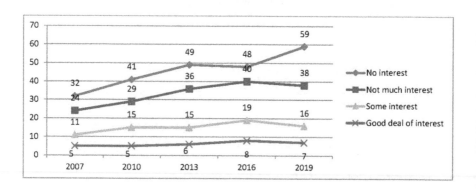

Sources: AES 2007–2019 "Whose policies, the Labor Party's or the Liberal-National Coalition's, would you say come closer to your views on (Global warming)?" "Generally speaking, how much interest do you generally have in what's going on in politics?" All figures are percentages.

Annexure 26: Did not know there was a difference in major party industrial relations policy and interest in politics

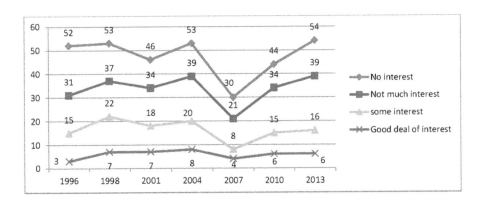

Sources: AES 1996–2013 "Whose policies, the Labor Party's or the Liberal-National Coalition's, would you say come closer to your views on (industrial relations)?" "Generally speaking, how much interest do you generally have in what's going on in politics?" Question not asked prior to 1996 or in 2016. All figures are percentages.

Annexure 27: Did not know there was a difference in major party policy for the Iraq war and interest in politics

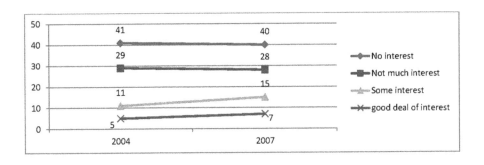

Sources: AES 2004, 2007 "Whose policies, the Labor Party's or the Liberal-National Coalition's, would you say come closer to your views on (Iraq war)?" "Generally speaking, how much interest do you generally have in what's going on in politics?" All figures are percentages.

Annexure 28: Age and political uninterest

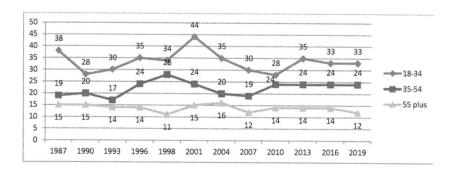

Sources: AES 1987–2019: "When were you born?" "Generally speaking, how much interest do you usually have in what's going on in politics?" All figures are in percentages.

Annexure 29: Education and political uninterest

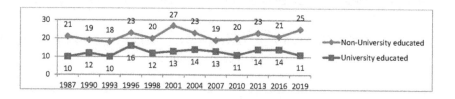

Sources: AES 1987–2019 "Have you obtained a trade qualification, a degree or a diploma, or any other qualification since leaving school? What is your highest qualification?" "Generally speaking, how much interest do you usually have in what's going on in politics?" All figures are in percentages.

Annexure 30: Income and political uninterest

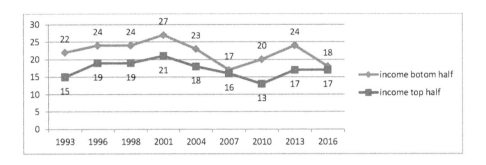

Sources: AES 1993–2019 "What is the gross annual income, before tax or other deductions, for you and your family living with you from all sources?" "Generally speaking, how much interest do you usually have in what's going on in politics?" The income question was not asked prior to 1993. All figures are in percentages.

Annexure 31: Place of residence and political uninterest

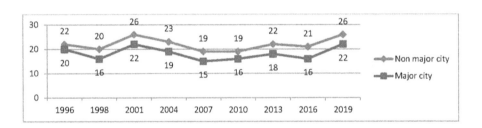

Sources: AES 1996–2019 "Would you say you live in a rural area or village, a small country town (under 10,000 people), a larger country town (over 10,000 people), a large town (over 25000 people), a major city (over 100,000 people)?" "Generally speaking, how much interest do you usually have in what's going on in politics?" Note: the responses differ prior to 1996 and have not been used. All figures are in percentages.

Annexure 32: Gender and political uninterest

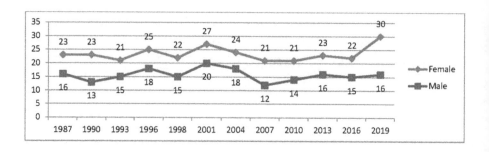

Sources: AES 1996–2019 "What is your sex?" "Generally speaking, how much interest do you usually have in what's going on in politics?" All figures are in percentages.

Annexure 33: Aboriginal/Torres Strait Uninterest contrasted to uninterest within the broader polity

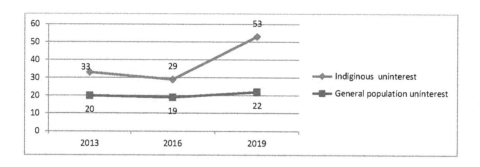

Sources: AES "Do you identify yourself as Aboriginal or Torres Strait Islander?" "Generally speaking, how much interest do you usually have in what's going on in politics?" All figures are in percentages.

Annexure 34: English speaking ability combined with firstly,
uninterest and secondly did not care who won the election

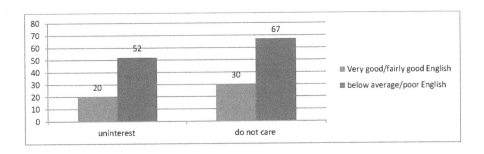

Source: AES 2013 "In day-to-day life, how good are you at speaking English when you need to? Generally speaking, how much interest do you usually have in what's going on in politics?" "Would you say you cared a good deal which party won the Federal election or that you did not care very much which party won?" The language question was only asked in 2013. All figures are percentages.

Annexure 35: Individuals who do not support a political party and political uninterest

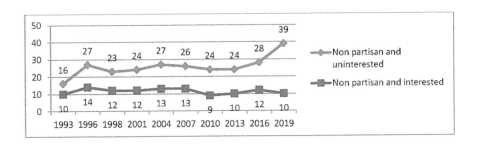

Sources: AES 1993–2019 "Generally speaking, do you usually think of yourself as Liberal, Labor, National or what? Generally speaking, how much interest do you usually have in what's going on in politics?" All figures are in percentages.

Annexure 36: Government run by big interests

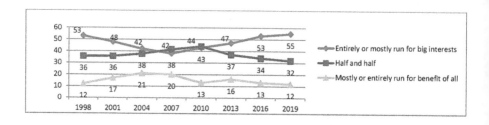

Sources: AES 1998–2019 "Would you say the government is run by a few big interests looking after themselves, or that it is run for the benefit of all people?" The question was not asked prior to 1998. All figures are percentages.

Annexure 37: Discussed politics and interest in politics

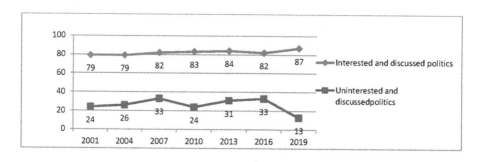

Sources: AES 2001–2019 "Did you discuss politics with others in person during the recent election?" "Generally speaking, how much interest do you generally have in what's going on in politics?" The question was not asked prior to 2001.
All figures are percentages.

Annexure 38: Satisfaction with the way democracy works in Australia

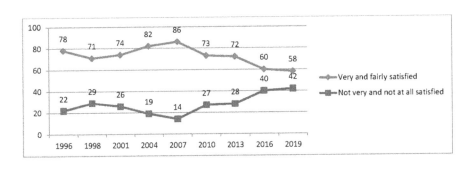

Sources: AES 1996–2016 "On the whole are you very satisfied, fairly satisfied, not very satisfied or not at all satisfied with the way democracy works in Australia?" All figures are percentages.

Annexure 39: Unsatisfied with how democracy works in Australia and political interest

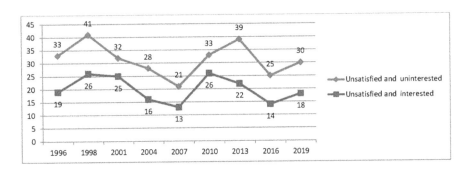

Source: AES 1996–2019 "On the whole are you very satisfied, fairly satisfied, not very satisfied or not at all satisfied with the way democracy works in Australia?" "Generally speaking, how much interest do you generally have in what's going on in politics?" All figures are percentages.

Year	2 to 4	5 to 7	8 to 10	11 to 13	14	16
1987	4.7	5.7	6.5	0	0	0
1990	2.8	3.4	5	0	0	0
1993	2.8	3	3.2	0	0	0
1996	2.8	3.1	3.6	3.6	0	0
1998	2.8	3.6	4	5	0	0
2001	3.6	4.5	5.8	5.4	0	0
2004	4.3	4.7	5.6	7.1	11.8	0
2007	4.4	4.4	4.5	3.7	0	0
2010	6.1	5.3	6.5	8.8	0	0
2013	0	5.5	6.2	5.8	0	6.0
2016	4.7	4.6	6.1	9.7	0	0
2019	3.9	5.1	6.1	11.2	0	0
Average	3.6	4.4	5.3	6.7	11.8	6.0

Sources: AEC

The reason only 6 per cent voted informally in 2013 when there were 16 candidates on the ballot is because this was the electorate of Melbourne. Melbourne is a highly interested and educated electorate to such a degree they are the only electorate represented by the Greens.

Annexure 41: Makes a difference who people vote for

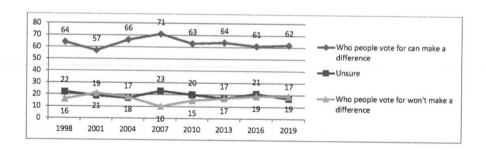

Sources AES 1998–2019 "Some people say that no matter who people vote for, it won't make a difference to what happens. Others say that who people vote for can make a big difference to what happens. Using the scale below, where would you place yourself?" The scale was 1–5 where 1 was made a big difference and 5 was made no difference from 2007 to 2013. Between 1996 and 2004 the scale was the reverse. The top two and the bottom two scales have been combined for visual clarity. The question was not asked prior to 1996. All figures are in percentages.

Annexure 42: Two-party preferred outcome of election overall and two-party preferred outcome if uninterested had not voted

Election Year	ALP vote	Coalition vote	Uninterested impact	Two-party preferred if uninterested had not voted	
				ALP	Coalition
1987	50.8	49.2	3.8 to Labor	47	53
1990	49.9	50.1	equal	49.9	50.1
1993	51.4	48.6	2.5 to Labor	48.9	51.1
1996	46.4	53.6	0.3 to Labor	46.1	53.9
1998	51	49	3.6 to Labor	47.4	52.6
2001	49	51	0.9 to Labor	48.1	51.9
2004	47.3	52.7	1.3 to Coalition	48.6	51.4
2007	52.7	47.3	0.6 to Labor	52.1	47.9
2010	50.1	49.9	1.4 to Labor	48.7	51.3
2013	46.5	53.5	0.9 to Labor	45.6	54.4
2016	49.6	50.4	0.8 to Labor	48.8	51.2
2019	48.5	51.5	1.1 to Labor	47	53
Average	49.4	50.6	1.2 to Labor	48.2	51.8

Sources: AEC, AES 1987–2019 All figures are percentages.

Annexure 43: Number of seats affected by uninterested votes

Year	ALP Seats	Coalition seats	Uninterested impact	Seats decided by uninterested	Seats won if uninterested had not voted	
					ALP	Coalition
1987	86	62	3.8 to Labor	21	65	83
1990	78	69	equal	0	78	69
1993	80	65	2.5 to Labor	17	63	82
1996	49	94	0.3 to Labor	2	47	96
1998	67	80	3.6 to Labor	15	52	95
2001	65	82	0.9 to Labor	0	65	82
2004	60	87	1.3 to Coalition	7	67	80
2007	83	65	0.6 to Labor	3	80	68
2010	72	72	1.4 to Labor	6	66	78
2013	55	90	.9 to Labor	3	52	93
2016	69	76	1.8 to Labor	8	61	84
2019	68	77	1.1 to Labor	9	59	86
Average	69	77	1.2 to Labor	8	63	83

Sources: AEC, AES 1987–2019 The table concentrates on seats won by the two major parties and does not take account of independents. All figures are percentages.

Annexure 44: Corangamite details

Source: AEC

Annexure 45: Number of electorates affected by donkey votes

Year	Number of electorates won by one per cent or less	Winner above the loser on ballot
1987	5	3
1990	6	4
1993	12	3
1996	10	6
1998	16	6
2001	5	0
2004	10	8
2007	12	10
2010	5	2
2013	5	3
2016	7	6
2019	6	4
Average	8	5

Sources: AEC 1987–2019

Annexure 46: Impact of preferences

Year	Number and per cent of electorates decided by preferences	
1987	54	(36%)
1990	91	(61%)
1993	63	(43%)
1996	65	(44%)
1998	98	(66%)
2001	87	(58%)
2004	61	(41%)
2007	75	(50%)
2010	85	(57%)
2013	97	(65%)
2016	96	(64%)
2019	106	70%)
Average	79	(53%)

Sources: AEC 1987–2019

Annexure 47: Voters who do not know or cannot remember which party they preferred

Year	House of Representatives	Senate
1996	24	25
1998	24	27
2001	24	27
2004	22	24
2007	19	24
2010	19	24
2013	28	37
2016	24	30
2019	25	21
Average	23	27

Sources: AES 1996–2019 "If your first preference was for (a minor party) in the end, which of the two major parties, the Liberal-National Coalition or the Labor Party, did you give your preference to in the House of Representatives? And in the Senate?" The above table is a compilation of those who answered Not sure/Don't know. All figures are in percentages. Note the AES did not ask about preferences prior to 1996.

Annexure 48: Voters who do not know or do not remember who they preferenced in the House of Representatives Average 40–18

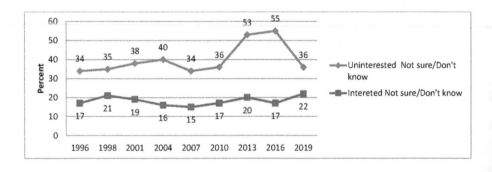

Sources AES 1996–2019 "If your first preference was for the Greens or other minor party: In the end which of the two major parties, the Liberal-National Coalition to the Labor Party, did you give your preferences to in the House of Representatives?" "Generally speaking, how much interest do you usually have in politics?" All figures are percentages. Note: The AES did not ask respondents who they preferenced prior to 1996.

Annexure 49: Election swings 1987–2019

Year	Swing	Did it change government
1987	1.0 against government	No
1990	0.9 against government	No
1993	1.5 to government	No
1996	5.1 against government	Yes, Howard
1998	4.6 against government	No
2001	1.9 to government	No
2004	1.8 to government	No
2007	5.4 against government	Yes, Rudd
2010	2.6 against government	No
2013	3.6 against government	Yes
2016	3.1 against government	No
2019	1.2 Coalition	No
Average	2.7	

Sources: AEC All figures are percentages.

Annexure 50: Number of voters required to change their vote from the winning major party to the loosing major party in the most marginal electorates to change the election outcome

Year	Number of votes deciding outcome	Total votes	Percentage of votes to change election outcome
1987	14,834	9,227,772	.16
1990	2,378	9,899,674	.02
1993	2,131	10,569,454	.02
1996	39,922	10,834,873	.37
1998	3,438	11,043,840	.03
2001	1,332	11,474,074	.01
2004	25,499	11,714,835	.22
2007	9,739	12,419,863	.08
2010	386	12,402,363	.003
2013	35,499	12,914,927	.27
2016	7,752	14,262,016	.05
2019	16,639	16456,054	.1
Average	13,296	11,934,979	.11

Sources: AEC, AES. Note: figures provide for a one vote majority in each seat as well as a one seat majority for government. In cases where it is not clearly apparent who independent members would support, they have been placed with the government.

Annexure 51: Actual election swings contrasted against uninterested swings

Year	Actual election swing	Uninterested swing
1990	.9 to Coalition	7 to Coalition
1993	1.5 to Labor	6.7 to Labor
1996	5.1 to Coalition	5.9 to Coalition
1998	4.6 to Labor	8.6 to Labor
2001	1.9 to Coalition	7.5 to Coalition
2004	1.8 to Coalition	4.8 to Coalition
2007	5.4 to Labor	4.5 to Labor
2010	2.6 to Coalition	2.3 to Labor
2013	3.6 to Coalition	2 to Coalition
2016	3.1 to Labor	1.5 to Coalition
2019	1.2 to Coalition	.07 to Labor

Sources: AES 1990–2019. All figures are percentages.

Annexure 52: Number of seats that changed from one party to another

Year	Number of seats that changed from one party to another	Percentage of seats to change
1987	8	5
1990	17	11
1993	18	12
1996	38	26
1998	23	16
2001	10	7
2004	13	9
2007	27	18
2010	16	11
2013	23	15
2016	19	13
2019	12	8
Average	19	13

Sources: AEC

References

(1) Insiders, ABC. 29 July 2018.

(2) Chaples, E. (1997). The Australian voters. In R. Smith (Ed.), *Politics in Australia*. Sydney: Allen and Unwin.

(3) Tranter, B. (2007). 'Political knowledge and its partisan consequences'. *Australian Journal of Political Science*, 42, 73–88.

(4) Macpherson, C. B. (1977). *The life and times of liberal democracy*. Oxford: Oxford University Press.

(5) Jones, A. H. M. (1957). *Athenian Democracy*. Oxford: Basil Blackwell.

(6) Finley, M. I. (1973). *Democracy ancient and modern*. New Jersey: Rutgers University Press.

(7) Samons, L. J. (2004). *What's wrong with democracy: From Athenian practice to American worship*. Berkely: University of California Press.

(8) Plato, Lee, H. D. P. S. & Lane, M. S. (2007). *The Republic, Vol. 2*. London: Penguin.

(9) Corcoran, P. E. (1983). The limits of democratic theory. In G. Duncan (Ed.), *Democratic theory and practice*. Cambridge, Cambridge University Press.

(10) Lipset, S. M. (1981). *Political man: The social base of politics*. Baltimore: The Johns Hopkins University Press.

(11) Sutherland, K. (2008). *Wealth of Nations*. Oxford University Press.

(12) Mill, J. S. (2010). *Considerations of Representative Government*. Cambridge: Cambridge University Press.

(13) Hitler, A. (1992). *Mein Kampf*. London: Penguin Books.

(14) Oldfield, A. (1994). *Australian women and the vote*. Cambridge University Press.

(15) Twomey, A. (1994). *The Constitution: 19th century Colonial Office document or a People's Constitution?* Parliament of Australia.

(16)   Wright, C. (2018). *You daughters of freedom*. Melbourne: Text Publishing.

(17)   Goot, M. (2006). 'The Aboriginal Franchise and Its Consequences'. *Australian Journal of Politics & History*, 52, 517–561.

(18)   An act: To provide for an Uniform Federal Franchise. http://www.foundingdocs.gov.au/resources/transcripts/cth5i_doc_1902.pdf.

(19)   Brett, J. (2019). *From secret ballot to democracy sausage*. Melbourne: Text Publishing.

(20)   New Zealand History, New Zealand turns down federation with Australia. 1901. https://nzhistory.govt.nz/page/nz-says-no-aussie-federation.

(21)   Botsman, P. (2000). *The great constitutional swindle: A citizen's view of the Australian constitution*. London: Pluto Press.

(22)   Hirst, J. (2002). *Australia's democracy: A short history*. Sydney: Allen and Unwin.

(23)   Bennett, S. (2008). *Compulsory voting in Australian national elections*. Canberra: Parliamentary Library.

(24)   Jaensch, D. (1995). *Election! how and why Australia votes*. St Leonards: Allen and Unwin.

(25)   Morris Jones, W. H. (1954). 'In defence of apathy: Some doubts on the duty to vote', *Political Studies*, 2, 25–37.

(26)   Bennett, S. E. (1986). *Apathy in America, 1960–1984: Causes and consequences of citizen political indifference*, New York: Transnational Publishers, Inc.

(27)   Chen, K. (1992). *Political alienation and voting turnout in the United States, 1960–1988*. San Francisco: Mellen Research University Press.

(28)   Delli Carpini, M. X., & Keeter, S. (1989). *What Americans know about politics and why it matters*, Yale University Press.

(29)   Lau, R. R., & Redlawsk, D. (1997). 'Voting correctly'. *American Political Science Review*, 91, 585–598.

(30)   Trends in Australian political opinion: Results from the Australian Election Study, 1987–2007. http://aes.anu.edu.au/publications/aes-trends.

(31)   Somin, I. (2013). *Democracy and Political Ignorance: Why Smaller Government Is Smarter*. California: Stanford Law Books.

(32)   Johns, G. (1998). 'Does Compulsory Voting Distort Electoral Outcomes?' *Agenda*, 5, 367–372.

(33)   McAllister, I. (2001). 'Elections without cues: The 1999 Australian Republic Referendum', *Australian Journal of Political Science*, 36, 247–269.

(34)   Dye, T., & Zeigler, H. (1970). *The irony of democracy*. California: Duxbury.

(35)   Rethinking democracy. http://www.project-syndicate.org/commentary/dani-rodrik-examines-the-root-causes-of-political-malaise-in-advanced-and-developing-countries.

(36)   Schumpeter, J. A. (1965). *Capitalism, Socialism and Democracy*. London: Unwin University Books.

(37)   Faulkner, J., & Jones, B., (ed.) (2006). *Apathy and anger. In Coming to the Party: where to next for Labor?* Carlton, Vic: Melbourne University Press.

(38)   Sartori, G. (1987). *The theory of democracy revisited*. New Jersey: Chatham House Publishers.

(39)   Aitkin, D. (1982). *Stability and change in Australian politics*. Canberra: Australian National University Press.

(40)   Hasham, N. (2016). Election 2016: Voter turnout lowest since compulsory voting began in 1925. *Sydney Morning Herald*.

(41)   Killestyn, E. (2016). Federal Direct Enrolment and Direct Update. AEC.

(42)   Goot, M. (1985). Electoral systems. In D. Aitkin (Ed.), *Surveys of Australian political science*. Sydney, Allen and Unwin.

(43)   McAllister, I., Makkai, T., & Patterson, C. (1992). *Informal voting in 1987 and 1990: Australian federal elections*. Canberra: Australian Govt. Pub. Service: Office of Multicultural Affairs.

(44)   Young, S. & Hill, L. (2009). 'Uncounted votes: Informal voting in the House of Representatives as a marker of political exclusion in Australia', *Australian Journal of Politics and History*, 55, 64–79.

(45)   AEC, Election Day and the Scrutiny: Australian Electoral Commission website, 2001.

(46)   Jackman, S. (1999). 'Non-compulsory voting in Australia?: What surveys can (and can't) tell us'. *Electoral Studies*, 18, 29–48.

(47)   ABC, Gruen Transfer, 2013.

(48)   No Land Tax support, the Donkey Vote and Informal Voting. http://blogs.abc.net.au/antonygreen/2015/07/no-land-tax-and-the-donkey-vote.html#more.

(49)   Wynne, E. (10 Dec. 2019). Scandals, division and voter apathy blamed for lack of interest in running for local council. ABC.

(50)   Real Aussies prefer science to sport. www.csiro.au/communication/mediarel/mr1997/mr97120.html.

(51)   Citizens' Agenda survey: voters tuning out, have little faith in politics. http://www.thecitizen.org.au/news/citizens-agenda-survey-voters-tuning-out-have-little-faith-politics.

(52)   Essential poll. (2019). Majority of voters think Bill Shorten will be the winner on Saturday.

(53)   Kinninment, M. (21 November, 2013). By-election caught some napping. *Northern Star*.

(54)   *The Australian*. (30 July, 2018). Questions for AEC after low voter turnout. 30 July 2018.

(55)   Aston, H. (3 April, 2014). Clive Palmer spends to the end in WA. *Canberra Times*.

(56)   Denemark, D. (2002). 'Television effects and voter decision making in Australia: A re-examination of the Converse model'. *Journal of Political Science*, 32, 663–690.

(57)   Young, S. (2010). *How Australia Decides: Election Reporting and the Media*. Cambridge: Cambridge University Press.

(58)   Roy Morgan. (14 June, 2016). The 10 most (and least) politically engaged electorates.

(59)   ABC. (2019). Australia Talks.

(60)   Manning, P. (2006). *US and Them*. Milsons Point: Random House.

(61)   Megalogenis, G. (2006). *The Longest Decade*. Melbourne: Scribe.

(62)   Latham, M. (2005). *The Latham Diaries*. Melbourne: Melbourne University Press.

(63)   Bowden, T. (21 July, 2010). Masterchef phenomena bumps Gillard and Abbott. *7.30 Report*. ABC.

(64)   Dahl, R. (1956). *A preface to democratic theory*. Chicago: University of Chicago Press.

(65)   Dalton, R. (2002). *Citizen politics: Public opinion and political parties in advanced industrial democracies*. New York: Chatam House Publishers.

(66)   Wilson, C. (1969). 'Western, J. S. Participation in Politics: A Preliminary Analysis'. *Australian and New Zealand Journal of Sociology*, 5, 98–110.

(67)   Western, J. S., & Wilson, P. R. (1973). Politics: participation and attitudes. In H. Mayer & H. Nelson (Eds.), *Australian politics: A third reader.* Melbourne: Cheshire.

(68)   Jaensch, D. (1997). *The politics of Australia*, Melbourne: Macmillan Education Australia.

(69)   Rapana, J., & Frost, C. (6 November, 2015). Revolving PM's too much for patients. *Daily Telegraph.*

(70)   Taylor, L. (13 September, 2014). Who is Warren Truss? Poll reveals holes in Australians' grasp of politics. *Guardian.*

(71)   Sheridan, J. (20 September, 2009). Celebrities yes, but politics? Don't ask. *Sydney Morning Herald.*

(72)   Huntley, D. (11 August, 2018). Michael McCormack's homophobic slurs re-emerge amid postal plebiscite controversy. *Newcastle Herald.*

(73)   Clennell, A. (30 May, 2014). Even this invisible man can still beat the ALP. *Daily Telegraph.*

(74)   Clennell, A. (16 March, 2015). Baird Builds. *Daily Telegraph.*

(75)   McAllister, I. (2011). *The Australian Voter: 50 Years of Change*, Sydney: New South Publishing.

(76)   History of Western Civilisation: Politics within the Revolutionaries. 2017.

(77)   How do voters vote when they have no ideology? evidence from Spain. https://www.academia.edu/1487391/How_do_voters_vote_when_they_have_no_ideology_evidence_from_Spain 2015).

(78)   Rodon, T. (2015). 'Do All Roads Lead to the Center? The Unresolved Dilemma of Centrist Self-Placement'. *International Journal of Public Opinion Research*, 27, 177–196.

(79)   MacCallum, M. (2007). *Poll Dancing: The Story of the 2007 Election.* Melbourne: Black Inc.

(80)   Stayner, T. (8 October, 2019). Malcolm Turnbull blasts Liberal party for being 'incapable' of climate change action. SBS.

(81)   Bean, C., & McAllister, I. (2013). Documenting the inevitable: Voting behaviour at the 2013 Australian election. In C. Johnson, J. Wanna & H.-A. Lee (Eds.), *Abbott's Gambit: The 2013 Australian Federal Election.* ANU Press.

(82)   Leigh, A. (2015). *The luck of politics.* Melbourne: Black Inc.

(83)   Harrington, S. (2009). Public knowledge beyond journalism: Infotainment, satire and Australian television; Doctor of Philosophy: Queensland University of Technology.

(84)   Coorey, P. (30 April, 2011). Rudd was beheaded and it was all for nothing, Tanner laments. *Sydney Morning Herald*.

(85)   Bean, C., & McAllister, I. (2012). Electoral behaviour in the 2010 Australian federal election. In M. Simms & J. Wanna, (Eds.), *Julia 2010: The caretaker election*. Canberra: ANU Press.

(86)   Baird, J. (2004). *Media Tarts*, Carlton: Scribe Publications.

(87)   Middleton, K. (2019). Fresh documents in Morrison's sacking. *The Saturday Paper*.

(88)   7.30 Report. (14 November, 2019). The Quiet Australians. ABC.

(89)   Coorey, P. (14 September 2009). The greatest game of all: politicians pretending to be sports fans. *Sydney Morning Herald*.

(90)   ABC Insiders. (30 May 2007).

(91)   ABC Insiders. (15 September, 2013).

(92)   Kenny, M., & Aston, H. (29 June, 2013). Rudd poll bounce boosts Labor. *Sydney Morning Herald*.

(93)   Smith, R. (2001). *Australian political culture*. Sydney: Longman.

(93a)   Bishop, B. (2008). *The Big Sort: Why the Clustering of Like-Minded America Is Tearing Us Apart*. Mifflin Company.

(94)   Emy, H., & Hughes, O. (1991). *Australian politics: Realities in conflict*. Melbourne: McMillan.

(95)   Victorian Aboriginal Legal Service. Submission delivered to the Electoral Matters Committee at a Public Hearing relating to the 'Inquiry into the Conduct of the 2006 Victorian State Election and Matters Related Thereto' on 28 August 2007 titled 'Voting, the law and Aboriginal people—a long story'. Victorian Aboriginal Legal Service Co-operative Ltd. 2007.

(96)   Hunt, D. (2013). *Girt*. Black Inc.

(97)   Franklin, M. N. (2004). *Voter turnout and the dynamics of electoral competition in established democracies since 1945*. Cambridge: Cambridge University Press.

(98)   Lazarsfeld, P. F., Berelson, B., & Gaudet, H. (1948). *The peoples choice: How the voter makes up his mind in a Presidential campaign*. New York: Columbia University Press.

(99)   Minchin, N. (1996). 'Compulsory voting and perceptions of Parliament'. *Legislative Studies*, 10, 15–19.

(100)   Creating the active citizen? Recent developments in Civic education; Library (1999). P. O. A. P. Canberra: Parliamentary Library.

(101)   Evans, M. (14 May, 2013). Why do Australians hate politics? *The Conversation*.

(102)   Grattan, M. (4 July, 2010). With sleeves rolled up, the PM makes elegant U-turn and quickly moves on. *Sydney Morning Herald*.

(103)   Saha, L., Print, M., & Edwards, K. (2005). Report 2: Youth, political engagement and voting: Australian Electoral Commission website.

(104)   Latham, M. (2014). *The political bubble: Why Australians don't trust politics*. Sydney: Macmillan.

(105)   Coorey, P. (6 September, 2012). Honesty the best policy: Turnbull swipes at Abbott and 'deficit of trust'. *Sydney Morning Herald*.

(106)   Warren, M. E. (2004). 'What does corruption mean in a democracy', *American Journal of Political Science*, 48, 328–343.

(107)   Humphries, M. (25 December, 2019). Barnaby Joyce says he is 'sick of the government being in my life' in Christmas Eve video. *The Guardian*.

(108)   Norris, P., & Sawyer, M., (ed.) (2001). *Confidence in Australian democracy. In Elections full free and fair*. Federation Press.

(109)   Bean, C., & Denmark, D. (2007). Citizenship, participation, efficacy and trust in Australia. In D. Denemark, G. Meagher, S. Wilson, M. Western, & T. Phillips, (Eds.). *Australian social attitudes 2: Citizenship, work and aspirations*. Sydney: UNSW Press.

(110)   Errington, W., & van Onselyn, P. (2007). *John Winston Howard*. Carlton: Melbourne University Press.

(111)   Henderson, G. (4 December 2004). Anti-climax for an excited left. *Sydney Morning Herald*.

(112)   Rawson, D. W. (1961). *Australia votes: the 1958 federal election*. Melbourne: Melbourne University Press.

(113)   Leighley, J., & Nagler, J. (2014). *Who Votes Now? Demographics, Issues, Inequality, and Turnout in the United States, Vol. 1,*. Ringgold Beaverton.

(114)   Hay, C. (2007). *Why We Hate Politcs*. Cambridge: Polity Press.

(115)   How and why has civics education developed to its current situation?

(116)   Civics and citizenship education: An Australian perspective. http://www.abc.net.au/civics/democracy/ccanded.htm Accessed 22/1/10.

(117)   Solomon, D. (1981). *Australia's Government and Parliament, 5th ed..* Melbourne: Thomas Nelson.

(118)   Murphy, D. (9 September, 2013). Detours ahead as minor parties claim Senate balance. *Sydney Morning Herald.*

(119)   ABC. (13 September 2006). Rotating ballots 'cut' donkey votes.

(120)   ABC. (30 March, 2006). Electoral reform group voices donkey vote concerns.

(121)   Colbatch, T. (5 October 2013). How mistaken identity and luck won on the day. *Sydney Morning Herald.*

(122)   Blake, S. (6 September 2013). Men of many parties have Lib in their sights. *Daily Telegraph.*

(123)   Bean, C. (1997). 'Australia's experience with the alternative vote'. *Representation*, 34, 103.

(124)   Goot, M., & Watson, I. (2001). 'One Nation electoral support: Where does it come from, what makes it different and how does it fit?'. *Australian Journal of Politics and History*, 47, 159–191.

(125)   Dinham, A. (10 September, 2020). Melbourne tower residents speak out on Pauline Hanson's attempted stubby holder delivery during lockdown. SBS.

(126)   Farr, M. (13 November, 2017). One Nation leader Steve Dickson's grubby 'strap-on' lie. *Queensland Times.*

(127)   Backhouse, A. (10 November, 2017). Pauline Hanson backs candidate amid sex shop furore. *Queensland Times.*

(128)   Rappolt, C. (1998). Maiden speech by Charles Rappolt MLA, Member for Mulgrave.

(129)   Katter, B. (2013). *Katteronia: The wit and wisdom of Bob Katter.* Melbourne: Black Inc.

(130)   Swan, J. (5 December, 2013). I am a bogan, says Clive Palmer (12) dismissing a 'voters are bogans' email leak. *Sydney Morning Herald.*

(131)   Steketee, M. (12 January, 2008). Swings and roundabouts. *The Australian.*

(131a) Stayner. (12 January 2021). Asked about MP's spreading COVID misinformation, Michael McCormack says 'facts can somethimes be contentious'. SBS.

(131b) Mills, S. (1986). *The new machine men: Polls and persuasion in Australian politics.* Penguin.

(132) Throsby, E. (2013). 'Engaging the disengaged: Swinging voters, political participation and media in Australia', Platform. *Journal of Media and Communication*, 5, 97–106.

(133) Campbell, A., Converse, P. E., Miller, W. E., & Stokes, D. (1966). *Elections and the political order*. New York: John Willey.

(134) Jensen, E. (2019). The Prosperity Gospel: How Scott Morrison won and Bill Shorten lost. *Quarterly Essay.*

(135) Tanner, L. (2011). *Sideshow: Dumbing Down Democracy*. Melbourne: Scribe.

(136) O'Malley, N. (14 July, 2012). Radicals push members out on a wing. *Sydney Morning Herald.*

(137) Lawrence, C. (2006). *Fear and politics*. Melbourne: Scribe Short Books.

(138) Do, A. (June, 2019). Brush with Fame. ABC.

(139) Bean, C. (1994). 'Issues in the 1993 election'. *Australian Journal of Political Science* , 29, 134.

(140) Gittins, R. (14 December, 2009). Abbott's populism may be making of Rudd. *Sydney Morning Herald.*

(141) McAllister, I., & Bean, C. (2000). 'The Electoral Politics of Economic Reform in Australia: The 1998 Election'. *Australian Journal of Political Science*, 35, 383–399.

(142) Lagan, B. (2005). *Loner: Inside a Labor Tragedy*. Crows Nest: Allen and Unwin.

(143) Goot, M., & Watson, I. (2007). 'Explaining Howard's Success: Social Structure, Issue Agendas and Party Support, 1993–2004'. *Australian Journal of Political Science*, 42, 253–276.

(144) Rootes, C. (2014). 'A referendum on the carbon tax? The 2013 Australian election, the Greens, and the environment'. *Environmental Politics*, 23, 166–173.

(145) Joyce, B. (2 December, 2009). Speech in Parliament.

(146) Oakes, L. (30 June 2012). Clowns laugh as we cry out for a leader. *Daily Telegraph.*

(147) Lowy Institute Poll 2015.

(148) Coorey, P. (6 September, 2012). A plague on both your sides of the house. *Sydney Morning Herald.*

(149) Stiglitze, J. (2 September 2013). Cheer up, Australia, you've got it good. *Sydney Morning Herald.*

(150) Warhurst, J. (2014). 'Grinding the face of the poor'. *Eureka Street*, 24, 43–45.

(151) Hartcher, P. (9 June, 2012). Merchants of doom, beware. *Sydney Morning Herald*.

(152) Koukoulas, S. (17 October, 2013). Why isn't Abbott acting on the 'budget emergency'? ABC.

(153) Aubusson, K. (4 May, 2016). Leigh Sales grills Scott Morrison on 7.30 in first post-budget interview. *Sydney Morning Herald*.

(154) Jericho, G. (4 June, 2015). Joe Hockey may call me a clown, but GDP growth hasn't been 'terrific'. *Guardian*.

(155) Kenny, M. (23 June 2016). Federal election 2016: Medicare and boats—who not to believe? *Canberra Times*.

(156) Gartrell, A. (17 June, 2016). Malcolm Turnbull says Bob Hawke's Medicare ads part of "disgraceful" Labor scare campaign. *Canberra Times*.

(157) Benson, S. (6 July, 2016). Innovation flatlined as mediscare spoke to the voters. *Daily Telegraph*.

(158) Emerson, C. (21 November, 2003). Wedge watch. *Sydney Morning Herald*.

(159) Charlton, P., & Solomon, D. (2002). Tampa: The Triumph of Politics. In D. Solomon (Ed.), *Howard's Race*. Sydney: Harper Collins.

(160) Solomon, D. (2002). Election race or race election. In D. Solomon (Ed.), *Howard's Race*. Sydney: Harper Collins.

(161) *Daily Telegraph*. (30 March 2015). They said it.

(162) McAllister, I. (2003). 'Border protection, the 2001 Australian election and the Coalition victory'. *Australian Journal of Political Science*, 38, 445–463.

(163) (Atkins, D. (2002). Beazley's campaign. In D. Solomon (Ed.), Howard's Race. Sydney: Harper Collins.

(164) Brett, J. (2007). Exit Right: The Unravelling of John Howard; 28 ed.; *Quarterly Essay*.

(165) Crabb, A. (2005). *Losing It*. Sydney: Picador.

(166) Jupp, J. (2012). Immigration issues in the 2010 Federal Election. In M. Simms & J. Wanna, (Eds.), *Julia 2010: The caretaker election*. Canberra: ANU Press.

(167) Hartcher, P. (19 November, 2011). Ugly game of race baiting. *Sydney Morning Herald.*

(168) Coorey, P. (1 November, 2012). Thomson turns his back on Labor. *Sydney Morning Herald.*

(169) Wroe, D. (4 June, 2015). Senators reveal scant interest in terrorism. *Canberra Times.*

(170) The Conversation. (4 August, 2017). Transcript of Trump-Turnbull call shows just how hard it'll be to deal with the president. *The Conversation.*

(171) Hunter, F. (1 March, 2018). Victorians scared to go to restaurants at night because of street gang violence: Peter Dutton. *Sydney Morning Herald.*

(172) Horin, A. (6 October, 2007). Too busy with smear tactics to note worker's real needs. *Sydney Morning Herald.*

(173) Johnson, P. (13 October, 2020). Anthony Albanese refuses to call for Gladys Berejiklian's resignation and defends Opposition tactics during pandemic year. ABC.

(173a) Bavas, Josh. (1 January 2020). Queensland Government warned of climate change amid political turmoil, 1989 cabinet documents reveal. ABC.

(174) Zhou, N. (9 May, 2019). PM says bill that mentions testing makeup on animals is 'action' on extinction crisis. *Guardian.*

(175) Khalik, J. (14 May, 2019). Why you can't sue a political party for misleading advertising in an election. *Crikey.*

(176) Project. Channel 10, (10 December 2020).

(177) Gartrell, T. (1 June, 2004). 2004 Election Analysis. Australian politics.

(178) McGregor Tan Research. (2011). Local government election survey: final report: Local government association of South Australia.

(179) Jaensch, D. (1994). *The Liberals.* St. Leonards: Allen & Unwin.

(180) Hartcher, P. (19 May, 2007). Rudd: I'll stamp out ad abuse. *Sydney Morning Herald.*

(181) Ramsey, A. (26 May, 2007). Titanic spending is first-class hypocrisy. *Sydney Morning Herald.*

(182) Murphy, K. (28 May, 2010). Rudd treats us like mugs with latest backslide on government ads. *Sydney Morning Herald.*

(183) ABC (17 July, 2011). Gillard defends carbon tax ad spend.

(184) Knott, M. (9 December, 2014). Government launches ad campaign to sell its uni plans, cost unknown. *Sydney Morning Herald.*

(185)   ABC (19 July, 2010). Gillard defends 'moving forward' mantra. ABC.

(186)   Cassidy, B. (2010). *The party thieves*. Melbourne: Melbourne University Press.

(187)   Banham, C., & Delaney, B. (2 February, 2003). Fridge door terror kit a $15m 'waste'.

(188)   Matthewson, P. (1 May, 2013). Abbott's image: an everyman for the everyday voter. ABC.

(189)   Taylor, L. (21 July, 2012). Labor boxed in over the price of pies and pizzas. *Sydney Morning Herald*.

(190)   Cited in Glenday, J. (3 November, 2013). Opinion polls explained: How to read them and why they matter. ABC.

(191)   Hartcher, P. (23 July, 2013). Stop the boats but not the people. *Sydney Morning Herald*.

(192)   Alcorn, G. (24 October, 2013). Tony Abbott can't ride out the expenses scandal. *Sydney Morning Herald*.

(193)   Hartcher, P. (13 February, 2016). Class clown: Barnaby Joyce has centre stage to prove himself. *Sydney Morning Herald*.

(194)   Bacon, W., & Jegan, A. (2020). Lies, Debates, and silences: How News Corp produces climate scepticism in Australia.

(195)   Cooke, R. (May, 2019). News Corp: Democracy's greatest threat. *The Monthly*.

(196)   Baker, N. (6 January, 2020). How a climate change study from 12 years ago warned of this horror bushfire season. SBS.

(197)   *Guardian*. (26 March, 2019). One Nation attempts to secure millions from NRA to soften Australia's gun laws—video.

(198)   Cox, L. (7 December, 2019). Leading scientists condemn political inaction on climate change as Australia 'literally burns'. *Guardian*.

(199)   Kenny, C. (11 November, 2019). 'Sick and irresponsible' green left politicians using bushfires for 'political gain. Sky News.

(200)   Baker, N. (11 November, 2019). NSW mayor slams deputy PM's 'insulting' climate change attack during bushfires. SBS.

(201)   Tan, S. (7 January, 2020). UK Meteorologist Shuts Down Aussie MP After He Calls Her An "Ignorant Pommy Weather Girl". https://www.pedestrian.tv/news/meteorologist-laura-tobin-responds-craig-kelly-weather-girl-comment/.

(201a) Bonyhady, N. (21 January 2020). Prime Minister says hazard reduction burns as important as emissions. *Sydney Morning Herald.*

(202)　Australia deliberates: A Republic—Yes or No. www.ida.org.au/australia/releases.php.

(203)　Metherell, M. (5 March, 2007). Fear of Muslims declines when all sides put their case. *Sydney Morning Herald.*

(204)　Fowler, G. (14 June, 2015). Socio-economics make big difference in study outcomes. *Canberra Times.*

(205)　Hutchens, G. (17 July, 2015). Mount Druitt v Potts Point: Analysis reveals true impact of Abbott governments two budgets. *Canberra Times.*

(206)　Price, J. (19 September, 2013). Tony Abbott, minister for women? No thanks. *Sydney Morning Herald.*

(207)　Lasswell, H. (1936). *Politics: Who Gets What, When, How.* Mcgraw-Hill.

(208)　Fukuyama, F. (1992). *The End of History and the Last Man.* New York: Free Press.

(209)　Wike, R., Simmons, K., Stokes, B., & Fetterolf, J. (2017). Globally, Broad Support for Representative and Direct Democracy. But many also endorse non-democratic alternatives. Pew Research.

(210)　Hansard Society. (2019). Audit of Political Engagement 16: The 2019 Report. https://www.hansardsociety.org.uk/projects/audit-of-political-engagement.

(211)　WACC. (2018). Media bread and circuses. https://waccglobal.org/media-bread-and-circuses/2018.

(212)　Dudley-Nicholson, J. (28 October, 2019). Your Right to Know: whaling to foreign visas, these are the stories the government wanted to hide. *Daily Telegraph.*

(213)　Brennan, J. (2011). *The Ethics of Voting,* Princeton: Princeton University Press.

(214)　Serena, K. (2017). Could You Pass This Voting Literacy Test Designed To Disenfranchise African Americans?, https://allthatsinteresting.com/voting-literacy-test.

(215)　Harvard. (2014). Harvard Takes the 1964 Louisiana Literacy Test, https://www.youtube.com/watch?v=L44aX-pUTGE.

(216)　Sackman, S. (2009). "Debating 'Democracy' and the Ban on Political Advertising". *The Modern Law Review,* 72, 475–487.

(217) BBC (22 April, 2013). European Court upholds UK political advert ban.

(218) Stitt, N. (29 June 2016). Election 2016: Blackout on broadcast ads 'pointless' in internet age. ABC.

Ingram Content Group UK Ltd.
Milton Keynes UK
UKHW020033060423
419711UK00006B/168

9 781398 449435